Lecture Notes in Artificial Intelligence 1083

Subseries of Lecture Notes in Computer Science
Edited by J. G. Carbonell and J. Siekmann

Lecture Notes in Computer Science

Edited by G. Goos, J. Hartmanis and J. van Leeuwen

Springer

Berlin
Heidelberg
New York
Barcelona
Budapest
Hong Kong
London
Milan
Paris
Santa Clara
Singapore
Tokyo

Karen Sparck Jones Julia R. Galliers

Evaluating Natural Language Processing Systems

An Analysis and Review

 Springer

Series Editors

Jaime G. Carbonell
School of Computer Science, Carnegie Mellon University
Pittsburgh, PA 15213-3891, USA

Jörg Siekmann
University of Saarland
German Research Center for Artificial Intelligence (DFKI)
Stuhlsatzenhausweg 3, D-66123 Saarbrücken, Germany

Authors

Karen Sparck Jones
Julia Rose Galliers
Computer Laboratory, University of Cambridge
New Museums Site, Pembroke Street
Cambridge CB2 3QG, UK

Cataloging-in-Publication Data applied for

Die Deutsche Bibliothek - CIP-Einheitsaufnahme

Sparck Jones, Karen:
Evaluating natural language processing systems : an analysis
and review / K. Sparck Jones ; J. R. Galliers. - Berlin ;
Heidelberg ; New York ; Barcelona ; Budapest ; Hong Kong ;
London ; Milan ; Paris ; Santa Clara ; Singapore ; Tokyo :
Springer, 1996
  (Lecture notes in computer science ; 1083)
  ISBN 3-540-61309-9
NE: Galliers, Julia R.:; GT

CR Subject Classification (1991): I.2.7, H.3, I.2

ISBN 3-540-61309-9 Springer-Verlag Berlin Heidelberg New York

© Springer-Verlag Berlin Heidelberg 1995
Printed in Germany

Typesetting: Camera ready by author
SPIN 10513063   06/3142 – 5 4 3 2 1 0   Printed on acid-free paper

Preface

This book presents a detailed analysis and review of NLP evaluation, in principle and in practice. Chapter 1 examines evaluation concepts and establishes a framework for NLP system evaluation. This makes use of experience in the related area of information retrieval, and the analysis also refers to evaluation in speech processing. Chapter 2 surveys significant evaluation work done so far, in relation both to particular tasks, for instance machine translation, and to NLP evaluation methodology as such, for example as this bears on generic system evaluation. The conclusion is that evaluation strategies and techniques for NLP need much more development, in particular to take proper account of the influence of system tasks and settings. Chapter 3 develops a general approach to NLP evaluation, aimed at methodologically sound strategies for test and evaluation motivated by comprehensive performance factor identification. The analysis throughout the book is supported by extensive illustrative examples.

The book is a development and update of an earlier technical report (Galliers and Sparck Jones, 1993). The work for the report was carried out in the Computer Laboratory, University of Cambridge, under the UK Science and Engineering Research Council's Grant GR/F 35227, 'A Contextual Reasoning and Cooperative Response Framework for the Core Language Engine (CLARE)'. This grant was for a component of a much larger project, developing CLARE itself, which was conducted at SRI International's Cambridge Centre, and we are grateful to Dr S.G. Pulman, the Centre's Director, for providing us with the opportunity and push for our enterprise. We are also very grateful to many people who supplied us with reports, papers, and information about their evaluation activities, both for the original report and this successor book, and to our colleagues, notably Louis des Tombe, for thoughtful comments.

Computer Laboratory   Karen Sparck Jones
University of Cambridge   Julia Galliers

January 1996

v

Table of Contents

List of Figures ix

Glossary of terms xi

Introduction   1

1 The Framework : Scope and Concepts   3

1 Systems 3
   1.1 Language processing 3
   1.2 Systems and subsystems 6
   1.3 System settings 11
   1.4 NLP system example 15

2 Evaluation 19
   2.1 Evaluation levels 19
   2.2 Information retrieval experience 20
   2.3 Applicability to NLP 28
   2.4 NLP evaluation example 30
   2.5 Speech processing illustrations 46
   2.6 Evaluating generic systems 49
   2.7 Evaluation tools 55
   2.8 Evaluation from the social science point of view 59

2 NLP Evaluation : Work and Strategies   65

1 Evaluation so far 70
   1.1 Machine translation (MT) 70
   1.2 Message understanding (MU) 87
   1.3 Database query (DBQ) 97
   1.4 Speech understanding (SU) 109
   1.5 Miscellaneous NLP task evaluations 115
   1.6 Text retrieval 118
   1.7 Cross-task issues 120

2 General developments 125
   2.1 Evaluation workshops 125
   2.2 Evaluation tutorials 155
   2.3 EAGLES 157
   2.4 Particular methodologies 163
   2.5 Corpora, test suites, test collections, and toolkits 167
   2.6 Generic NLP system evaluation 180
   2.7 Mega-evaluation 185
   2.8 Speech evaluation 188

3 Conclusions on evaluation to date 189

3 Strategies for Evaluation   **193**

   1 General recommendations 193
     1.1 Question framework 194

   2 Evaluation illustration 196
     2.1 Illustrative examples: scene setting 197
     2.2 Examples: evaluations 201

   3 Conclusion 218

References   **219**

Index   **226**

List of Figures

Chapter 1

1 Illustrations of language, material and processing terms   5
2 Illustrations of system types and elements   7
3 Illustrations of setups and systems 12
4 NLP system and setup example : 'Motorbikes' 16
5 Illustration of IR system variables and parameters 24
6 NLP evaluation example: 'Motorbikes' 31-34
7 Diagram of setup and system relations for NLP evaluation example 35
8 Speech evaluation illustrations 47

Chapter 2

1 Summary of MT criteria, measures and methods 72
2 Falkedal: Summary of MT criteria, measures and methods 82
3 EAGLES Translation Memory (TM) feature checklist example . 88
4 Summary of MUC-3 criteria, measures and methods 90
5 Summary of database query criteria, measures and methods . . . 99
6 Summary of ARPA speech understanding criteria, measures and
  methods 113
7 Summary of FRUMP criteria, measures and methods 116
8 Summary of EAGLES evaluation methodology (EAGLES, 1994) 158
9 Summary of quality characteristics for software, ISO Standard
  9126 (ISO, 1991) 159

Chapter 3

1 Framework questions for evaluation scenario determining test and
  evaluation programme on subject 195
2 Summary of evaluation scenario for Example L 211

Glossary of terms

(assessment	= evaluation)
acceptability	class of performance criterion
activity	of user in setup
adequacy evaluation	ends-oriented evaluation
AI	artificial intelligence
aims	of user
angle	viewpoint in evaluation linked to subject's ends
annotated corpus	corpus with labels
answer	output system should supply
antecedent variable	usually environment variable
apparatus	equipment other than system in setup
application	(system for) task in specific domain
architecture	infrastructure specification for NLP system
argot	very restricted sublanguage
attribute	pertinent to quality characteristic
baseline	performance floor from simple system
behaviour	of user
benchmark	established performance norm
black box	input/output-only evaluation
bound	area of evaluation - wide or narrow
broad scope	of setup
catalogue	fact list on evaluation subject
category	of user e.g. casual
checking collection	controlled test collection
checklist	evaluators' aid for featurisation
class	of performance criterion - efficiency etc
complexity	of system
component	part of system
composite	evaluation subsuming several measures
constitution	of evaluation subject
consumer	of evaluation findings
context	of evaluation subject
corpus	of test material
coverage corpus	corpus with all phenomena
criterion	for evaluation
customer	interested/consuming party for evaluation
data sort	kind of test/evaluation material
data source	e.g. corpus
decomposition	of setup working or system operation
design	for/of evaluation
design goal	system specification for objective
development data	working data for whole community
(diagnosis	= evaluation)
diagnostic evaluation	analytical evaluation

dialogue	user-system interaction involving NL
distribution corpus	corpus giving phenomena distribution
division	between l-system and n-system
domain	area or field of task
dry run	of evaluation procedure to check out
eccentric	idiosyncratic system performance
effect	of system, including output
effectiveness	class of performance criterion
efficiency	class of performance criterion
ends	system objectives/functions or setup purposes/functions
environment	setup from system's point of view
environment factor	variable as factor affecting performance
evaluation	of system or setup performance
evaluation data	data used for evaluation
evaluation methodology	methodology for evaluation
evaluation procedure	for carrying out test
evaluation standard	requirements for evaluation criteria etc
exemplar	baseline or benchmark performance
exigent processing	thorough NLP
experiment	to explicate system/setup performance
extrinsic criterion	for evaluating wrt embedding setup
factor	see performance factor
feature	attribute, attribute value
featurisation	feature choice for evaluation
field evaluation	evaluation in real-life situation
form	of evaluation yardstick as attainable/ideal etc
full processing	complete NLP
function	role of system in setup (or one setup in another)
general-purpose system	system for any application
generic system	system independent of application
glass box	internal operation evaluation
goal	of evaluation
granularity	of parameters under evaluation
grid	design style for test/evaluation
guidelines	for evaluation
hybrid system	with both l- and n-subsystems
indicator	of performance, variable or parameter
informativeness	of evaluation about system or setup
interactive system	with user-system dialogue
interface	system for user interaction involving NLP
interest	category of evaluation requester e.g. developer

intervening variable	usually system parameter
instance	of input in test data
intrinsic criterion	for internal system/setup evaluation
investigation	to determine system performance
IR	information retrieval
kind	of evaluation as experiment/investigation
l-system	see language system
language	natural language
language system	(sub)system doing NLP
legitimacy	of data for test/evaluation use
linkage	of variables, parameters, objectives, effects, and measures
measure	of performance, instantiating criterion
mega-evaluation	large-scale, long-term, multi-task evaluation
method	of applying measure
methodology	for test/evaluation
metric	= measure
mode	of evaluation as qualitative/ quantitative/hybrid
motivation	stimulating reason for evaluation
n-system	(sub)system not doing NLP
narrow bound	of area of evaluation
narrow scope	of setup
NL	natural language
NLP	natural language processing
non-interactive	system without user dialogue
norm	performance requirement (benchmark or target)
objective	what system itself is for
observation	of system/setup, preceding evaluation
operation	of system
orientation	of evaluation as extrinsic/intrinsic
p-setup	setup for individual user
parameter	of system
partial processing	incomplete NLP
performance	of system/setup wrt objective/purpose
performance exemplar	from baseline or benchmark
performance factor	any system/setup element affecting performance
perspective	aspect under which evaluation subject seen e.g. financial
pretest	test of evaluation measures, methods
programme	set of related tests/evaluations
progress evaluation	improvement, development evaluation
pseudo-language	not actually natural language
purpose	what setup is for
qualitative	holistic, non-numeric performance measure

quality characteristic	(general) desired property of evaluation subject
quantitative	numeric performance measure
quasi-language	sublanguage with own life
range	of NLP system, especially generic
rationale	for performance comparison
reality	of data for test/evaluation use
reasonable	fair performance, given environment
references	data including answers supporting evaluation
reliability	consistency of performance measure
remit	of evaluation
reportable attribute	for evaluation customer
representativeness	of data for test/evaluation use
richness	of language
role	of user in setup e.g. data input
run	of system giving performance measure
scenario	test and evaluation plan
scope	of setup - broad or narrow
separation	of system from user
serious material	complex natural language material
setting	of parameter
setup	system plus operational context
simple processing	rudimentary NLP
sort	of test/evaluation data e.g. test suite
source	corpus for data
standards	requirements for test/evaluation conduct
status	of test/evaluation data for e.g. representativeness
strategy	for conducting evaluation
style	of evaluation as exhaustive/indicative etc
subject	of evaluation, i.e. component/(sub)system/ setup
sublanguage	of natural language
substitute	honed answer in reference data
subsystem	l- or n- part of system
system	software+hardware entity
system factor	parameter as factor affecting performance
target	for performance
task	what system does
terminal	I/O manifestation of interface
test	investigation or experiment
test bed	application for exploring system design
test collection	data, with references, especially for experiment
test data	data for tests

test methodology	methodology for tests
test program	for doing runs, scoring performance, etc
test set	data subset used for system testing
test suite	designed test material
tool	for evaluation, i.e. data or program
toolkit	processing tools e.g. software for test/ evaluation
training set	data subset used for system development
transcription	test collection of transcribed speech
transportability	of system
trivial material	simple natural language material
tuning	of system to application
tweaking	of system to evaluation conditions
type	of evaluation as black box/glass box
user	of system in setup
utility	operational setup-oriented criterion
validity	propriety of performance measure
value	of variable
variable	property of environment affecting system
wide bound	large area of evaluation
working	of setup
working data	system input material for testing
yardstick	nature of performance for comparison

Introduction

How does one evaluate natural language processing (NLP) systems? What kinds of question can one ask about their scope and performance, and what kinds of answer can one hope to get? What sorts of test do these require?

The report, Galliers and Sparck Jones (1993), from which this book follows was originally stimulated by evaluation issues for particular systems, SRI Cambridge's CLE and CLARE. These are generic systems, to be customised for individual applications, and there are special problems in evaluating such systems apart from any application.

However we found on investigation that while NLP evaluation is vital, there was little prior art. We therefore decided to undertake a broad study, attempting both a thorough analysis of what NLP evaluation involves and a comprehensive review of what has so far been done. NLP evaluation has indeed become a topic of interest in recent years, with considerable activity promoted by the US DARPA, now ARPA, initiatives. But we believe much more work is needed to develop proper methodologies, and much more attention needs to be paid to evaluation by all those working in the field.

This was the conclusion we reached on completing our report in 1993. Since then there has been further progress with the ARPA evaluation programme, and increasing interest in evaluation in the context of, for instance, European Commission and national research programmes. However though this experience has heightened awareness of the importance of evaluation and improved actual evaluation practice, there is still a great deal more to be done in developing and applying evaluation technology. Thus while this book includes the report's earlier review, it concentrates on evaluation issues and principles, illustrated via detailed examples, that remain relevant to evaluation now. At the same time, the review element of the report has been updated to take account of the most salient effort and references in the past two years.

The book is divided into three parts. Chapter 1 establishes the framework for a more specific treatment of evaluation techniques by introducing relevant concepts and terminology, first in relation to systems themselves as the subject of evaluation (Section 1), and then to evaluation itself as applicable to systems (Section 2). The discussion in each section is filled out by extended examples, and the introduction of evaluation concepts is amplified by comparisons with the evaluation problems and techniques of two areas related to NLP, namely information retrieval (IR) and speech processing (SP). We also address the problems of generic system evaluation. The distinctions we regard as most important for evaluation are between system and what we call setup, namely the system plus its operational context; between system factors and environment factors within a global set of performance factors; and between evaluation criteria, evaluation measures, and evaluation methods in defining performance.

Chapter 2 examines work done so far in evaluating NLP systems. In Section 1 we consider evaluation for particular tasks, for instance machine translation; in Section 2 we review general developments, including those represented by workshops dedicated to evaluation methodology as such, and by work on test corpora and tools. Section 3 draws conclusions from this survey on the state of the art. The main findings are that both theory and practice are very patchy, and that evaluation in general is not rigorous enough and is too narrowly focussed.

In Chapter 3 we present what we believe is a rational approach to evaluation motivated by performance factor identification and leading to evaluation programmes based on grid designs. We do this primarily through a series of related examples.

All *defined terms* are given in the Glossary.

Chapter 1

The Framework : Scope and Concepts

This chapter introduces some notions and distinctions relevant to the overall topic of NLP system evaluation. The first section, 1, establishes a frame of reference for systems in the context of evaluation, partly by reference to other, related areas and partly through NLP examples, concluding with a more extended description of an illustrative example. The second section, 2, provides a comparable analysis of the various generic concepts involved in evaluation. It uses information retrieval and speech processing as areas for comparison, and also relates the evaluation notions that have been developed to NLP in a follow-up with the illustrative system of Section 1.

1   Systems

For NLP evaluation purposes it is necessary to make careful distinctions with respect both to the nature of the systems themselves - for instance is a system entirely or only partially dedicated to NLP, - and to the nature of the larger setting in which the system is used - for instance is the system interactive or autonomous? These distinctions are developed in the first part of Section 1 below. However it is necessary as a preliminary to indicate what is taken here as the scope of language processing.

1.1   Language processing

Both the current limitations of NLP, and the new possibilities for information communication and management that automation has provided, make it necessary to state what constitutes natural language for the purposes of this report. We will therefore set some bounds and adopt some terms as follows.

We will use *language* (and hence *linguistic*) to refer to natural language unless explicitly indicated. This covers *sublanguage* in the conventional NLP sense, but

3

not *pseudo-language* (a defined artificial language which happens to use natural language terms, as many command languages do). This book is not about processing pseudo-languages (e.g. program specification languages), or about how much these may share properties with natural language. It is also not directly about the relative merits of natural language and non natural languages (pseudo languages, formal languages, menus, or whatever), though NLP evaluation may bear on the propriety of choosing one rather than the other, say for interactive purposes as in database query, and may also have to consider the use of natural language within structures like menus. The book is also not concerned with the use of natural language text, especially for system output, in canned (or text template) form where there is no NLP to be done by the system, however much system users may understand canned text for real, though again evaluation may have to allow for systems with some canning. One general aspect of evaluation, predominantly but not exclusively in the interactive case, is that all kinds of mixes of natural language with other types of communicative device characteristic of HCI as a whole may be in question. But though contrasts between and combination of natural language and other communication media or modalities are important both in individual applications and in relation to the potential or actual general value of NLP, we will not be addressing these large questions in this book.

Though the term "sublanguage" may be taken to imply that the language referred to is a more or less specialised subset of ordinary language, sublanguages have a life of their own which makes it difficult to be sure of this. The term will therefore also be taken to cover *quasi-languages* where these have a strong but not subset relationship with given natural languages (as in "quasi-English") and are not, alternatively, pseudo-languages and, especially perhaps, poorly defined ones.

We are making these distinctions because assessing the qualitative characteristics of the language material with which a system has to deal is itself a factor in evaluation. NLP may be intended in principle to deal with full natural language, but the state of the art, not only in NLP but in AI generally, means that the language a system can be expected to deal with is much more limited. [1] The boundary between demanding and rudimentary natural language material is not well-defined, but material may be so limited it may be doubtful whether it is worthy of being labelled natural language material at all. We will not, however, attempt to define natural language: we will take it that it is characterised by variety and expressive power, and that natural language material is generically characterised from a processing point of view by non-trivial ambiguity presupposing substantive non-deterministic operations depending on a range of types of information - about syntax, semantics, pragmatics, and the world, - but leave the boundary between *serious* and *trivial material* open. It is nevertheless important, for evaluation, to determine how restricted a sublanguage is, and in particular whether it is so restricted, in relation to the presuppositions on which

---

[1] Systems however need to be able to deal with full natural language even when their NLP capacities are restricted, in the sense of coping appropriately with their failures.

evaluation is based, that it is better treated for evaluation purposes not as natural language but rather as what can, for want of a better term, be labelled an *argot*.

We will also refer to *exigent* or *simple processing*, which may concide respectively with *full* and *partial* processing, though again the precise boundary between these two concepts has to be left open. This distinction is important for evaluation because however thoroughly natural language has been exploited to produce the material a system has to deal with, it does not follow that the system itself has even notionally to process it in a comparable way. Natural language may, in particular, have been fully exploited to produce serious material, but this need not imply that the system has a task requiring a similar level of language processing. Thus while NLP may be taken as in principle concerned with fully-understood interpretation or generation, much less rigorous processing, e.g. by template matching or phrase selection, may in practice be in order. This report will exclude minimal processing of the kind represented by basic keyword indexing (whether by vocabulary reference or on a statistical basis). But identifying the level of processing, whether more or less exigent, required in a given situation is a factor in evaluation, and one which is logically independent of the nature of the material being processed. From this point of view it is worth emphasising that some human uses of their language do not involve exigent processing.

```
(natural) language    : eg   what this report is written in

(full) language       :      weekly magazine

sublanguage           :      medical reports

serious material      :      scientific articles

trivial material      :      food label ingredients list

exigent processing    :      summarising

simple processing     :      scanning

full processing       :      database query interpretation

partial processing    :      noun group extraction
```

Fig. 1. Illustrations of language, material and processing terms

The nature of the language use in question is important because, just as with the nature of the material, it cannot be assumed that the goal is machine use of a natural language like English which is as close as possible to the human use of languages. Current inadequacies in the state of the art make this an unrealistic goal. But involving computers in natural language communication creates new contexts for language use, and hence allows for the possibilities of distinctive languages, materials and uses. Thus it is essential in evaluation to be clear about the way in which, and the extent to which, the situation should properly be regarded as emulating language communication among humans. The distinctions made here about languages, materials, and processing are summarised, with examples, in Figure 1.

1.2   Systems and subsystems

As NLP presupposes a system for doing it, it is necessary for evaluation purposes to identify this system. However systems may not be exclusively devoted to NLP, so it is also necessary to determine system tasks, and in many cases to decompose systems to separate out the language subsystems and components. The functional and structural characterisation of a system in its own right may be very complex, so this section introduces a set of distinctions referring to system function and structure which can support this characterisation. These are also illustrated in Figure 2.

We will use *system* to refer to the entire automatic software and hardware entity in the situation of interest. A system carries out a *task*. This can be intrinsically or primarily linguistic, as in translation, or primarily or intrinsically non-linguistic, as in industrial plant control. A system for translating newspapers is essentially linguistic, even if it exploits non-linguistic knowledge in doing this; a system for managing a chemical plant is essentially non-linguistic, even if it has a natural language interface for its human monitors. There are many intermediate cases in the knowledge based / expert systems area, depending on how dependent on the user the system is, on how substantial, whether necessarily or naturally, the natural language dialogue with the user is, and on how complicated the system's own internal operation is. Thus with query access to a conventional database mangement system through a natural language interface, the system cannot function without the user, the user's contribution is in principle linguistically substantial, and the system's internal operations are not too complicated. With a current state expert system, say for monitoring a patient, on the other hand, with an interface for a doctor as user, the system may function without reference to the user and the dialogue may be linguistically elementary, but the system's internal operations may be quite complex. The relations between what can be labelled *separation* from the user, *richness* of the language, and *complexity* in the system, can be both very intricate for any one system and very different across systems.

It is convenient from the NLP point of view to distinguish *interactive* and *non-interactive* systems, since the former may (though they will not necessarily) impose different NLP requirements, like those characteristic of *dialogue*. But

6

```
task                       : eg summarising

application, in domain :   translation of weather forecasts

system                     :   holiday advisor; style checker

hybrid system             :   holiday advisor

l-subsystem               :   NLP part of holiday advisor

n-subsystem               :   expert system part of holiday advisor

l-system                  :   style checker

component                 :   sentence generator; flight optimiser
                                  for holiday advisor

general-purpose system :   none such l-systems

generic system            :   NL analyser with 'common vocabulary'
          component        :   parser

interactive system       :   programming teacher

interface                 :   subsystem conducting interaction
                                  in teacher subsuming NL inputs
                                  or output

non-interactive system :   message router

terminal                  :   X-windows
```

Fig. 2. Illustrations of system types and elements

while exigent NLP may stimulate or be stimulated by complex internal operations in the interactive case, this is not necessarily so: exigent NLP may be associated with simple underlying operations, as in translation between very different languages, and equally, simple NLP may trigger or be triggered by complex internal operations, as in expert system explanation. It is further the case that non-interactive as well as interactive systems may be primarily non-linguistic, as in a data recording and analysis system which also generates reports, for instance about the weather. (Interaction here refers to 'primary' interactive language use;

interaction may have 'secondary' uses for e.g. disambiguation or checking.)

For evaluation it is essential to be clear about the status of NLP in relation to the system's overall task. Is the task itself an NLP task, however many non-linguistic resources are needed to support this, as summarising is? Or is it a non-linguistic task, with the overall system embedding a language processor which may be more or less vital to the system's action, say by invoking it as in a consultation system, and/or more more or less enmeshed in the system's operation, say by determining the way its operational concepts are characterised, as in an advice system?

We will use *l-system* (short for *language system*) for that part of a system which engages in language processing. In a translation system the whole system is thus an l-system. In other cases the l-system may be a *subsystem*. Thus as already indicated with expert systems, for instance for equipment fault-finding, there may be substantial non-linguistic processors which are invoked by, but are minimally concerned with, language. Thus a diagnostic processor may be stimulated by a user inquiry ("What is the patient's disease?") and further assisted by language inputs ("The temperature is normal"), but the diagnostic processor itself reasons independently on a distinct knowledge base. At the same time, there may be more to the language processing than 'just' lexical, syntactic and semantic operations. We will use *n-system* (short for *non-language system*) for (that part of) a system which does not engage in language processing. We are using "l-system" and "n-system" rather than perhaps more obvious terms like "front end" and "back end" for two reasons. One is to avoid the implication that the two can always be viewed as essentially independent systems which are in effect just butted together with a small communication channel between them, and also any further implication that language processing is typically a relatively shallow and surface affair. The other is to avoid any suggestion that language processing is specifically to support interaction with the user as in the database inquiry case. We can indeed in principle envisage NLP operations not confined to the system's input and output, but as applying internally for communication and data transmission between processors in complex, multi-purpose information management systems: it cannot be taken for granted that internal operations will always be on meanings.

However while it may be useful to refer to l-systems and n-systems respectively, this should not be taken to imply that they are, or can be, separated except by definition. Thus it should not be supposed that a system's use of language can always be decoupled from the rest of what it does. In reacting to language inputs, and responding by language outputs, the system's l- and n-processing may be functionally interdependent, regardless of the details of the system's structural and operational architecture and especially of its modular organisation. The one crucial issue in evaluating NLP where the system's task is not itself exclusively an NLP one, is in establishing the *division* between l-system and n-system. If the separation between the two is weak, it is hard to establish and evaluate l-system performance independent of n-system performance. Obvious cases of interdependence are those where word definitions in the lexicon used by the language processor are geared to the way the corresponding concepts figure in the domain model exploited for reasoning by the non-linguistic processor, or where semantic sentence representations are minimalist and left for full fleshing out by reference to the domain model.

Thus the problem for evaluation is not essentially (though it may be effortful in practice) in allocating data or operations to the l- or n-system elements of a *hybrid* system, i.e. in descriptively separating these elements, and in knowing, for instance, that parsing is an l-system function and diagnosis an n-system one, so parsing and diagnosis failures can then in principle be attributed to the l- and n-system components respectively. Individual component performance, however this is characterised, cannot be taken as equivalent to overall system performance, which is what really matters. At the same time, when the performance of a complete system, like a language-driven consultation system, as a whole is evaluated, if responses to inputs are joint functions of two such components, depending for instance on shared responsibility for establishing input word or sentence meaning, the problem is how to relate overall performance characteristics to individual components which are designed to be partial processors depending on others. This is nothing to do with the directionality of processing. The point is rather that, if something comes unstuck, say, with the way an input word is interpreted, is it legitimate to blame this on the inadequacies of a language processor when this is designed to do only part of the input processing work? It may indeed be legitimate to attribute individual data or process faults to a specific component like a language subsystem: the serious problem is in the generic partitions the system embodies, and thus in whether it is meaningful to tie overall performance to the consequences of having a partition in one place rather than another.

For convenience where the distinction does not matter, "l-system" may be used to refer indifferently to the cases where a system's entire task is NLP, and to those where NLP is done by a subsystem. "System" and "subsystem" will normally be interpreted generally, as they have been used so far (though in contexts dealing entirely with NLP they may be used informally to refer to NLP systems or subsystems). It is also convenient, in interactive contexts, to refer to an *interface* as an l-subsystem allowing the human user to interact with some task system in natural language. This will normally be within a system with substantial non-linguistic components, like a medical expert system, but can refer to a system primarily engaged in NLP, with a subordinate specialised data access subsystem: some document indexing and retrieval systems may be of this sort. It is also necessary in some contexts to distinguish what we will call the *terminal* in order to refer to the interface as manifest to the user for input and output purposes. The way information is presented on screens and so forth may interact with what is presented, affecting the user's perception and use of the system, so the properties of terminals may have to be taken into account in system evaluation (menus as vehicles for information display and gathering are good examples of the way terminals can influence the use of natural language in interfaces, and the same applies to mixed media terminals). The matters here include, however not only properties of the terminal from what may be called the information display point of view just mentioned, but also the nature of generic screen management software and hardware matters like screen resolution and legibility: Hypercard on a Macintosh, for instance, shows how interrelated all these aspects of the terminal can be.

All of the foregoing refers to individual systems, i.e. systems for carrying out some task in some *domain*. We will refer to any such system as an *application* (system). However while it is generally important to evaluate individual systems, it may also be desirable to (attempt to) evaluate *generic systems*. Generic systems may be roughly equated with expert system shells. They are normally designed for some task or perhaps, more broadly, for a task type, and while they may incorporate domain-independent knowledge bases, do not include domain-specific resources. In the expert system case, generic knowledge may include 'common knowledge', for example about time or human beings, or may be rather more restricted but still useful across individual expert systems, as e.g. an anatomical knowledge base could be for a range of medical expert systems. In the NLP case, a generic l-system may include a general-purpose syntactic grammar of some language, and a 'core' lexicon of common words, but not a domain-specific vocabulary. As it is impossible to evaluate a system fully unless it has all the resources required for its application, it is correspondingly difficult to evaluate a generic system fully, and especially to evaluate an uninstantiated generic l-system fully. Generic system evaluation thus presents challenges which will be examined in detail later. Thus, for instance, it is not sufficient to extrapolate performance from some one specific application to another. It does not, however, follow that nothing can be done to evaluate a generic system in the sense of providing some decent grounds for predicting future application performance: part of the problem is the useful grain size for prediction, since although even with one application system it may not be wholly sound to predict performance for any future use, this can be done reliably enough for all practical purposes. It should be emphasised that a generic system is not the same as a *general-purpose* system intended to be directly usable, without further tailoring, for an application: these do not exist even for any one NLP task, let alone a range of tasks. [2]

Evaluation is also relevant below the system level, and specifically below the l-system level, for individual *components*, whether these are data sources or processors, e.g. grammar, parser. These are subject to the same incompleteness problem for evaluation as l-subsystems, and there are links with the evaluation of generic systems where these subsume individually complete components. There are some differences from the point of view of NLP evaluation, in that the partitioning is entirely within the l-system. But the essential problem is the same, in that while it may be possible to obtain some performance data for an individual component, what this means has to be properly related to the intended purpose and operational experience of the system as a whole, or at least of the l-system

---

[2] As indicated earlier, basic statistical indexing systems for example, which can be general-purpose, are not taken here as NLP systems.

as a whole. It is also necessary to allow for different scales and complexities in components: thus an English analyser may subsume e.g. both syntactic and semantic components, but itself be a component in a translation system.

It may be argued that these concerns about subsystem or component dependence are not well taken, in that in any theoretically well-grounded system the partitions are well-motivated and the modules have well-defined autonomies: thus in an l-system, syntax and semantics are properly different and definable, so the precise nature of there dependencies is understood and can be taken into account in evaluation. But this is a very strong claim which, whether it holds for some specific system being evalated, cannot be deemed to hold for any NLP system being evaluated. Moreover, though the boundaries between and responsibilities of, the components of l-systems may be deemed uncontroversial and known, this is less obvious where the boundary between l-system and n-system is concerned.

As mentioned earlier, examples illustrating the various notions relevant to systems are given in Figure 2.

1.3 System settings

The subsystem and component dependencies, or interdependencies, just considered are not the only ones affecting evaluation: systems themselves operate within larger envelopes. Though NLP systems are being taken here as the prime focus of attention for evaluation, they cannot in general be effectively or usefully evaluated in isolation. It is necessary to consider them in relation to their settings, and thus also to address evaluation as applying to system and setting as these together constitute a 'setup'. It is thus important to separate the objectives and properties of systems from the purposes and properties, including the properties of system users, characterising setups as wholes. Two complete, integrated examples covering the concepts discussed here are given in Figure 3: this shows how they apply in a financial data processing situation and in a translation one respectively.

Thus a message processing system like the TICC traffic message system for example (Allport, 1988), may be intended to supply selected kinds of information to different classes of people, and to do this very rapidly. Here the system proper, which can be deemed an l-system, has to meet not only strictly NLP requirements to extract the required types of information; it also has to do this rapidly and has to be connected with data gathering and distribution mechanisms which involve various kinds of people and rely on miscellaneous processing and communication equipment including, for instance, mobile radio. In an informal sense the whole is a system, but particularly since people are an integral part of this larger whole, we will refer to such larger wholes as *setups*. [3] Thus while the message processing system is the system proper as far as its *objective* 'message processing' (however specified in detail) is concerned, it is also part of a larger setup, involving its *users* and any other *apparatus*, which in turn has its own encompassing *purpose(s)*,

---

[3] We are reserving the obvious terms "environment" and "context" for other uses.

11

```
EXAMPLE (1) :  financial data processing

setup           :      stockmarket service
    purpose        :      investment recommendations
    working        :      considering, checking, advising ...
system          :      transaction scanning, analysis and digesting
    objective      :      trend and event reporting
    function       :      convenient current data for investment
                            advisors
    operation      :      aggregation, comparison, selection,
                            generation
apparatus       :    data collection machinery
users           :    investment advisors
    role           :      transaction advisors, bulletin writers
    category       :      habitual
    aim            :      please customers, enhance status
    activity       :      advising, surveying
    behaviour      :      reading, browsing, searching (digest file)


EXAMPLE (2) :  machine aided translation

setup           :      government department translation office
    purpose        :      official document translation
    working        :      assembling, translating, disseminating ...
system          :      translation assistant
    objective      :      linguistic processing and data provision
    function       :      support human translator
    operation      :      parsing etc, lexicon display etc
apparatus       :    document printing
users           :    translators
    role           :      translators
    category       :      habitual
    aim            :      produce quality translations
    activity       :      translation
    behaviour      :      directing, assessing, revising
```

Fig. 3. Illustrations of setups and systems

namely to manage road use, etc, and within which the system has a *function*. Even if the limits on the system proper (as also of the other elements of the setup and indeed the setup as a whole) have something of the arbitrary, there can clearly be real distinctions between embedded systems and embedding setups which are marked by the differences between their respective objectives and purposes. It is nevertheless the case that, while the system's message processing capabilities can be evaluated on their own terms, it has also to be evaluated in terms of whether what it does suits its environment, i.e. whether it serves its intended function. This might be deemed to be an irrelevant concern if the system matches its specification: but one important goal in evaluation is to study and refine specifications.

We are labelling as "users" any humans involved with the system's operations, and not just the consumers of its services, though these are often seen as most important, for example those seeking information from databases. Users also include designers, data suppliers, and run-time operators, e.g. as in machine-aided translation. Cutting across these functional *roles* are other *categories*, often the focus of concern in explicit user modelling, which refer to such user properties as being experienced or a novice, being a habitual or casual user, and so forth. These classifications again may or may not refer to users engaged in natural language interaction, depending on the task or application. It is fair to pay special attention to those users engaged in natural language interaction, as l-systems are frequently intended precisely to provide this means of access to a system, but evaluation should not necessarily be confined to these users even in setups with natural language interaction. As we are using "task" to refer to what the system does, we will use *activity* for what the individual user does. Thus in machine-aided translation the system's task may be to manage and display lexical data, where the user's activity is translation. Evaluation has to take account of the relative ambits and responsibilities of the system and the user as these relate to their local setup within any encompassing one. We will call such a personal setup (typically, in fact, for a class of users) a *p-setup*. Thus in an institutional setup with the purpose of providing translations there would be p-setups for the actual translators whose p-purpose is to do translations. In this case the institutional and personal do not seem very different, but even here as far as evaluation is concerned, literature coverage and translation cost, for instance, apply only at the institutional level, while working convenience, for instance, applies at the personal level.

While distinctions in relation to users may be in order for evaluation purposes, we are using "apparatus" rather broadly to subsume any non-human constituents of a setup, assuming that these are distinguishable, and are distinguished, from the system which is taken as the main focus of concern.

It is clearly crucial for evaluation to decide whether this is narrowly interpreted as concerned only with the system (or l-system) and with how well it meets its objective, or more widely, as concerned with the setup and its purpose. Thus while, for example, the system's task may be translation, its purpose in its wider socio-economic context may be to provide translations of official documents which have legal status. The NLP system cannot itself directly engage with notions of legal status, i.e. determine whether a candidate translation is legally viable, even if the way the translation system works is intended to meet some standards of accuracy which its designers have taken as implying legal viability. Thus while evaluating the system itself will be directed at discovering whether it does meet the standards of accuracy required - and the object of the evaluation is precisely to establish that the notion of accuracy has been properly operationalised, and indeed was previously properly defined, - evaluating the system in its setup in turn depends on having got the right view of accuracy in relation to legal viability. This may be deemed to be a matter of system specification and thus of no concern for system evaluation, but in general evaluation cannot be restricted in this way, both because systems are not independent of their ulterior purposes, and also because what a system delivers can affect its specification. Thus in the translation case, how it turns out in practice to be possible to define translational accuracy, either as a notion independent of machine attainment or as unavoidably modified by the limitations of machine systems wanted for other, for instance economic, reasons, will interact with the notion of legal viability.

It is at the same time clear that the *scopes* of setups can differ from one case to another, and that a setup's scope may be wide and its boundary hard to draw. Thus it may be difficult in relation to users, especially where natural language interaction is concerned, to decide whether they fall inside or outside the setup. This may be somewhat arbitrarily decided in terms of the system's design and user dependency. For instance in machine-aided translation, the human translators are clearly part of the system's setup. But with a fully automatic translation system, are the optional readers of its output part of its setup or not? One is inclined to say not, but the system's objective and design may nevertheless be based on some assumptions about what the readers of its output are like, even if they are free to read or not. This suggests that while setup may be a somewhat relative notion, and any individual setup be hard to determine, what a system's setup is is not arbitrarily definable. It also follows that it is crucial for evaluation purposes to be clear about what a system's setup is taken to be. It may then be useful in individual cases to allow explicitly for both narrower and broader setup scopes, say in the machine-aided translation case on the one hand by confining it to the actual translators, and on the other extending it to the whole translation department. Both of these setups may be relevant to, because they have different interests in, the system evaluation. Similar distinctions would apply in a database case, between on the one hand staff actually engaged in conducting database inquiries, and on the other the staff of a company's whole database department.

Finally, just as it is necessary to distinguish the system's task from the user's activity in relation to a setup, and correspondingly between system objectives and users's *aims*, it may be necessary to distinguish various behaviours: the system's *operation*, the user's *behaviour*, and the setup's *working*. These have to be observed to provide the data for evaluation.

Figure 3 shows how the concepts for setups, users and systems, their respective purpose, objectives and aims and so forth apply for the two example situations. All of it may seem very complicated, and unnecessarily so, though the figure shows clear distinctions, suggesting these are well motivated. Further justification for the various distinctions can be seen by considering, informally, what might follow from asking various evaluation-motivated questions about a system. These include not only obviously evaluative questions like "How well is it working?", "Does it work better with Factor X?", "Does it work better than System Y?", but also the *observational* questions which evaluative questions presuppose and which are logically distinct from these, for instance "How is it working?", "Does it work differently with Factor X?", "Does it work differently from System Y?". Both types of question are relevant to evaluation even if a more obviously evaluative term like "perform" is naturally substitutible for "work" only in the first three. The need to evaluate does not in fact remove the need to observe, and also the need, as will be seen later in an analysis of information retrieval, to keep the two notions distinct. Thus in the retrieval case, we may observe that the system retrieves 2 relevant documents and 5 non-relevant ones, but evaluatively, according to different criteria, we can say it worked well because it retrieved 2 relevant documents, badly because it retrieved 5 non-relevant ones, or relatively well because it retrieved 2 relevant for 5 non-relevant.

1.4 NLP system example

In the discussion so far many individual concepts and distinctions have been introduced, but the supporting examples have been largely independent of one another. In this final part of Section 1 we will illustrate these concepts in more detail, and show how they relate to one another, by describing a single, more elaborate case. This hypothetical setup and system will also be used later, to indicate how the evaluation notions that will be introduced in the next section are related to the system concepts introduced in this. This example is also summarily shown in Figure 4.

Thus to illustrate the potential role in evaluation of the many distinctions introduced so far, consider a database query system with a natural language interface, intended for use in the one plant of a company that manufactures custom motorbikes. We suppose further that the system consists of a natural language subsystem communicating via a query in a conventional data query language like SQL with a conventional database management system (DBMS). Whether this is a rational system design is not the point: that's the way things are, for the historic reason that the DBMS came before the natural language interface. The database contains information about orders for bikes and stocks of parts and materials, where the former are characterised not only by obvious properties like their nature and customer, but also by phases like 'design', 'construction', 'testing', 'finishing' ..., and the latter about nature, supplier, quantity in stock, replacement time, ... The system is designed to provide information for three classes of people in the plant, namely workshop staff for their work organisation, warehouse staff for their stock control, and financial staff for their cash position

NL database query within a company plant for producing custom motorbikes, providing information on warehouse stocks and progress of orders for warehouse, production floor and finance office

```
TASK              :  database query
DOMAIN            :  motorbike production
LANGUAGE
  - sublanguage   :  motorbike parts, orders
material
  - trivial       :  question, command and statement forms;
                        mainly single sentences/fragments
                        limited sequences/exchanges
processing
  - exigent       :  input interpretation, output generation;
      (fairly)          simple speech acts
                        mainly object-level
                        fragments, limited sequences/exchanges
  - full          :  complete input analysis, output generation
SYSTEM            :  database access
  - hybrid
    subsystems
      l-system    :  NL interpreter/generator
      n-system    :  data retrieval, database management
  - interactive   :  NL interface
      terminal    :  NL with commands, graphics: text, tables
                  :  quality screen, keyboard, mouse
objective         :  answer data queries
function          :  meet data needs
operation         :  query determination and answer provision
l-system
  - components    :  grammar (syntax, semantics, reference)
                        lexicon, domain model, data model
                        parser, generator, resolver, mapper
                        dialogue manager
SETUP             :  database utilisation
purpose           :  decision support
working           :  need identification, information consideration
users             :  warehouse, workfloor, office staff
role & category   :  queryist, habitual
aim               :  obtain information, make sensible decisions
behaviour         :  query forming, revision, information extraction
```

Fig. 4. NLP system and setup example : 'Motorbikes'

16

analyses. This imaginary system can handle questions about orders like "Where is Robinson's order?", "Has Heath's order reached finishing yet?" "What parts were used for the Smith order?" and "Did O-9 use a VV or WW handlebar?"; and questions about stocks like "How many Double V handlebars are there?", "Is there a stainless mudguard flange in stock?", "When was our last batch of styrofoam seatpads received?" and "How much did Grubbins Mouldings charge for the Z-2380 hubs?" The system itself is only for queries about the state of stocks and progress of orders, so internal requisitions for parts or materials from the warehouse for the workshops, and external orders to suppliers of goods, or invoices to customers who have ordered bikes, are quite separately handled. The justification for having the system cover both bike orders and stocks is that though the database itself has two constituent parts, the same person may ask questions of either and, as the third and fourth questions show, orders and parts are related, as they will be seen to be in the detailed breakdown of charges in bills to customers, for example. As a system it may seem messy, but it is thus quite realistic.

The system task is thus database query in the motorbike domain. The language used is a sublanguage, in that while it handles ordinary words like "use" in ordinary senses, it does not exploit their full range of meanings, and it is essentially restricted to dealing with motorbike parts and orders. It has a quasi-language aspect associated with the specialised vocabulary of part names. In the sense of "trivial" being used in this report the material is trivial as it is restricted to a limited range of discourse, sentence and fragment forms and functions: individual inputs and outputs are typically single sentences (or fragments), and apart from system-driven clarification dialogues is confined to simple input/output pair exchanges: the system relies on a longer memory only in a very limited way to handle anaphora and ellipsis. The processing is moderately exigent: inputs have to be interpreted into meaning representations, and outputs may have to be generated from these in association with retrieved data. However inputs can be treated relatively simply as speech acts (questions map onto queries, and so do commands), and are taken at the object level of the database: the system's ability to handle meta-level language is restricted to clarification dialogues under its own control. Generation has to present output data clearly, and system responses when showing input interpretations or seeking clarification have to be comprehensible, but can take advantage of a limited context. Processing is also full, in the sense that inputs are fully, not partially treated, and generation has similarly to be carried through completely from an underlying content representation, albeit sometimes with embedded data blocks.

The system as a whole is engaged in data access, and is thus a hybrid system with an l-subsystem for interpretation and generation between NL and the formal data search language SQL, and a data retrieval and database management n-system. The system is interactive, with an NL interface, which for the user has the form of a terminal using NL within the framework of a standard command system and in conjunction with a graphical display capability (e.g. for data tables), all depending on a conventional windows, keyboard and mouse machinery. The system's own objective is to answer database queries in a helpful way, whereas its function in relation to its setup is to meet data needs. Its operation essentially involves determining users' queries and providing answers to legitimate ones, or politely bouncing illegitimate ones. The l-system's components include linguistic and application knowledge resources: grammar (with syntactic, semantic and reference rules) and lexicon, and domain and data models; and processors: parser and generator, resolver and mapper; and overall dialogue manager.

The setup which encompasses the system is an abstract entity, for database utilisation. Its purpose is decision support, i.e. to allow decisions to be made on the workfloor about production, in the warehouse about parts stocking and supply, and in the office about the management of orders. Working, for the setup as a whole, is identifying needs for data and considering information obtained (including iteratively). The users are in different locations and may have different typical needs, but from the system's point of view they all have the same role, namely as submitters of queries, and category, as they are all habitual users. Their own aims are to obtain information and make sensible decisions. Their behaviour, within the setup, involves formulating queries, revising them, extracting information from the system's responses, and so forth. (Note that it is possible to extend evaluation so a setup *(i)* embedding a system is treated as a whole for evaluation within a further encompassing setup *(j)*; in this case it is reasonable also to extend the term "function" to refer to setup *i's* function with respect to setup *j*. Setup *i* becomes a kind of abstract 'system'. For example, in the motorbikes case the setup described, with its decision-support purpose offered by the embedded system together with its users, has the external function of allowing effective work flow and control for the company.)

Thus in our example, the system itself, the surrounding setup, and the part the system plays in the setup are all quite complex. It is possible to ask all kinds of evaluative questions: e.g. "Is the information the system provides useful?", "Does the system retrieve the correct data?", "Can the users understand the answers?", "Do they find the system easy to use?", "How well is the parser working?", and many others. Questions like these address different aspects of the whole; but they are also far from specific: what does asking about information utility or parser performance really mean? Before evaluation can proceed it is necessary, first, to be clear about precisely what is being addressed in a performance question: for instance does the question "How easy is the system to use?" refer to the ease with which a natural language question can be formulated, to the readiness with which the system accepts this, or to the simplicity of operation of the terminal during query submission; and second, to be clear about what any attempt to answer the question requires. The next section considers evaluation concepts in more detail.

2 Evaluation

This section introduces some basic, general evaluation concepts, using illustrations from information retrieval and speech processing as well as NLP itself to indicate their nature and implications for NLP evaluation. Thus the first subsection, 2.1, discusses levels of evaluation, and these are motivated by reference to information retrieval, where evaluation is rather better established than in NLP, in 2.2 and 2.3. In subsection 2.4 the illustrative system for database query just described is considered from the evaluation point of view, to bring out the complexities involved. Speech processing is then used in 2.5 to throw further light on the problems of, and possibilities for, NLP evaluation, while the next two subsections consider on the one hand the issues raised by any attempt to evaluate generic systems (2.6), and on the other the potential for evaluation, especially in relation to generic systems, of evaluation benchmarks and other common tools (2.7). The final subsection, 2.8, considers evaluation from the social science point of view, as potentially applicable to NLP systems with their human users.

2.1 Evaluation levels

It is necessary to recognise that different evaluation criteria may apply both to a system in itself and to a system in its setting, and also that evaluation, to be effective, has to be made increasingly precise and rigorous, so criteria have to be instantiated in performance measures and test methods. These points apply whatever the motive for evaluation: thus evaluation is of past performance, but its results may be exploited only for their retrospective information, or as a base for prediction about future setup working or system operation, or as a design and development aid for new setups or systems.

The *criteria* applied in performance evaluation normally fall under two major heads, intrinsic and extrinsic, and may also, under each head, be grouped into broad classes. *Intrinsic* criteria are those relating to a system's objective, *extrinsic* criteria those relating to its function i.e. to its role in relation to its setup's purpose. It is necessary to be careful not only about evaluation ambiguity between a system's intrinsic objective and extrinsic function, but also about ambiguity in relation to the embedding setup, since the setup in turn may be evaluated intrinsically in relation to its purpose, or extrinsically in relation to some other socio-economic concerns. Thus for a translation system, intrinsic criteria could be ones applying to the quality of the translation, and extrinsic criteria those applying to the ease with which post-editors could tweak these, while for the translation setup as a whole intrinsic criteria could refer e.g. to the speed of production of the final translation, and extrinsic criteria to the value/acceptability/utility of the final translations for some purpose such as literature scanning. (These examples emphasise the point made earlier to the effect that setups vary in scope, and that because, for example, classes of system users may fall inside or outside the scope of the evaluation, setup is a relative notion.)

While criteria may be very specific, they are usually more general or even vague e.g. convenience of use, ability to answer questions correctly etc. They thus need to be translated into, or replaced by, specific performance *measures* (in fact a very specific criterion is probably a measure in disguise). For example convenience of use of an interface might be measured by the number of commands per session. The main problem in evaluation is finding measures, i.e. concepts which are both instantiations of generic notions and are operable as measures. Thus for example a single criterion may have to be replaced by a collection of distinct measures. However there is a further necessary step, providing a test *method* for the application of the chosen measure(s). This includes all aspects of experimental design, e.g. how many sessions/people to get numbers of commands used for, and is where statistical issues of sample adequacy and result significance enter evaluation.

To illustrate the need both for these distinct levels in evaluation, and the problems with all of them, it is useful to take an example from a related information processing area where a test and evaluation methodology has been painfully developed over the decades (cf Sparck Jones, 1981; IP&M 1995). The area in question is information retrieval (IR), i.e. document or library retrieval. This illustration emphasises the fact that it may be more pointful to evaluate a setup than just its embedded system, but that even if it is not, it is essential to be clear about what the precise boundary between system and setup is as far as the system's objective goes, and how important it is to take account of the implications of the setup for the system. The illustration will also be used to introduce further evaluation notions referring to types of test, and to the specification of systems for test purposes in terms of the factors affecting system performance and of the system's design goals. Thus performance factors embrace both the system's environment factors determining the values of its data variables and the system's constituent factors as these are defined by its parameters and their settings. The system's design goals are therefore cashed in as the parameter settings intended to match given environment variable values.

2.2 Information retrieval experience

It appears obvious that the objective of a library system, or purpose of a library setup, is to give library users what they need, which may for convenience here be simply referred to as relevant documents. It then follows that the top-level evaluation criterion is that the system or setup succeeds in giving library users what they want. But this obvious aim proves not so obvious on inspection: as users are often seeking information about something they do not already know about, it may be more valuable to think about what they need rather than what they think they want. It is also the case that in general the users of an information service or library will be very varied and will have different types of need, some in fact genuinely well defined needs, i.e. 'I want book B', others much vaguer needs: 'something on topic T' (though part of the service function is to identify T, which may be a considerable distance from the initial expression of it). However it is not enough to specify needs: it is also important to discover

20

why users have these needs, as this bears on how they may be satisfied - this can be taken to imply a notion of real need e.g. two users may both have a need for documents on topic T, but for different contexts of use, so User 1's need becomes topic T modulo X, User 2's need topic T modulo Y. The notion 'need' therefore needs interpreting as 'real need'.

The fundamental problem in retrieval is that what makes a document relevant to a user's need is not a fully accessible and therefore objective fact about the relation between need and document: i.e. relevance is a primitive. This means that any way the system's objective can be stated in a sufficiently concrete form to serve as a base for system design is necessarily an approximation. However quite apart from the central, shared requirement for relevant documents, user's needs can differ in many ways beside those leading to differences in judging relevance based on document content. Thus the first problem which arises is that if users' needs are not merely different but of different types, can the performance criterion - giving users what they need - be unitary (for the evaluability of the service to achieve this), i.e. if need types are different enough, can they all be measured in the same way e.g. using speed of satisfaction? For example User 1 needs any document now, User 2 needs the best document by the end of the week, other users may need books on the shelves to browse through, may need books got by inter-library loan, may need up-to-date documents as soon as possible, and so forth.

These variations in need even under the general rubric 'give the user the documents he needs' clearly make it difficult to get measures for establishing how well a library system, like the automatic indexing and search apparatus of an online search service, or its embedding setup as a whole including e.g. the professional intermediaries conducting searches, is performing. This is not just because the need has to be characterised in a sufficiently concrete way to be accessible to translation into or substitution by a quantitative measure. It is also because measures force further precision, and hence sharper distinctions which may be difficult to assort with the essentially qualitative views users may have of what a system or setup should provide.

Thus suppose that it is accepted that the criterion to be applied in the evaluation of an online search service is its ability to deliver relevant documents given topic descriptions or rather, more strictly, to deliver bibliographic information including abstracts for documents such that judgements of relevance are made on these document surrogates: the question of access to the source documents is a separate matter, and so is, for example, the question of whether the users' topic is modified as the session goes on, etc. Is the system's delivery ability to be measured simply as the number of relevant documents retrieved, regardless of how many non relevant are retrieved, or as 'precision', i.e. the ratio between relevant and retrieved, or as 'recall', the ratio between the relevant retrieved and those (assuming this information is available) relevant but not retrieved? These three measures are quite different, but are equally plausible: thus the third is important because the user may assume recall is better than it is. Moreover, the questions asked so far are only the beginning: going further, should composite measures be used, for instance some function of precision and recall taken together; should there be decomposition e.g. if the system ranks search output, should figures be obtained for each rank level? It is possible to arrive at specific measures which are all individually sensible (intuitively and formally) but which differ as appropriate interpretations of the generic relevance need?

At the third level, given a choice of measure, there has to be a method for applying it. This covers on the one hand a characterisation of its data conditions (e.g. how many sessions, how many different people), and on the other the techniques for averaging, establishing significance, and so forth. In fact, the issues which arise here are as tough as those on the higher levels, e.g. how to establish the recall base when it is impossible to assess the relevance status of every document in the file, how to average across searches with different numbers of search terms, from just one to, say, ten.

The kinds of point involved in establishing an evaluation apparatus apply even if the evaluation is viewed solely as retrospective, but are naturally more important when the evaluation results are to be used predictively for system design, development or modification. They also apply where the performance is being evaluated in what may be labelled investigative or in experimental mode. An *investigation* is typically concerned with an operational system or setup and with establishing its performance characteristics; an *experiment* is designed to answer not the question 'what is happening?', but the question 'what would happen if so and so?'. The transition from one question to the other comes with seeking to answer the question 'why?', and in the accompanying requirement, if the answer is to be sound, for thorough control and comparison. However even if investigation may be less exigent that experiment, it still requires a proper methodology, and thus falls along with experiment under the general heading of *test*, with the consequences for careful definition and conduct that this implies.

The IR examples used hitherto have been drawn from what might be described as the core function of an IR system or setup, and indeed of a library one more generally. Even here, as library evaluation work has shown, evaluation is not only complex in itself, from any point of view: it can also be approached from quite different points of view, e.g. those of user classes, of library staff e.g. cataloguers, of administrators or funding bodies, and so forth. Further, while it may be useful to attempt to provide strictly financial cost/benefit analyses, it is important, quite apart from the difficulty of costing information use, to consider information requirements, goods and services in their own right. When the full range of activities that a library or information centre or service may support is taken into account, moreover, it is evident that performance evaluation can extend in all directions. It thus becomes very difficult to attach any meaning to highly abstract, aggregated, or averaged measures. For instance in many circumstances the notion of an average user is very uninformative.

The development of evaluation techniques for library and information retrieval systems and setups over the last forty years has sharpened the notions of criterion, measure and method while seeking to establish criteria and so forth which are appropriate to the IR case. This has been paralleled by the development of an appropriate descriptive framework and analytic methodology for carrying out evaluations centred on the notion of *performance factors*. This framework has been used to separate the system with its constituent *parameters* and their *settings* from the system's *environment*, i.e. from its setup as seen from the point of view of what is given as properties of or constraints on the system's inputs and outputs. From the test point of view these constraints are taken as data *variables* with *values* which have at least to be descriptively recognised as potentially bearing on test results, though the challenge in IR, as also in NLP, evaluation is not only to identify and describe variables at some generic level, but to capture variables and values in a form that can be directly tied to system working. Thus the distinction between variables and parameters is between external *environment factors* embodying givens from the system designer's point of view, and internal *system factors* embodying the designer's choices, which are together responsible for the system's *effects*. In an investigation of a current system there will in practice be no distinction as all is taken as given, but for experiment the distinction is important since parameter settings may be deliberately changed (as opposed to ensuring, for valid experiment, a good coverage of data variable values). It is often hard to determine what the environmental variables are, and what ranges of values they have, let alone how they interact with system parameters. At the same time, while environmental variables may be viewed as givens, because they interact with system parameters, one of the consequences of system evaluation may very well be modification in the embedding setup, leading to new givens.

A specific example

For example, suppose we have a so-called selective dissemination of information (SDI) - alias routing, filtering - system in a company. Describing this from the evaluation point of view gives us the following (summarised in Figure 5). The system is supplied with document titles and abstracts and uses standing interest profiles for staff members, searches titles plus abstracts for matching word stems, ranks output in descending order of number of matching terms, and circulates titles and abstracts for the top twenty documents to each user once a week. The environment variables here include the subject field of the documents, the journals from which material is taken, the size of the abstracts, the users' interests and their relevance or pertinence notions. Thus the value of the subject field is, say, biochemistry; the value of the journal set is some list of named journals; the value of the users' interests is some topic set, which has generic, range properties like more or less breadth as well as its specific topics, and is also of a particular type, the standing interest profile; the value of the pertinence variable is a range from high to tolerant, and so forth.

The system's parameters include the choice of text area to search, various parameters to do with the nature of the indexing including term form and grounds for selection, the matching coefficient used, the choice and style of output, and so on. The settings for these parameters may then be using abstract as well as title as search field; for indexing using all content words, using stems, stemming on

Selective dissemination of information (SDI) in a company

environment

```
 - variables :  subject      - value  : biochemistry
                literature            : journal
                                        J Biochem Soc,
                                        Nature, ...
                form                  : titles and abstracts
                interests             : standing profile
                                        broad
                                        P1 = 'enzymes', P2 ...
                relevance             : high to moderate
```

system

```
 - parameter :  search field   - setting : title plus abstract
             :  index style
                word form                 : stem (type t)
                word selection            : all non-function
             :  matching mode             : counting common terms
                                             & ranking
             :  output form               : top twenty, titles
                                             and abstracts
 function    :  supply documents with information relevant to
                needs
 objective   :  deliver best documents for queries
 design goal :  at least one good document in top five
```

Fig. 5. Illustration of IR system variables and parameters

some particular basis; taking a simple count of common terms as the matching coefficient and ranking by score; limiting output to the best matching twenty; providing the user with abstract and title to inspect.

There are other variables and parameters. For evaluation all have to be specified, and with the necessary degree of preciseness, for example the particular area of biochemistry if there is one: part of the evaluation effort is precisely in establishing environment and system factors so proper coverage and specificity is achieved, for instance what is the language makeup of the document file, does the user get the best twenty in rank order or just as a set? The illustrative parameter settings seem rational, but there are many other superficially plausible, or in fact well-motivated ones: these include fine-grained differences, e.g. concerning

24

stemming, or coarse-grained ones like the choice of search field (using abstracts as well as titles can improve the recall measure at the expense of the precision one). Some system factors, like term weighting, subsume both, as in the choice of one formal coefficient rather than another, and of one information base for weighting rather than another. It is also easy to see that the environment values could be not merely different in fact, but could be deliberately altered, say to change journal coverage.

The challenge of attributing features of performance to variable values or parameter settings is well illustrated by the subject area variable: what does it mean for system design and performance to have biochemistry documents? Can this variable be precisely characterised, presumably decompositionally into the nature of the language used, the homogeneity or heterogeneity of the documents, etc? What are the language subvariables? What does it mean to refer to the language as technical: does it mean words have only one sense? If the documents are homogeneous does it mean they use the same language or are about the same things, or have the same style? Is there a relationship, and if so precisely what is the relationship between, say, the homogeneity of the documents and the forms of indexing and matching that influences performance, and if so how does it influence performance? For instance, is there some relationship between homogeneity and the exhaustivity (length) of index descriptions which implies that making them more or less exhaustive would improve performance? Would it always improve performance or only for some user's types of need or views of relevance?

The experience of IR, especially that following from the attempt to do indexing and retrieval automatically in novel ways, has also served to emphasise the need for fully characterised *design goals*, representing the specific interpretation, for system implementation, of a system's objective(s). Thus if a system's objective is the generic one of delivering documents relevant to users' needs, this may be interpreted as a design goal, for a system delivering document citations in rank order of matches between a request and document descriptions, to mean: deliver at least one relevant citation in the top five ranks. The evaluation criterion when applied as a measure of system performance has then to explicitly ask whether this goal has to be met for *every* request. Constructing the system to meet the design goal, however, is where a decision about the matching coefficient to use is made. There is thus an intimate relationship between objectives and their restatements as design goals on the one hand, and criteria and their instantiations as measures on the other, since the outcome of evaluation feeds back into the characterisation of objectives.

The test methodology established in the IR field has resulted in reasonable test practices (even if they are less than ideal and not always adopted) in relation to the needs for variation and comparison on variables and parameters, and for adequate sampling. These practices refer to individual tests (or rather groups of subtests): practices have also been developed, though they again are far from ideal and are not always followed, which are designed to promote consistency and comparability on the larger scale, through the use of, for instance, common measures, common *baselines* or *benchmarks* (e.g. 'rock bottom' or 'par' indexing and searching strategies) or other paradigms (e.g. 'standard human professional results'), which can be used as performance *exemplars* or *norms* for comparison when alternative or new automatic systems are proposed. Both are combined in the widespread use of *test collections*, i.e. sets of documents, requests, and relevance assessments, which has obvious parallels in the idea that test corpora should be used for NLP system development and evaluation.

The experience obtained in IR is also valuable in another respect. The contrast between between environment variables and system parameters, raises a most important issue in evaluation, namely its *granularity*. This is most clearly seen in experimental comparisons. What is it that is being changed to make the comparison? Is it the least change, namely the setting of a single parameter, or the largest change (assuming there is still no difference in the environment)? In IR it is easy to see different grains, for instance from different bases for stemming keywords to larger ones affecting the whole style of indexing, for example simply coordinated extracted words to assigned complex subject headings. However as the grain size becomes larger what was formerly external environment is internalised: for instance comparing an automatic indexing system with a manual one could mean that the indexing base was changed, the automatic system working from abstracts, the manual from full text; and when automatic and manual searching are also compared this may make it difficult to ensure even the literature seeker's needs are a fixed environment factor for both.

The environment/system contrast has obvious connections with the conventional contrast between *black box* and *glass box* evaluation, where the former considers only system input-output relations without regard to the specific mechanisms by which the outputs were obtained while the latter examines the mechanisms linking input and output. However it is important to emphasise that while black box testing may be more concerned with the effects of changes to environment variable values where glass box testing focusses on the consequences of altering system parameter settings, either form of evaluation refers to both environment variables and system parameters.

It is convenient to think, though only informally, of different grain sizes as representing different levels in a parameter tree, so fine-comparisons are at the leaf level and coarse-grain ones refer to higher levels in the tree. This also has the advantage of fitting with the way factors may fall into classes, for instance in IR for requests or for documents. The tree analogy emphasises the point, already noted in Section 1, that it is essential to be clear, in drawing conclusions about the results of comparisons, about exactly what is being compared or, in other words, about where the boundary between environment and system is. It is vital, in particular, not to draw more specific conclusions than the grain of the comparison will warrant. Thus in the IR case, it was learnt that it was not legitimate to conclude that manual indexing was superior to automatic just by comparing whole retrieval 'systems' since these could differ in many ways apart from the manner of indexing. All that could be concluded was that the results were associated with having 'systems' that differed in *all* the parameter settings where they did. But given the dependencies among parameters, it was impossible to attribute responsibility more precisely. Moreover, even the global conclusion was contingent on whatever the actual environment was, say the same document collection (and hence subject matter etc). It was clearly necessary then to make further comparisons against different values of these environment variables. Thus research designed to gather sufficiently precise information about retrieval system behaviour through comparative evaluation came to combine two things: pushing further down the parameter tree for a factor of interest with systematically ranging over different values of what were now environment variables in the rest of the tree. It was then possible to establish what differences in parameters and in variables were associated with real performance differences (or, equally importantly, were not associated with any performance effects), and therefore to design systems suited to any specific, independently determined environment variables, like the nature of a subject literature, where these affect performance.

All this led naturally in IR testing, and especially in laboratory experiment, to the notion of a *run*, namely carrying through whatever a system's (or its manual analogue's) process is, for instance of complete search for a literature request under a particular set of environment constraints and parameter settings. In fact runs were normally for sets, notably request sets, since individual request results are of no value as system performance indicators: run results and performance measures were therefore averages. Clearly, the notion of run relates to whatever level of distinction is involved in some comparative evaluation. The important point, however, is that proper IR experiment required whole series of complementary runs: changing system parameters against constant environments, and changing environments while holding the system constant, in a *grid* design for a set of tests. The challenge in experimental design was therefore of minimising the number of runs needed to guard against the effects of hidden variable or parameter dependencies: this stimulated the construction and use of test collections, for example to allow comparisons between indexing in physics and in philosophy. It is of course not always possible to hold systems absolutely constant, for instance the actual subject classes when indexing in different areas like physics and philosphy: constancy here means working with classifications for physics and philosophy constructed and applied on the same principles.

The applications of these ideas to NLP are obvious. For instance given a translation system, a low-level parameter change might be to the treatment of adverbs in the grammar, a higher level one the substitution of one whole grammar for another, a yet higher-level one a quite different division of interpretive effort betwen syntax and semantics or a quite different form of meaning representation. The grain size would be further enlarged, and invade the environment associated with this system, if the system along with its low-profile human post-editors were compared with a full-scale machine-aided translation setup: as this example makes clear, enlarging the grain size may naturally lead to setup rather than system comparison. Alternatively, reverting to the original translation system, comparisons between different environments depending on the nature of its intended application could be on the one hand between translating titles (not normally 'running text') and abstracts (as running text), and on the other between translating food handling regulations and translating employment legislation.

2.3 Applicability to NLP

It seems clear, especially when considering library or information setups as wholes and from the point of view of the properties of their user communities, that the concepts and methodologies of economic and social research are relevant, whatever problems there may be in capturing and quantifying information. At the same time, both much of the system and setup characterisation that is needed to underpin economic and social evaluation, and all the more particular characterisation of objects (e.g. books) and processes (e.g. indexing) needed to evaluate the central distinctive area of information system and setup performance, depend on the development and application of concepts that are appropriate to this particular field, for example of information need and indexing function.

But though there are clearly distinctive elements in IR evaluation, there is much to be learnt for NLP evaluation from the experience of performance evaluation in the library and information area, particularly the latter. Evaluating library services, as expensive invisibles, has long been a matter of concern. Performance evaluation for computer-based information services has grown with the development of these services, since the benefits and costs of doing things in new ways call for assessment, and though the techniques used are far from perfect, and are often imperfectly applied, there are sufficient similarities between the information management and NLP area for it to be worth taking advantage for NLP evaluation of any experience gained in information management evaluation, which has a longer history.

The recent explosion of information provision on the Internet, and growth of end-user information seeking, is indeed posing new challenges for IR evaluation which attempts to cover, rather than exclude, the effects of user interaction. But though there is less established evaluation expertise to refer to here, the longer IR evaluation history (including as is does some observation of manual searching) suggests that IR may precede NLP in developing methodology here too which will be pertinent to the many interactive applications in which NLP will be involved in the future. At the same time, this IR experience will be of value in drawing attention to the fact that in the information technology world the tasks change their shapes for users, and that assumptions about environments based on non-automatic versions of tasks need to be rooted out and system environments freshly and carefully analysed.

Overall, the similarity between information management and NLP task(s) lies not so much in the common use of natural language (though this may be one underlying cause of the resemblance), as in the character of the tasks involved. This is well illustrated by abstracting, which is a challenging NLP task but is related to indexing, a key information management task: indexing or document description can be seen as a very simple form of abstracting, though it has to meet other requirements for document access as well.

The challenge for indexing is that it has to ensure that documents are retrieved that are relevant to some future unspecified and quite possibly underspecifiable need. Evaluating retrieval system performance in principle calls for the users' judgements about relevance, which, whether or not they can be objectively characterised in that context, are essentially transient, as they refer to the users' then state of need and knowledge. Relevance judgements are thus especially precarious in online search situations. Evaluating abstracting, and so systems for automatic abstracting, presents the same problem as IR, but in spades (Sparck Jones, 1990). The nature of the need an abstract is intended to meet, or actually meets, is as vague as or even vaguer and is at least as transient as a retrieval need; at the same time, an abstract is intrinsically more complex than an index description, so principles for obtaining a good abstract (e.g. 'pick up key concepts') are very vague and therefore difficult to operationalize. Further, attempting to discover those elements of an automatic abstracting system that are responsible for observed specific features of the abstract produced is a challenge, even assuming these features can themselves be identified as responsible for properties of measured performance. (The analogy in indexing would be with an analysis of the effect of individual terms.) Thus from an experimental point of view in particular, carrying out enough tests in a sufficiently controlled way to establish how an automatic abstracting system is working, and why it is working in this way, is a major enterprize. The investigation of FRUMP (DeJong, 1982) was more substantial than most that have been done for NLP systems, certainly until recently, but was still very informal, relying heavily on intuitive judgements about whether key concepts in sources were (adequately) captured in the summaries, and there was no setup evaluation with real users.

Given these general relationships between NLP and IR derived from the fact that both deal in language, meaning, information and communication, there are two possible ways in which IR experience might be exploited for NLP evaluation. One is to seek to make direct use of any worked-through analyses and operationalised interpretations of key 'entities' and processes like information content, need, or searching wherever they might seem to be applicable. Where NLP has been advocated for document retrieval purposes, e.g. for indexing, the results have to be evaluated strictly from the IR point of view. But there may be other forms of information characterisation and retrieval, for instance in message processing for information extraction, which may need their own specific forms of evaluation but in which the nature of needs and their satisfaction can be approached using library and information retrieval experience as a starting point.

The other potential use of IR experience is in applying test methodologies and especially those developed for controlled experiments, for instance in decomposing system environments into their constituent factors insofar as these refer to linguistic material and in establishing data samples, say for the adequate coverage of text types. Similarly, IR findings about the size and character of samples of information requests would apply in many interactive NLP situations, for example with database query.

2.4 NLP evaluation example

It will be evident now that for any individual NLP system and its setup, evaluation can be approached from various points of view with varied implications for the conduct of any evaluation and the lessons to be drawn from it. The third chapter of this book will consider these problems in detail, but it is useful to give a first indication of the complexities involved now. This section therefore takes the illustrative system described in Section 1.4 and considers it from the point of view of the evaluation concepts introduced so far. This extended discussion will be particularly concerned with the way what is to be evaluated changes with the progressive reduction of the scope of the setup in which the system is embedded.

Thus in an evaluation situation, as in the illustrative case, there are several potential evaluation *subjects*. There is a setup which can be taken as a whole for evaluation, either intrinsically in relation to its specified purpose or extrinsically in relation to criteria derived from some extraneous requirement. A setup may also be evaluated in either black box or glass box manner, but if the focus is on the performance of the setup as a whole, the automated system within it will be just one element among many in the whole. However as soon as the system itself becomes the prime focus of attention this brings a shift of perspective. The system can again be evaluated either intrinsically in relation to its specified objectives or extrinsically in relation to the embedding setup. However the setup has now to be viewed as providing the environmental data variables which constrain the system.

The sequence of views of the illustrative NLP system we will consider here shows how intricate the relations between the system and the other constituents of its setup in evaluation are; how criteria can change with changes in setup (and indeed also system), either because quite different criteria are appropriate or because, when one setup is included in another, there are transformation effects as criteria are reinterpreted are applicable to a particular setup, for instance when 'outer' criteria are reapplied as 'inner' ones. However while it may seem natural in many cases to think of a series of setups centred on a system as if they were simply included in one another, and the illustration will start with a progression inwards from wider-scope setup to narrower-scope setup in this way, it will become apparent that this is far too simple an approach.

The entire example is summarised in Figures 6 and 7. It cannot be emphasised too strongly, however, that all the specific instances of purposes, objectives, criteria and so forth given below are only a few selected illustrations, and that the way they are characterised in the figure is necessarily very brief: any actual evaluation along the lines indicated would involve both far more elements and a far more detailed breakdown of each. (It should be noted that any setup inclusion relations in Figure 7 refer only to users, not to setup purposes and functions.)

The treatment below is relatively informal. In Chapter 3 we return, after surveying work on evaluation, to illustration with a more systematic presen-

NL database query within a company plant for producing custom
motorbikes, providing information about warehouse stocks for
warehouse, production workfloor and finance office

SETUP 4

```
system          :  entire dbms with various interfaces,
                     subsuming NLP database query system
(objective      :  manage data)
(function       :  meet information needs)
users           :  people involved in any way with dbms,
                     subsuming users making NL database queries
setup purpose   :  a) assist warehouse management
                   b) assist bike production
                   c) assist financial control
int criteria    :  a) utility for warehouse management
                   b) utility for bike production
                   c) utility for financial control
measure         :  c) 10% ratio stocks to current orders
method          :  c) applied 9 am each Monday

(ext criteria   :  effectiveness for company policy making)
```

SETUP 3

```
system          :  dbms with NL query interface
users           :  those using NL interface in warehouse,
                     workfloor, office
(objective      :  answer data queries)
(function       :  meet data needs)
setup purpose   :  a) assist smooth production workflow
                   b) provide convenient inquiry for users
                   c) provide informative data to users
int criteria    :  a) promotes timely parts arrival on workfloor
                   b) provides information whenever needed
                   c) makes inquiry easy
                   d) gives comprehensible data
measure         :  a) consistency for workfloor parts requests
                         and arrivals
                   b) proportion occasions system down
method          :  a) matching on random 10% of pairs
                   b) random user sample
```
                                                   / CONTD ...

Fig. 6. NLP evaluation example: 'Motorbikes'

SETUP 2

2A)   data query aspect

```
system            :  dbms with NL query interface
users             :  those submitting queries from workfloor
(objective        :  answer data queries)
(function         :  meet data needs)
setup purpose     :  a) satisfy information needs
                     b) provide correct information
                     c) provide convenient inquiry
                     d) provide comprehensible data
                     e) give job satisfaction
int criteria      :  a) meets information needs
                     b) gives correct information
                     c) offers convenient inquiry
                     d) shows data fully and clearly
                     e) promotes positive attitude
measure           :  c) number of preliminary exchanges per
                           database search
                     e) percent query time users whistle or sing
                           cheerily
method            :  c) logging at random terminals on random days
                     e) recording Monday mornings, Thursday
                           afternoons

environment variable  :  amount of user training
```

2B)   data entry aspect

```
system            :  dbms with entry interface
users             :  data inputters (in warehouse)
setup purpose     :  provide correct data
int criteria      :  have correct data
measure           :  correspondence of database with warehouse
                        holdings
method            :  check random parts classes on random days
```

/ CONTD ...

Fig. 6. NLP evaluation example: 'Motorbikes'

SETUP 1

```
  system          :  dbms with NL query interface
  users           :  those submitting queries from workfloor
 (objective       :  answer data queries)
 (function        :  meet data needs)
  setup purpose   :  a) satisfy information needs
                     b) provide convenient inquiry
                     c) provide comprehensible data
                     d) provide timely response
  int criteria    :  a) meets information needs
                     b) offers convenient inquiry
                     c) shows data in suitable language
                     d) responds in timely fashion
  measure         :  b) questionnaire
                     d) start query time to answer time
  method          :  b) all users
                     d) random sessions

environment variable    :  database correctness
```

SYSTEM

```
  system          :  dbms with NL query interface
  objective       :  answer data queries cooperatively
  function        :  meet data needs
  environment     :  = Setup 2A, users, queries etc
  ext criteria    :  a) success in meeting data needs
                     b) is cooperative
  measure         :  a) agreement stated needs and assessed
                           answers
                     b) paraphrase requests, by query types
  method          :  a) week's sessions, inspector filtered
                     b) random sample
  int criteria    :  answers queries appropriately
  measure         :  proportion queries suitably answered
  method          :  only queries after clarification
```

/ CONTD ...

Fig. 6. NLP evaluation example: 'Motorbikes'

L-SUBSYSTEM

```
subsystem      :  NL interface
objective      :  interpret input, generate output
function       :  support NL data seeking
environment    :  a) users in Setup (e.g. Setup 1)
                  b) data retrieval n-subsystem
ext criteria   :  a) handles language
                  b) conducts dialogue
                  c) produces acceptable datalanguage queries
measure        :  a) proportion linguistic outputs accepted
method         :  a) observer checking
measure        :  b) incidence datalanguage failures
method         :  b) random days
int criteria   :  construct smooth text output for data
measure        :  percent 'missing' pronouns
method         :  all answers, typed by complexity
```

L-COMPONENT

```
component      :  lexicon
objective      :  provide word data
function       :  support interpretation and generation
environment    :  rest of l-system
ext criteria   :  meets parser needs
measure        :  percent parsing failures due lexical data
method         :  inspection random sample failed parses
int criteria   :  correct lexical retrieval
measure        :  percent input word lexical entry mismatches
method         :  trial using all words in vocabulary with
                     sense specified
```

Fig. 6. NLP evaluation example: 'Motorbikes'

tation of a different example using a more explicit list of analytical headings. These cover an evaluation *remit* and evaluation *design*, especially referring to the former where, for instance, informal notions like point of view (on evaluation) which we have so far used without a definition are broken down. These later examples further illustrate the general idea of evaluation subject *decomposition* in the *unpacking* process which embodies an evaluation *strategy* and delivers the *scenario* for an evaluation.

```
********
* syn  *
* sem  *                                        comp
*  etc *
*      *
*******************************                 system
* 1-  * n-              *                        (NL rel)
*  sys * sys            *                        subsys
*      *                *
*********************************************************************
* stat  * NL    * term * retr * data  * update *
*  rout * inter *      * rout * base  *  rout  *                system
* &     * face  *      *      *       * &      *                (global
* interf *      *      *      *       * interf *                 dbms)
*       *       *      *      *       *        *
*********************************************************************
*********************************************************************
*      ***              **      **
*      ***   e.g. comms **      **              apparatus
*      ***              **      **
*********************************************************************
*      ***              **      **
*      ***   SETUP 1    **      **
*      ***              **      ** work-
*      *******************************  ** floor
*      **               *        ** (ware-
*      **      SETUP 2   *        ** house)
*      **               *        **
*      ***********************************  setups
*      *                *        *
*      *       SETUP 3   *        * work-
*      *                *        * floor
*      *******************************  * ware-
*      *                          * house
*              SETUP 4            * office
*                                *
****************************************************
```

Fig. 7. Diagram of setup and system relations for NLP evaluation example

35

Surrounding setups

Thus we suppose that we have, as in Section 1.4, a system for natural language database query in a plant for producing custom motorbikes. We will, however, assume here that the system deals only with warehouse stocks, and not also with the progress of production orders. As before, the system's own objective is to interpret and answer questions like "Are there any chrome pedals in stock?", coming from various places including the production workfloor: this is not just a 'database department' system. The system's function in relation to any encompassing setup is to provide information about the state of the warehouse's stocks, where the setup in turn can have its own internal purposes (and also external functions) within the whole plant and company in relation not only to the actual manufacturing operation itself where parts are consumed, but also to the ordering of new parts for the warehouse from the suppliers, and to policies and operations concerned with cash flow etc.

Setup 4

Now starting with a broad-scope setup, Setup 4 in Figure 6, one might imagine extrinsic criteria refering to general company policy (e.g. profitability). But more realistically, taking criteria intrinsic to the setup but independent of the system, these might still not bear in any direct way or at all on the users actually submitting natural language queries, but apply to concerns of financial staff interested in the balances between orders and stocks who actually access the database through some other aggregative, statistical software package. Thus the database query system is seen as one system resource among several serving the financial department whose activities are within the setup. Other criteria could concern both NLP users and other staff because of their implications, for instance those relating to workflows and the implications of inefficiencies in these for company finances: these would be extrinsic criteria for the system.

Setup 3

Limiting the setup to those who are actually NLP users, shown as Setup 3 in Figure 6, can still invoke extrinsic or more importantly intrinsic criteria applying to a whole larger set of activities together defining the working setup, for instance the maintenance of workflow in the workshop. These criteria might cover all aspects of the DBMS including its data correctness, completeness and currency, since database queries concerning parts required for the workshop and the replies received bears on workflow and may have consequences as idle time in the workshop if parts are not to hand when needed. But we will suppose here that the setup's purpose is to be able to obtain information when needed, so insofar as the DBMS is concerned, this means software and hardware reliability with respect to database state maintenance and retrieval operations and well as the reliability of the query system proper. At this setup level, however, reliability means having people capable of using the natural language interface sensibly as well as having a crash-free system. It is also possible to consider criteria more strictly relating to the query system's setup but still extrinsic to it: these include, for instance, ease of use, since user hostility to a system can clearly have implications for management, and also criteria concerned with whether the user correctly understands, or misunderstands, what the system is doing, since errors leading, for example, to wrong parts reaching the production line can be costly.

The important point in these possible different setups is that they subsume other activities, and in particular other human activities, which depend on human query interaction with the database but do so only contingently and typically very indirectly. The setups are relevant because the database query system has a functional role within them, but the contingency makes whether it serves its function properly in making its contribution to whatever any setup's purpose very hard to determine. Any performance evaluation of a setup involving the query system will be a complex matter in which it is necessary first to factor out the database-using setup from other aspects of the manufacturing and management operations constituting the relevant area of the organisation's operations e.g. all the company's day-to-day financial management operations. There will then be the challenge of defining appropriate evaluation criteria refering to the setup's purposes, for instance for Setup 4 of assisting the production process of getting motorbikes made, or assisting financial control, and specifically here with helping in warehouse stock management from a cash flow point of view. Thus one instrinsic criterion for the latter in Setup 4 could be that the DBMS as a whole, with the query facility as one constituent but also with the actual database as another, allows optimal warehouse stockholding. There is then the further challenge of providing specific measures of optimal stockholding, etc, and of methods for applying these: for example optimality could be defined as not having more in the value of held stock then ten percent of the value of current orders, and the method of applying the measure could be by determining these two values as at 9am every Monday. Similarly for Setup 3, given the setup's purpose of maintaining a smooth workflow, this could be interpreted as a measure by checking for consistency between the orders for parts transmitted from the workfloor to the warehouse as a result of the answers to workfloor queries about the stocks held, and the parts received; and the method of applying the measure could be by inspecting a randomly chosen percentage of pairs. In both of these examples the criteria are intrinsic to the setup but not extrinsic to the system since non-system elements are directly involved, e.g. in the latter case the people doing the part delivery. However for the setup's purpose of providing information whenever needed, a measure of this could be the proportion of time users sought information and the system was down, applied to a random sample of user approaches, suitably trapped. This would be an extrinsic criterion for the system alone.

Setup 2

Now focussing more narrowly on the immediate database-using setup and, we will suppose, on the workfloor only, from the intrinsic evaluation point of view this has three major elements: the people involved, the equipment, including both the system and other apparatus, and the data. These will have to be characterised in detail to provide the setup's internal factors, both to motivate the choice of evaluation criteria and to support the detailed investigation of the setup's working, for example the experience of the users, reliability of the apparatus (e.g. here, the plant communications network). These will be dependent on environment factors for the setup itself, like staff training or funding for equipment, or on the transmission of stock arrival information from the warehouse receiving dock.

The analysis of the database-using setup would naturally look at the properties of the users submitting queries, for instance the types of user needs stimulating queries. Criteria here would thus refer to the satisfaction of types of user need; again, for different types of user (e.g. frequent or casual) evaluation could address ease of system use, including many aspects of the terminal as the point of user-system communication: this can cover germane properties of the hardware, for example screen legibility on the workfloor, as well as strictly NLP-related screen content affecting the comprehensibility of the system's output, for example. If we suppose that one purpose of the setup is to provide a convenient mode of inquiry about stocks, so one evaluation criterion is that the system is easy to use, then one measure of this could be the number of exchanges between user and system before the database is actually searched, assuming longer exchange sequences mean more difficulty in query submission. The associated method could be random logging of terminals designed to avoid individual user biases. This would be an intrinsic criterion for the setup, and an extrinsic one for the system: the assumption on which the actual measure is based would of course have to be justified by reference to the system design for the conduct of dialogues, as long exchanges could mean something quite different.

But now if we are assuming that the purpose of the setup just described includes that of providing correct data, then even though we are adopting a quite restricted view of the database-using setup, we cannot in fact confine ourselves to the query mode only, even if this covers correct interpretation of and hence response to queries. Being concerned with data quality implies that the database query system cannot really separated from the management of the database as a whole, i.e. from the provision of its content, so evaluating the database setup, even if this is quite narowly defined, would have to cover the data entry side (in the warehouse) and would have to address ways of determining data correctness and currency. However it would then also, as it analogously does for the query community proper, have to look at the resources provided for data entry, for example format displays. We thus have a setup, Setup 2 in Figure 6, with the two constituents labelled 2A and 2B, which is not simply included in Setup 3: even its query side, 2A is not so included, as providing correct data is not a stated purpose of Setup 3. If it was, then Setup 3 would also have to be extended to cover the data entry side, and it would then include Setup 2.

It is thus clear that even on a fairly narrow view of the database-using setup, characterising it as a whole in sufficient detail to support rigorous evaluation is not a trivial matter. It is already clear that even with a restricted setup like the database one, global statements about overall performance, however intuitively informative, can only be very general, and that at this level of evaluation single numerical measures of performance are essentially meaningless. It is also clear that while one may have wide or narrow scope setups, one may at the same time have *wide bound* or *narrow bound* evaluation, [4] where there may not be any simple relationship between breadth of scope and of bound. And it is further clear that there may be very complex relationships between the purposes even of setups with much in common, and similarly between their respective evaluation criteria. There is in particular no simple trend towards more specific purposes and more refined criteria as setups become 'smaller'. Even with a limited setup like the database one, investigating performance involves decomposition into subworkings that are causally related but have their own distinct character and subcriteria. Thus while the purpose of the database query setup is to correctly provide correct data when sought, looking at the correctness of the data leads to an investigation of the data entry activity and may have to engage with the behaviour of those 'users' doing data entry. Clearly the purpose of that subsetup will be just to provide a correct, current etc database, i.e. will be different from that of the query-only subsetup, and it is evident that the specific study of this setup will be quite different from the detailed study of the query subsetup. The example brings out the fact that any idea of concentric setups is a gross oversimplification: Setups 3 and 2, and the two constituents of Setup 2 have all kinds of overlap, even at the system level where they may share parts, but not all, of the complete DBMS system, as the query users and data entry uses have distinct interfaces.

The example also emphasises the fact that evaluation can be conducted from very different *angles*, and hence with very different *goals*. The presumption so far has been that for whatever system or setup being considered, performance can be evaluated in relation to some obvious stated objective or purpose, and can also be taken as referring to some broad notion of 'effectiveness' or, perhaps, 'efficiency'. But while the evaluation of the database setup as a whole might, as one possibility for Setup 2 above, consider only the reliability of the database information provision, an alternative evaluation could be from a different angle and adopt the different criterion of providing job satisfaction, and look at the (i.e. a) purpose of the database setup as encouraging a feeling of understanding and being responsible for the company's activities. Thus it is important to allow, though this may in fact imply different characterisations of purpose, that evaluation of a setup can be from very different angles, as well as for the fact that whatever the top-level angle is, evaluation may require decomposition into subsetups with their own different flavours.

At the same time, it is useful to recognise that there can be different *perspectives* on evaluation, i.e. aspects under which the subject of evaluation is seen, for instance financial or scientific; and there may be different *interests* in evaluation associated with different categories evaluation promoters, e.g. developers, funders, as well as classes of *consumer* of the evaluation results, e.g. users, researchers. There may of course be overlap among these, e.g. a system developer can be both promoter and consumer, but all three can affect the choice of evaluation criteria as well as of what about the system or setup is submitted for evaluation.

---

[4] Not the same as black box and glass box evaluation.

Setup 1

Suppose, however, that we now do confine ourselves only to the yet narrower setup for query from the workfloor, so database provision is an environment factor for this. We have to look in detail at the properties of the query user community like information needs or familiarity with the database material, at properties of the terminal used for interaction, and for the evaluative investigation, study users behaviour in conducting their activities as well as the system's own operation. If the purpose of this specific setup is to provide the appropriate (supposedly correct) answers to the questions representing the users needs, and to do this in a convenient way, one aspect of how the query setup performs in relation to its purpose will thus refer to such matters as comprehensible dialogue mechanisms for query checking, clarification and repair. But it is clear that measures and methods for determining how helpful recovery dialogues are are not easily devised. Is measurement to be by reference to the user's view, with a questionnaire as the method? This is suitably comprehensive, but not very precise. Or is it to be by, say, looking at the relationship between the system's requests for query paraphrases by the user and query sessions, for a suitable sample of sessions?

Timely response may also be a purpose. It seems an obvious one: provide information quickly when it is needed on the workfloor; and it looks easy to translate into an evaluation criterion and find a suitable measure, for instance average time from submitted query to answer. But perhaps it is better to take the time from the beginning of a user query formulation session to the time of answer, to allow for the user's not getting an acceptable question first off. The method problem here, however, if this is to be done by automatic logging, is being able to clearly identify the session associated with a single query or, alternatively, need: it might even be difficult to identify a single, permanently connected and open terminal.

Timeliness illustrates the main issues about evaluation very well. It may or may not be a declared setup purpose, for example for Setup 4 it might not be. At least, it may not be a purpose from the general angle being adopted in evaluation, for instance it might or might not be so in an evaluation devoted to job satisfaction. Timeliness is not necessarily very easily defined, as just indicated, and may have quite different interpretations in different setups, for example in the finance office and on the workfloor. Nor does it follow, with a wide scope setup or wide bound evaluation, that it will be a vague notion or alternatively one requiring disaggregation into more specific notions. While there may often be a process of increased specialisation as setups or evaluations become narrower, in general each setup and evaluation has to be treated as independent, with its own purposes and criteria. At the same time the examples so far show that in each case, global criteria like effectiveness have to be given a precise meaning, which may not be easy and in particular may lead to the use of a whole collection of more particular criteria and measures which are not easy to combine in a valid or informative way, for example convenience and time in the database query case.

System proper

We now come to the evaluation of the system proper. For this we have to separate the properties of the user community from those of the system, and to treat properties of the user community (or perhaps communities) as environmental variables. The properties of the community may include, for example, literacy (because this may give rise to spelling mistakes), frequency of use (because of habituation to language forms), and work need (because of query types). They have to be sufficiently precisely defined to make the connection, through the system's design goals, with its parameter specification. Thus needs may be treated as query types, but these have in turn to be characterised in some system-relevant way, for instance in terms of the complexity of their entity-attribute descriptions. These environmental factors will appear as both input and output variable values constraining the system's effects. User properties may have quite remote consequences, for example literacy or ignorance of the database content: thus illiteracy can lead to undetected wrong answers through query misintepretation. [5]

In fact, environments are a matter of choice: for instance in evaluation even from the query point of view, where it may seem obvious that the system environment should include a specification of the properties of the database in terms of its expected correctness, completeness and currency (as well as of its more obvious properties like size and density), it need not do so: as we have seen, evaluation of query management from some points of view can simply treat the database as whatever is held in the DBMS and focus on the system's responses to actually submitted queries regardless of the presumptions these embody about the correctness of the file? The important point here is that the notion of environment is more rigorous than that of setup: in order to understand the system's operations within its setup, the setup has either to explicitly subsume or explicitly exclude, database supply in relation to the evaluation of system performance from the query point of view.

Thus suppose we take the environment for the system to be that associated with Setup 2: then the environment variable for query type will include the value simple, for such cases as "Have we any saddles?" or "Have we two P41 footrests?" We have to define the system's objectives, for example to supply correct answers to questions, which may include not only specific questions of the kind just given but ones of a 'display' type giving whole files as for "What engines have we?"; and also to support natural language interaction in cooperative way, which of course requires a more precise definition, e.g. always to offer a constructive response however awful the input.

The system's function in its setup is to provide the user on the workfloor with the information he seeks. Extrinsic criteria would therefore refer to the sys-

---

[5] This remoteness is more obviously seen in the possible consequences of carelessness in data input, which could affect query interpretation through the lexicon, if the lexicon incorporated data values, as well as produce wrong responses.

41

tem's success in doing this, where the measure could be, for example, agreement between the user's initial statement of need before submitting a query to the system and the answer supplied by the system, for needs independently judged 'legitimate' given the scope of the system. If the system's function is to provide the user with easy access to the database, extrinsic evaluation will address much the same points as clarificatory dialogue as intrinsic evaluation for Setup 1, but now in a tighter way with explicit reference to different values of the environmental variables, for example breaking down queries into different types. On the other hand if the system's function is to provide the user with uptodate information, this cannot cover data input: it can only be interpreted, to be valid for the system proper, in relation to e.g. data file updating as a software action.

Turning now to intrinsic criteria, we have again to apply these against constant environmental variables in terms of user properties and data supply conditions. Thus in terms of the system's objective of supplying appropriate (notionally correct) answers, this now refers to actually submitted user queries, not to their underlying needs as the latter apply in the extrinsic evaluation; that is the query properties are taken in their own right as embodying value(s) for the system's query type(s) environmental variable. The evaluation may look at all submitted queries, or only at 'legitimate' ones, say excluding ones 'bounced' by the system or, perhaps more reliably, filtered out by some human inspector, and check these for the appropriateness (i.e. correctness given the database) but without assigning failures to defects in the language processing, data retrieval or database elements of the system, or indeed without investigating whether processing aborted or was carried through with a formally viable but wrong interpretation. Thus a simple measure, for either definition of the scope of input queries, would be the proportion of queries receiving their appropriate answer, or more strictly an appropriate answer, since there could be no reference to what the user intended. The precise form of the measure, and also of its application method, would, however, have to take the system's specific objectives relating to its intended way of dealing with non-straightforward inputs into account, i.e. how is an initially illegitimate query which is successfully blocked and explained to the user to be handled?

There are other methodological questions about e.g. sampling queries for the user population, and also ones concerned with establishing what the answers for a large database ought to be. It is certainly not enough to simply look at the actual answer, because this gives no information about what the answer does not say. Unfortunately, it may be far from easy in practice to establish what the answer ought to have been. In IR this problem has led to the use of relative rather than absolute recall as a measure, and in some database contexts it might be necessary to accept that whatever method was used to identify what the answer ought to have been (for example by using a direct search for an independently-contructed formal query) might only provide a relative, not absolute, standard: much would depend on the specific properties of the database and database software, and also of the latter as exploited by, but independent of, the language processor.

These questions would arise for any particular environment, like that treating all the users as a single population. It might also be useful to proceed to a finer-grained evaluation with different classes of users, distinguishing them as (for the workfloor) habitual or occasional users, and thus obtaining performance measures for a series of separate runs. Again if evaluation was in relation to timeliness as a system objective, which might be interpreted as providing rapid answers, an intrinsic criterion might refer to absolute time - answers to be obtained within 20 seconds, where an extrinsic one would look at times set with reference to workfloor needs, for example speeds required to avoid production delays. Of course, it would be surprising if the system's own internal time objective was not chosen as a design goal on the basis of the system's intended function, illustrating the close connection between objective and function; but the two could nevertheless be stated differently, for example in the one case as a specific fixed time and in the other as 'never causing a production delay', and would thus be reflected by distinct evaluation criteria and methods.

Subsystems and components

L-system

The penultimate step is to separate the language and non-language components of the system, i.e. the l-subsystem from the n-subsystem(s). This involves deciding not only what side of the boundary a domain model should be placed (which is not necessarily a simple matter as it may be a relatively clearly-demarcated module or may be embedded in the lexical and semantic resources of the language processor, even assuming it is obvious what types of knowledge are in principle linguistic or non-linguistic; and in some cases the lower-level data model may be similarly encapsulated in mapping rules). The evaluation criteria which apply to the l-system are obviously those referring to the interpretability of inputs. They also refer to the delivery of answers if the system packages these in natural language, which we assume may be the case depending on the nature of the answer and also, sometimes, in properly generated as opposed to template form. But it is necessary not only to distinguish the l-subsystem from its 'back-end', and to define the essential parameters for this n-system with respect to the l-subsystem one. It is also necessary to separate out the terminal elements of the complete system insofar as they interact with the use of NLP, i.e. to establish the l-subsystem's environmental parameters in relation to external communication with the user.

Thus the situation is complex because we can consider either the l-subsystem function in relation to the user, or in relation to the other parts of the system, i.e. to the n-system. The l-system objective is correctly interpreting input queries and packaging output data, as well as conducting clarification dialogues. This objective reflects its function with respect to its users of accepting natural language queries and delivering natural language answers in a cooperative way, i.e. through natural language dialogue. Thus extrinsic evaluation criteria will refer to its ability to accept natural and deliver natural language, and to conduct dialogue. The former now will have to address the range of language forms and expressions which can be handled, the latter the ability to plan and execute recovery dialogues. The very difficult issue about how the scope of a language processor is defined with respect to 'illegitimate' or 'off-board' inputs is considered in more detail in relation to generic system evaluation in Chapter 2. For the moment we will suppose the l-system has to conduct clarification dialogues relating to inputs which are deemed to fail on lexical or syntactic grounds. Then a measure of performance for the extrinsic criterion of accepting natural language inputs from users might be what proportion of user inputs of any sort are linguistically interpreted, or linguistic outputs are accepted by the user. The latter illustrates the problem of methodology here, as one measure of success, but clearly only apparent and undiscriminating with respect to l-system and n-system, would be no user follow-up seeking explanation: it might therefore be necessary to engage in human checking of the user's perception of the linguistic character of an output e.g. as to what a prepositional phrase modifies.

Intrinsic criteria, on the other hand could include one refering to the system's ability to generate output sentences for retrieved data: could it actually construct the necessary or a proper or a smooth text? This might be measured by the percentage of replies for which the system had to offer raw data because it could not package them (for those replies which would not be served raw anyway) or, for smoothness, by failures to substitute pronouns for full noun phrases. The evaluation method here would have to take account of how taxing the source questions were in terms of retrieving data which was easy or difficult to handle in generation. Evaluation for the l-system with respect to the n-system would look at the extent to which linguistic inputs when transformed into formal search specifications were actually acceptable to the retrieval routines, i.e. were syntactically and semantically sound in datalanguage terms. An obvious environment variable here, operating as a constraint on the l-subsystem's output, would be search specification complexity. Other evaluation criteria and measures here might have to do with the efficiency of the formal specification, measured perhaps by retrieval time compared with independently-constructed formal queries for the original language inputs.

At this level of evaluation, environment variables may be characterised in a fairly specialised and detailed way, for instance for the l-subsystem in relation to its user inputs in terms of types of syntactic form, or the prevalence of heavy compound nouns which can present interpretation problems; input in the form of sentence fragments would be another variable value.

L-components

Finally, considering the internal structure of the l-system alone, we have to decompose it into its component modules, the syntactic component, the semantic component, and the pragmatic component and domain model (insofar as these are deemed part of the l-system), and so forth. We have then, to evaluate any one of them, to specify the environment the others define for it. But again, extrinsic evaluation may be quite multifacetted: for instance one function of the lexicon is to accept input words from the user, and it would then have to be evaluated from the point of view say, of input lexical coverage (by word type or token). However another function of the lexicon, external to it but not internal to the system, is to deliver lexical data to the parser: it can therefore be evaluated in terms of the extent to which it actually delivers the required data about words, and here, further, according to whether the lexicon design is correct, say for classes of words, or the data for some individual word is faulty (for whatever reason). Intrinsic evaluation of the lexicon, on the other hand, would be directed towards the organisation of the lexical data, both from an informational and an access point of view, which could be measured by checking for correct lexical retrieval. Alternatively, given the objective of good coverage, the lexicon could be evaluated by comparison with a large random sample of input vocabulary obtained by a Wizard of Oz experiment with users of a simulated system. (Again, intrinsic and extrinsic criteria could be very similar here, since this objective is very like a system function where performance could be evaluated in a very similar way, but with real inputs, though the latter would raise additional method points about dealing with e.g. misspellings.) Similarly, a pragmatic component intended to support inter-sentential pronoun resolution insofar as this could be done on purely linguistic grounds could be extrinsically evaluated by reference to the proportion of pronouns handed on by a semantic analyser it could resolve, intrinsically by whether, on its own principles, it did the job correctly, i.e. its principles were properly translated into specific rules adequate for the actual inputs encountered. The measure for the latter could either using a reduction in alternative candidates, or unique resolution.

Conclusion on example

In all of the foregoing, as we have been imagining we are dealing with a running database-using system, we have been engaged with an investigation, i.e. with determining what the performance of the system is, and hence, insofar as performance quality can be adequately rated just by comparison with stated objectives and purposes reformulated as criteria, with how good the system's performance is. But as evaluation in IR has shown, this may be very misleading. Thus while the purpose of an IR system may be to deliver all and only relevant documents, so 50% precision and 50% recall does not seem very good, this stated purpose appears unattainable in the real world. It is thus desirable, quite apart from having more realistic norms, to obtain some idea of whether a system's performance is *reasonable* rather than *eccentric*, i.e. whether it is fair given its environmental constraints or is due to idiosyncratic features of the system design. This may not seem necessary if performance in relation to the stated criteria is high, and the criteria are well-accepted; it is much more important if performance seems poor or uninisipired. In this case it is normally necessary to proceed from investigation to experiment, which can be less or more extensive in scale, ranging from within-system component changes, for example of the grammar, to wholesale ones, for example using a completely different l-system. These studies should naturally also extend themselves to comparisons where changes are made to relevant environmental parameters instead, for example, testing different styles of clarificatory dialogue with different user classes.

Finally, though the database case taken here as an example NLP task does illustrate all the essential points about NLP evaluation, testing and evaluation will naturally be rather different for other tasks, like translation. What it may involve for other tasks is, however, conveniently illustrated by the discussion of evaluation work done so far in Chapter 2. Further points about the evaluation of generic systems are also, as mentioned earlier, considered there.

2.5   Speech processing illustrations

An alternative view of the problems evaluating an NLP system can present is provided by considering possibilities in relation to speech processing (SP), where, as noted earlier, evaluation has long been an issue. Looking in detail at this shows the refinement needed at all levels (or over all scopes) of evaluation. In what follows we look at successively more challenging cases, summarised in Figure 8.

Illustration A

Here we suppose the task is transcription of read text. In this case the words are already known, so it is reasonable to interpret a general system criterion called 'accuracy' as the specific measure: percent of words correctly transcribed. If transcribing read text was a genuine external purpose, one would expect a wider contextual evaluation for the setup as a whole to cover e.g. recording convenience and so forth. In the other direction, methods for applying the percent of correct measure would include sampling across repeated readings by the same reader, different readers, different texts and so forth. This covers the essential environmental variables. This type of evaluation is typically a laboratory style one, so comparative experiments would control for different aspects of the speech process (e.g. voice sampling rate, word boundary demarcation strategies etc).

The main evaluation design issue which arises is in establishing clearly the design goals the system is supposed to have, as these define the systems objective in the specific way which is a prerequisite for evaluation, and which is needed to choose sensible criteria, measures and methods. For example, is the system meant to cope with any speaker (e.g. a non-native one?). Again, for wide bound evaluation, as adopted in SUR (Klatt, 1977), performance criteria may be intentionally adopted which make no reference to internal system design: thus it is possible to imagine (for the purposes of illustration) an approach to the read text task which identified word boundaries by acoustic indications, and so did not require a lexicon. A wide bound evaluation would deliberately not consider whether two competing transcriptions systems did or did not use a lexicon. On the other hand, in a narrow bound evaluation for a lexicon-based system, reference could be made to a design goal setting a target percent of words to be captured given an assumed vocabulary coverage in the lexicon: i.e. for a text system it might be expected that some words would never have been encountered before (either as wholes or as morphologically decomposible). Similarly

EXAMPLE A

```
setup        :  (laboratory experiment)
environment  :  text types, speaker types
task         :  transcribe read text
measure      :  percent words recognised
method       :  several readers, several readings
design goal  :  adult speaker, no punctuation
```

EXAMPLE B

```
setup        :  individual in office
environment  :  speaker clarity
task         :  transcribe dictation
measure      :  percent compared human transcription
                  (words only)
method       :  several persons, several dictations
design goal  :  omit coughs
```

EXAMPLE C

```
setup        :  e.g. individual with hands occupied
environment  :  speaker training
task         :  transcribe natural sentences
measure      :  agreement human observed sentences
method       :  several sessions, several observers
design goal  :  word sequences, bound as sentences
```

EXAMPLE D

```
setup        :  e.g. telephone inquiry
environment  :  random speakers, equipment noise
task         :  interpret and respond to inputs
measure      :  dialogue success as absence of 'dead end'
                  "Sorry" stops
method       :  human subjects informed of system data scope
design goal  :  convergent query identification and reply
```

Fig. 8. Speech evaluation illustrations

while focussing on word transcription, it is necessary to have goals about the 'recognition' of coughs and about the treatment of punctuation i.e. of pauses etc: is the transcription to be literally of sounds presumed words only, or to include the provision of punctuation based on e.g. pause length, or to cover the interpretation of spoken punctuation e.g. "comma", of spelled-out words etc (these are requirements, not presumptions about how these will be done)?

Illustration B

Now modify the task slightly, to careful dictation. The immediate methodological issue here is that there is no absolute a priori standard for establishing correctness: there can only be a human transcription (by the dictator or someone else).

There is then a conceptual point for the definition of design goals, namely that normal human transcription will omit coughs or restarts, supply punctuation etc: is this to be a requirement of the automated speech recognition system too, or is its designed goal simply to be to get words down? Dictation is also a more real task than reading, so consideration of setup factors is more significant (as with the Alvey Speech Word Processor Project (cf LD 006, 1985): how is reading and editing of the transcript etc done?). Goals for the treatment of punctuation are a good example of the challenge design goals present and of the need for careful attention to them for evaluation purposes.

Illustration C

Suppose now we consider transcription of natural speech. Whether or not this is a sensible system function for real applications, it may be a reasonable function during system development, or for intermediate technology approaches to speech interpretation/understanding, where this is done as an n-stage process. Even as a freestanding application it presents evaluation problems about design goals and evaluation *standards* for dealing with e.g. false starts, punctuation etc. But it is also evident that when transcription is just a component process in a larger system, evaluation becomes more complex because of the nature of the overall application system task, and of the encompassing setup's purpose and characteristics. For example does the system have to determine the meaning of speech inputs? Is this for human user-system interaction, which may affect discourse chunking for speech interpretation purposes and also notions of grammaticality? Even if the evaluation is focussed on the transcription itself, what performance levels are to be attained which depend on these other factors e.g. on how much meaning may be determined, and hence words identified, from pragmatic/domain world factors: if further work is to be done by the rest of the system, transcription in itself may not have to be of such high quality. Environmental variables mentioned earlier will be even more important e.g. assumptions about user training for the system (say about how carefully they speak).

Illustration D

Finally, suppose we have a task where speech interpretation/understanding is required (i.e. even if processing is two-stage, the concern is with evaluating overall performance, not not just the first transcription-only phase). As in the earlier non speech examples, it is necessary to consider both characteristics of the setup as a whole, and then those of the system more narrowly. For example, suppose we have a speech-driven train inquiry system like VODIS (Young, 1989). It is necessary to consider its function in its complete setup: for instance is it a facility for use as part of a travel agent's business, so how does it contribute to the effectiveness of that business e.g. is using it more efficient than using printed guides or speaking to human inquiry agents (compare the Speaking Timetable). Thus even for the system itself, there will be different environment variable values for the user community according to whether it has travel agents using it regularly or the general public using it occasionally.

However attempting to interpret natural speech presents even harder problems for system evaluation than before, because there are more variables and parameters. This holds even if the overall system task is quite specific e.g. database inquiry, in ways which usefully constrain evaluation criteria, simply because the system as a whole has more to do. Thus for example one criterion for evaluation could be mapping spoken questions onto the same database search specification as corresponding typed inputs (L Hirschman, personal communication, 1991) But this may be too limited, as in the general one would not expect identical spoken and typed behaviour, so success with spoken interpretation without the direct comparability is more difficult to establish. It has to be with any form of the same question content as typed, but then, depending on the nature of the formal query language, optimization etc, one might get different but equivalent formal query expressions, so identical responses and specifically retrieved data might be a better standard. There is a further possibility that if the system allows clarificatory dialogue to establish input meaning unambiguously, 'first off' correct interpretation may not be a very useful performance indicator: one has then to look, e.g., at incidence of the need for clarification. (Note that the experimental methodology required to establish a common agreed question content to be offered to the system either typed or spoken is itself not trivial.)

This last speech case illustrates two further issues. One is evaluating a generic subsystem or component independent of a specific application context, for example the speech component alone if it was an embedded general-purpose transcriber. The complementary problem is how to evaluate any part of an integrated system for the effectiveness of its own contribution.

2.6 Evaluating generic systems

As already noted, there are no existing general-purpose NLP systems, i.e. ones capable of carrying out any task. *Generic systems* are application-independent, and indeed while not task-independent may be designed for a wide range of similar tasks e.g. for supporting interactive inquiry and not just database query. At the sentence processing level they may in fact verge on the general-purpose, though this is partly a matter of definition in relation to the *range* of a language processor in dealing with pragmatics, as discussed further below.

The SRI Core Language Engine (CLE) (Alshawi, 1992) is intentionally a generic NLP system, and the more recently developed Core Language And Reasoning Engine (CLARE) (Alshawi et al, 1992) has a similar status with processing extended to domain reasoning, especially for pragmatic purposes. Though the distinction is essentially arbitrary, it is useful to make a working distinction, for evaluation purposes, between generic shells like the CLE, TEAM (Grosz et al, 1987), or Q&A (Harvey, nd), and generic components exemplified by the Alvey NL Tools (Briscoe, 1992), consisting either of knowledge resources like grammars and lexicons, or of processors like parsers. Generic shells are intended, when instantiated, to subsume all the NLP for a system, and may indeed extend to further task processing. This may cover much of database query bar the actual data store searching, for instance, or allow for substantive reasoning on a model world, as for CLARE.

The problem with generic shells is that it is impossible to evaluate them without a specific instantiating application, but one important practical motivation for seeking evaluative information about shells is in order to decide whether they are appropriate for a given task, or more specifically, application. In so far as a generic shell includes a 'default' content in the form of, for example, a general-purpose lexicon or grammar, it may be possible to do some systematic, if limited, evaluation. However the real difficulty is that proper evaluation requires a well-specified environment and this is just what a generic system lacks, so even intrinsic evaluation presents problems.

The motivation for generic systems is purely practical: it is to save effort by being able to use the same software for different applications. The crucial issues, therefore, are what the range of a generic system is, and also whether there are any costs associated with having one. These are not so much operational costs, though generic systems may not be computationally optimal for any individual application, as costs associated with ensuring that the connectivity between the generic subsystem and the rest of the system is correctly achieved. This may require special effort in characterising the nature of the application-specific information and processes in the way required for the generic system (though it is typically assumed that this explicitness is beneficial all round), and in acquiring the actual application detail: TEAM illustrates these points well.

As suggested earlier, it is reasonable in the current state of the art to see an inverse relationship between generic and general purpose: the more limited the range of a generic system, the more likely it is to be able to function as a general-purpose component, as the comparison between a database front end and a parser suggests. The focus in this section is on generic subsystems intended to carry out a significant part if not all of the NLP for the system as a whole, though the points about generic systems and especially their connectivity requirements also apply to system components, however general purpose they are.

The underlying assumption with generic NLP systems is nevertheless that, within certain limits, or on certain assumptions about the range of language processing, they are essentially general purpose, i.e. they will serve language-processing needs within any task system. The only concession that is made is that some or all of the linguistic data used, e.g. grammar, lexicon, may be application dependent, where it is in turn assumed that the form this must take can be unequivocally specified and the necessary data reliably and perhaps even easily, acquired.

This position appears to be justified as follows. First, if we characterise language processing, and particularly interpretation, as delivering a meaning representation, then the belief seems to be that there is some correct, or at any rate uncontroversial, or even just adequate, representation to be found. The analogue within syntax is that there is a characterisation of syntactic structure and function with the same status.

The second assumption is that many if not all tasks requiring exigent or full NLP depend on this representation, if not exclusively at least substantially. In other words, that the processing for any serious task cannot be carried through without the help of this representation. Thus there is not only a 'true' representation but a generally useful one.

The third assumption is that much of the work of language processing for any task is covered by obtaining (or in generation, working from) this representation, i.e. that its contribution is not merely necessary but large.

Taken together these three assumptions, however practically motivated, may be described as embodying the grammarians' view of language processing. However they have different implications for evaluation. The first claim could be justified by having some independent (humanly established) normative or benchmark representation against which some individual generic shell's performance could be measured. One problem with this is that even within the supposedly better-understood syntactic area, the precise, correct characterisation of the syntactic structure and function of a linguistic object is not known and uncontroversial, and there is even less knowledge and agreement about semantic representation, if only because what falls within the scope of semantics is itself a matter for argument. The only, much more limited, way of approaching evaluation in this style is to have 'local' standards, i.e. to say that on some theory T of language processing and representation these sentences have these representations, and then to see whether a generic interpreter delivers the representations for the sentences, or a generic generator delivers the sentences for the representations. This may be something, but it is not perhaps so much. How informative it is in particular depends on the view taken of what representations are, and also of how much testing, even for these, requires some application-dependent lexical information.

The other two assumptions are of a different kind: they can *only* be established by a range of tests with actual tasks. Thus it is necessary to see whether the representation delivered for a common generic interpreter (or taken by a generator) will serve for different applications and also, though this will naturally vary somewhat with the task and is also hard to establish, whether the generic component does much of the total processing work.

Generic systems also make strong assumptions about modularity, or modularisation, i.e. that the informational interface with other components is well-defined, whether or not actual processing is serial or interleaved. However the danger here is that all the more challenging processing is actually pushed elsewhere, e.g. into the pragmatic or inferential component dependent on task and domain knowledge. It is one reason why the acquisition, in a suitably connecting form, of application-specific information is so important.

It is useful to compare generic processing in two other areas with generic NLP. (As noted earlier, a speech processor may be treated as a generic component, and is then open to the same problems of connectivity and distribution of effort.) In IR, global classifications are general-purpose indexing and searching resources, but statistical strategies, for instance, are generic ones. Thus the entire approach to obtaining and using term weights exploiting collection and relevance statistics is application independent, and is simply instantiated for the actual terms, documents and requests of a collection in a completely mechanical way. There is a general theory which claims that this approach is the right way to do things, but more significantly, the approach has been very exhaustively tested in very different environments and to some extent with different setups, though research is still needed on whether there are important environment constraints.

In work on expert systems, generic shells have long featured. In the limit these may be very minimal, e.g. backward-chaining reasoning mechanisms, so an expert system shell may have less 'content' than an NLP generic system. Where an expert system typology can be specified, a reasoning mechanism can be made more specialised, and general-purpose data resources analogous to grammars can be provided, for instance a knowledge base of human anatomy for all medical purposes. But in general having an expert system shell is not like having an NLP generic system: it is more like providing a parser and a set of grammar rule constraints. (The difficulties encountered in treating the substance of an expert system as general purpose, as when the attempt was made to use MYCIN for teaching, illustrate the problems of doing this.)

Generic NLP systems, like the CLE and CLARE, are in an important sense more substantial than either the IR technologies or expert system shells. But their real utility can only be established, as with these, by demonstrating that they perform satisfactorily when used for applications. This not only involves, however, all the apparatus of evaluation considered so far in this report. Because the whole point is to be able to predict that a generic system will be useful in the future, it is necessary to make an exceptionally careful and exhaustive analysis, in a relatively fine-grained way, of all the environment variables that have applied in past performance. It is then necessary to size future potential applications very carefully and systematically, as discussed by Bates and Weischedel (1987) for database query, for example, and as done for expert systems (P Nii, personal communication, 1982), and perhaps also to conduct Wizard of Oz simulations (as by Carbonell (1983) for instance). But as mentioned in the previous section, while it is essential to take any existing system to be replaced together with its setup, it is necessary to be careful about extrapolating from an existing to a new and necessarily different setup. Thus for instance for database query, while data about the frequency of query types in the past may be of some use, the Mobil experience with INTELLECT showed that a new resource enabled users to ask new types of question (EAF Peach, personal communication, 1985).

Whether there can, in the current state of the art, be task-independent generic systems which achieve significant coverage of all that has to be done in NLP is very doubtful (unless the scope of NLP is made a matter of definition in a favourable way). It may be useful here to distinguish purely linguistic systems from hybrid ones. However if we compare, for example, a message processing system with a summarising system, it is not clear whether processes and resources which will do much in the first case will do anything like as much in the second. But there are much more serious problems with hybrid systems. For example, as Frost (1989) found, there are great difficulties in separating the linguistic and the non-linguistic in designing a medical consultation system with a natural language interface, and the role of the NLP component is bound to be dependent on the non-linguistic elements of the system, and to contribute less to the overall task processing. Even extending an NLP generic system with reasoning may still mean its contribution is very limited: this is not so much where the reasoning has a restricted purpose, for instance to do discourse context reasoning to resolve anaphors during pragmatic processing as because, as the expert system case illustrates, it is the substance of the inference rules referring to the task and domain of the application, rather than their abstract form, which really matters.

Robustness

But the crucial issue for generic systems is robustness. This applies to all types of task, whether exclusively linguistic or not, and while it may not be a serious problem for any individual application, has to be faced up to in general. For example in message processing, the material may have all kinds of 'nonstandard' expressions in it, and the same applies to interactive systems. There may indeed, as in message systems, be sheer noise (as, analogously, in speech). It is not necessary here to elaborate on what 'ill-formed', 'non-standard' and so forth mean. What is meant, broadly speaking, is input falling outside the linguistic or application scope of the system, and whether or not, insofar as linguistic coverage is concerned, reference is to some supposed general language norms, or to those of a sublanguage. As the examples in Sparck Jones (1988) show, the problem about ill-formed input is that it is typically ambiguous, i.e. the nature of the errors is such that they are not easily, or even cannot be, determined. In general, insofar as error recognition and recovery is possible, it calls for the full resources of the entire application system: all that a strictly language processor can do in general is provide some candidate accounts of errors. However it is also necessary that processing should not grind to a halt and that, especially in interactive situations, as in database query, there should be some feedback, preferably of a cooperative sort, to the user. (Undetected error is a separate issue: it may be necessary to monitor performance for these.

There may also be applications, for example in text skimming, where it may be sufficient simply to bypass ill-formed material, but this is an application-specific strategy which has to be justified for the individual case.)

The problem, then, for a language processor, and hence for the resources provided by a generic processor, is what the system should do with an input it cannot handle. To put the question in its sharpest form: how much is it the job of a *language* processor to indicate what might be wrong with an input it cannot handle? How can a language processor understand an input sufficiently to be able to say, in a helpful way to the user, that it cannot understand it? It may be argued that, essentially by analogy with human capabilities, anything worthy of the name of language processor must be able to say something about what it cannot understand (A Copestake, personal communication, 1992). However it is essential to be clear here how much this can be legitimately required of a generic language processor without the support of general or domain world knowledge. It is then necessary, for the purposes of evaluating a generic system, to specify its required autonomous capabilities in detail. In particular, it is necessary to separate here what is required of the generic system in terms of its own capabilities from how the results, when the generic processor is embedded in an application system, might be delivered to the user.

This last point applies in principle whether the system is interactive or not. However it is clearly critical for the interactive case, and leads to another important point about generic system evaluation. This has to do with specifically with interactive system evaluation. Because the user has a significant role, maybe more or less trainable and more or less adaptable, the assumptions about user behaviour on which a generic interface design is based must be made quite explicit and exhaustively tested (as for instance in Carbonell's Wizard of Oz study (Carbonell, 1983)). Thus while it may be generally reasonable to assume humans can adapt quite readily to system limitations, i.e. can learn to inhabit their situations, it is necessary to be clear about what is being asked of them. This is a point where past setup evaluation becomes particularly important in relation to predictive assessment for future applications.

The conclusion about generic system evaluation is that intrinsic evaluation is of very limited value. As far as intermediate outputs, like syntax analyses, are concerned, this can be useful, especially in the design phase, but it must not be taken as contributing too much to a view of future application performance. Similarly, as far as specific operational strategies are concerned, like generating paraphrases back to show how an input has been interpreted, this may also be of mechanistic as well as test value, but is not necessarily very relevant to application operation and performance.

It is equally difficult to push extrinsic evaluation, i.e. evaluation designed to test a system's performance in relation to its function rather than objective, very far as an independent enterprise: this can only be done either by making quite extensive assumptions about what any application setup will require, or by simulation, both of which have their limitations. Of course this is not to say either intrinsic or extrinsic evaluation of the generic system alone, whether with such general-purpose knowledge resources like grammar and core lexicon it may possess or with ad hoc substitutes for application ones, is of no value. It can be of great value for development purposes. But it must be treated with great caution from the point of view of predicting application performance.

Moreover, even for the relatively limited, free-standing of generic systems, it is necessary to define, in a manner the evaluation can use, what the task orientation (if any) of the generic system is; what the scope of the NLP subsystem in any overall system is meant to be: what assumptions are being made about what the rest of the system will be doing, i.e. what the real as opposed to nominal distribution of effort is in relation, especially, to the determination and manipulation of meaning; and also what assumptions are being made about the feasibility of instantiating the generic system properly for any application. These points are particularly important for applications where there is no real restriction of domain, as in some types of message processing.

Then the evaluation itself, while it may include evaluation 'en detail' to establish local correctness, for instance by the analysis of individual outputs, must also include evaluation 'en gros' to establish consistency and coverage, so it is essential simply to conduct tests of quite extensive data, gathered as best it can be. It may well be possible to do better in evaluation than simply inspect intermediate results, like parse trees, on which judgements of only limited utility can in any case can be made; however assertions that a language system is doing alright because it includes a correct interpretation among ten incorrect ones, or because it has mapped the lexical item "street" onto the underlying predicate STREET, are still of only limited utility beyond that of internal system evaluation. Generic system evaluation has to progress beyond this to the more serious business of evaluating performance in applications in a way that can be extrapolated for future ones.

One source of information relative to a future application of a generic shell is of course some past instantiation. But as with IR examples e.g. of applying an indexing language to a different collection, this depends on very carefully gathered data about previous applications, and also about the intended one, which provide a fair base for legitimate prediction. This may still, moreover, be rather weak. For individual generic components, like a lexicon alone, evaluative scope is necessarily more limited, though equally only limited information may be of quite sufficient value for an intended new application e.g. the lexicon has never so far been found wanting.

For potential purchasers, or from a financial perspective generally, there is clearly also a rather different evaluation question, namely the effort and cost of customisation.

2.7 Evaluation tools

Evaluating generic systems or components is linked with the issue of common evaluation *tools*. One of the most important features of IR research has been the development not merely of acceptable but of common evaluation methodologies and tools. This has been particularly important for experiments, but has also played a part in investigations. If the aim is to demonstrate that indexing method A gives better retrieval results than indexing method B, say, in some environment, it is very useful to be able to take account of another comparison between these two methods in a second environment. These cross comparisons could of course in principle be carried out by any one team, but the range of environments and the cost of testing are both too large for this, so cross team comparisons are essential.

Similarly, it is useful to be able to take one team's comparison between A and B with another's between B and C. This requires not only a proper specification of the properties of the retrieval data itself; it also requires commonality in evaluation techniques at all levels. This has been in part served by the use of common retrieval data - the so-called test collections of requests, documents and relevance assessments, - and in part by the adoption not just of shared criteria but of common measures, even though this has not always been carried as far as common methods, and there are many difficulties in insuring commonality because different retrieval techniques may be intrinsically incomparable (e.g. it is not clear how to compare retrieval methods which are designed to rank search output with those that don't). The analogue here is what does it mean if parse trees from different grammar theories are different.

Shared evaluation methodologies, including criteria, measures etc, constitute tools in an abstract sense. From a practical point of view it is obviously useful to have concrete programs for manipulating system outputs and computing performance scores, and in using the term "tool" we will refer primarily to concrete means of assessing performance, and indeed running entire tests. Thus under the general heading of evaluation tool we include both *test data* and *test programs*.

In the larger area outside speech, there has until recently been very little serious use of, or even concern with, common evaluation tools, presumably because proper evaluation techniques, let alone shared ones, have hardly been established. The use of standard test data for testing speech processing systems has long been accepted, and (better) community data is under development (Pallett, 1992); and one feature of the US DARPA [6] evaluations is the use of common materials, for instance for message understanding in the MUC evaluations (see Chapter 2, Section 1.2) and also now for machine translation (Chapter 2, Section 1.1): though translation evaluation has long been a matter of concern, it has not had established common test data. The DARPA materials, like the MUC data, are used within the framework of a specific NLP task context, and some informal use of common data has been made by those engaged with other NLP tasks, e.g. the IBM White Plains questions used for database access (Damerau, 1980). It has also been argued, for instance by Flickinger (Flickinger et al, 1987) and by Sampson (1992), that research on grammars and parsing needs common sentence or text samples: how far these recommendations have been followed in considered in Chapter 2. Recent initiatives like those of the Data Collection Initiative (DCI), the Linguistic Data Consortium (LDC) (see DATA and Chapter 2, Section 2.5), and that leading to the British National Corpus (BNC) can

---

[6] as noted, now ARPA again

provide common test material as well as information sources: the test objective is explicit in the case of the LDC, for instance.

One implicit assumption in some of this data gathering is that it can be multi-purpose, though in practice there has so far been a distinction between material for component testing, which applies to the speech recognition case as well as to the parsing one, and material for task system testing. It has nevertheless in practice proved difficult to share test data, for example queries from one database application may be unamenable to another because domain differences imply lexical differences. It is also clear that attempts to provide properly-founded test data, of a well-understood, systematic and discriminating kind, have been hampered by the lack of any clear idea of what the test data is supposed to be representative of i.e. how valid it is in principle as test data. Even with data, e.g. corpus material, drawn from the real world, it is necessary to be clear about the nature of the variables it instantiates, as well as whether it does instantiate them in a statistically valid way, i.e. whether it does represent what it is supposed to be representative of, and so is in practice valid, before the question of whether the data is in principle appropriate as test data for the NLP system of interest can even be considered. Thus though a real corpus may be large and well-founded, it does not follow it provides suitable material for all purposes. An analogous situation currently applies with IR test collections where, for example, queries constructed from real search service operations cannot necessarily be used as test vehicles for new interactive searching techniques. The problem is as difficult, though perhaps in a different way, with 'artificial' test data. Sentence collections may have been gathered to test some particular system in a very adhoc way which makes them in principle suspect as general-purpose test data, and even if they are well founded in themselves, it does not follow they are appropriate for particular test purposes e.g. a body of well-formed sentences would not be a sensible test vehicle for an NLP system designed for processing the rougher 'ill-formed' material of telexes. Thus it is necessary both to fully characterise the test material in its own right and to show that it is appropriate material for the evaluation in which it is to be exploited. We return to the properties and uses of different forms of test data in Chapter 2, Section 2.

However it should be noted, in relation to test data, that comparative evaluation across different projects raises particular difficulties in the case of components, where only incomplete task processing is possible. For example when syntactic analysis is only one element in NLP as a whole but information is available for overall system performance, it may be possible to compare performance for two different approaches to the same global task e.g. database query, regardless of the internal constitution of the two systems, and hence regardless of differences in what their syntactic components deliver, i.e. to conduct a black box evaluation. It is more difficult if the attempt is made to conduct a glass box evaluation comparing only syntactic components when these deliver very different outputs e.g. ones based on different theories of what syntactic representations should be like, or more seriously, embody different views about the relative scopes of syntactic and semantic processing. There is a similar illegitimacy in IR about comparing different types of index description in themselves, when what matters is how they succeed in retrieving relevant documents. It is not obvious what can be learnt from looking for similarities betwen index descriptions as such, whether because different approaches to indexing will deliver different forms of description, or because to approaches may distribute effort differently between indexing and searching. It is certainly not enough to look at intermediate processing output for intuitive plausibility when inspected. Thus any attempt to provide, for example, a neutrally parsed corpus as *reference* data for evaluating other analysers and implicitly defining a performance *norm*, is fraught with problems. (Using the output of different syntactic analysers for the light they throw on syntactic theories is another matter.) Even where such a reference and norm may be acceptable, providing precise means of parse tree comparability is another problem, and is indeed a good example of the difficulty of devising satisfactory measures.

As this discussion suggests, under the heading of evaluation tools there are a number of related notions in the class labelled *test data* : these are discussed in more detail in Chapter 2.

There is also a second class of data tools, represented by various task performance levels and their manifestations for particular tasks or approaches: these include *baselines* and *benchmarks*, again further discussed in Chapter 2

In this context Hanks, Pollack and Cohen (1993)'s discussion of *test beds* as opposed to benchmarks in relation to experiment, in this case in artifical intelligence (AI), is very useful. They see the test bed as a challenging environment for studying what AI programs can do, which is exploited for controlled experiment and has research roles for exploration, confirmation, and generalisation. Hanks et al's notion of environment is strongly related to that used here, though their focus on test beds for studying intelligent agents emphasises simulated worlds as environments (because AI's capacity to deal with the real world is very limited). Test beds clearly raise issues of legitimacy, and in NLP the same issues arise in laboratory experiments relying on e.g. notional typical user database queries, or supposedly exemplary database domains, even if the actual behaviour in which agents engage, combined with the large simplification of the real world that our present understanding of agents requires, make AI agent test beds in important ways far more remote than even the most detached NLP system evaluation concentrating on glass box analysis via a test suite. Hanks, Pollack and Cohen's points about maintaining evaluation proprieties, in the form and of test beds, are thus relevant here.

Test beds and benchmarks both depend, for relevant results, on some justifying underlying theory of the process in question (e.g., for them, of agency). But benchmarks presuppose sufficient understanding of a task to make precise metrics appropriate, where test beds, in contrast, have a primary role in fostering understanding through guided exploration. The main problem they present, as with NLP test data especially before the days of large corpora, is in providing sufficient support for generalisation.

We should also note here the third class of tool, *toolkits* in the narrow sense, which include not only general-purpose processors like parsers when these support evaluation (e.g. of grammars), but more importantly evaluation tools like performance scoring programs: such results processing programs, especially when they apply widely-accepted criteria and measures (as in some IR cases), are evaluation toolkits in the proper sense.

As this discussion makes clear, the broad notion of test data, i.e. material to apply some task or subtask program to, subsumes the narrower one of *evaluation data* which provides desired ('correct') task output or *answers*, i.e. coupled inputs and outputs. It also makes it clear that there is normally a challenge in providing these answers, both intellectual in deciding what they should be and practical in obtaining them, especially without enormous cost. The data aspect of tool provision has naturally been the dominant one, and development in the provision of common test programs has been much slower, primarily because the evaluation concepts and procedures they should apply have not been agreed. However the DARPA evaluations have stimulated the production of standard performance assessment programs, and other test engines in the form of portable toolkits or with vanilla flavours are being made available. (This has been a noticable sevelopment in IR, for example.)

2.8   Evaluation from the social science point of view

In the discussion so far, the framework for evaluation has been built up by direct reference to NLP and kindred areas. In IR the attempt has been made both to conduct laboratory experiments with as much of the rigour of the natural sciences as is appropriate, but also, especially in work directly involving information users, by applying methods developed within the social sciences. In concluding this section, therefore, it is useful to take an account of evaluation from a social science point of view to see what additional light it throws on NLP evaluation. From this point of view a straightforward textbook account is helpful: we have considered several, but have made most use of Rutman (1984), and the discussion which follows is based primarily on this. We have also concentrated, since evaluation in the social sciences has an extensive field, on those concepts which seem most germane to our own concerns and can be transferred to NLP evaluation. The social science account which follows is, further, given as far as possible using terms we have already introduced, though it is appropriate in some cases to indicate the corresponding terms used by social scientists; and we have adopted theirs for additional notions it is useful to incorporate in our own analysis. We are couching the presentation specifically as dealing with the evaluation of computational systems: this is of course not what social scientists normally deal with, so we are making a more targeted application of their notions. However it naturally follows that much of what we say about system evaluation is also relevant to setup evaluation.

Rutman divides evaluation criteria into what we have called intrinsic and extrinsic, the former concerned with the system's own objective, the latter with its function in relation to its setup (and hence perhaps indirectly referring to the setup's purpose). These two classes of criteria have a somewhat different character. Intrinsic criteria in turn divide into what may be respectively described as 'whether'- and 'how'-type criteria, the former addressing the question "Does the system achieve its objective?" and hence leading to black box evaluation, the latter addressing the question "Does it achieve its objective in a certain way?", leading to glass box evaluation. In social science terms the distinction here is between 'outcome' and 'process'. Extrinsic criteria can be divided, in a way which is manifestly important in social science contexts, into *what* the system is for and *who* it is for, referring to different sorts of function or, in social science terms, 'stated goal'. In either case, in turn, whether- and how-type questions apply, for example "Does the system meet its functional specification for people P?" and "Does it meet it in a certain way?"

Whichever of these directions and types of criterion is in question, however, it is further possible to distinguish criteria according to whether they consider the system achieves its objective or function, i.e. its *ends*, *effectively* or *efficiently*. [7] We would further argue that it is also helpful in many cases to ask whether a system achieves its ends *acceptably*: this is particularly relevant in the interactive case, for example with a consultation system, where the system may perform effectively in reaching the right decision and also efficiently in reaching it quickly, and may still need to present this acceptably to the user (e.g. by not appearing to treat the user like a moron).

With respect to the measures through which the evaluation criteria are interpreted, it is necessary to distinguish reliability from validity, presupposing for both that there is a correct methodology (i.e. proper methods in our terms) for applying them. *Reliability* refers to the extent to which variation in measures is attributable to the nature of measurements themselves as opposed to the nature of the phenomena being measured: a reliable measure can be depended on to give consistent and stable results. *Validity*, on the other hand, refers to the degree to which a measure truly means what it is supposed to mean, i.e. captures what it is supposed to capture. Validity is thus associated with systematic or constant error, where reliability is associated with random error. Evaluation measures also normally presuppose some norm or *exemplar* for *comparison*. Thus while there might appear to be an absolute norm represented by some measure value like 100 percent, in many cases the natural comparison in the NLP context is between system and human performance (much social science comparison is of course only between human alternatives).

The evaluation criteria and measures have also to take proper account of all the relevant variables, including both *antecedent variables*, constituting the system's context, and *intervening variables*, which facilitate or impede the attainment of the system's ends. In relation strictly to the system the antecedent variables will all be environment variables, and the intervening variables will be the system's parameters, though it may be more natural in particular cases to think of the system's parameters and some environment variables as intervening, with other environment parameters as antecedent: this could occur, for

---

[7] We use "ends" as a general label also to subsume setup purpose.

60

example, where evaluation suggested changes in the environment conditions for the system. Clearly, both to justify the measures (and methods) and to conduct the evaluation, all the required connections must be made specifying the *linkage* between environment variables, system parameters, system objectives, system effects (especially outputs), and the performance measures.

In the social science context, the results of evaluation may be a *composite* of results from different approaches, since no one approach can provide all the types of information needed, i.e. satisfy all the different requirements subsumed under a general need for informativeness about performance. It is in particular possible on the one hand to adopt *quantitative* approaches defining output measures related to variations in the *indicators* represented by variables or parameters. Quantitative measures naturally involve statistical analysis both to establish significance and to indicate import, for instance that of the size of performance differences. *Qualitative* measures are based on observation or inteviewing, and are broadly designed to obtain a more holistic, less reductive or fragmented, view of a situation, which is also more naturalistic: quantitative measurement may interfere with natural behaviour in users in particular, and is more appropriate to laboratory experiments, though observation and interview can of course also disturb natural behaviour.

Both quantitative and qualitative approaches can be either goal, i.e. ends-oriented, focussing on discrepancies between performance results and previously stated system objectives or functions, or they may be ends-free, designed simply to record outcomes. However ends-oriented approaches have prior neutral observations as a base. Qualitative approaches often naturally fit an ends-free style.

This treatment of evaluation offers some further notions to develop our framework, even if the framework is already rather more detailed than that just presented. The additional concepts are most easily taken on board via examples, so this will be done briefly first for IR, where they are readily illustrated, and then for the extended NLP example.

Thus in relation to the three *classes* of criterion addressing effectiveness, efficiency and acceptability, with an on-line document retrieval system effectiveness is, for instance, finding relevant documents, efficiency is finding them quickly, and acceptability is providing the user with enough information in the proferred document descriptions for him to be able to perceive (probable) relevance. A measure like recall is an obvious quantitative measure of system performance, declared satisfaction a qualitative one (i.e. such a measure is qualitative even if the result of applying it to a set of users is some percentage figure). Recall is a valid (though not the only valid) measure, but it is not very reliable, both more superficially in that it can only be based for large document collections on sampling, and also because of intrinsic biases in user judgements arising from learning during scanning. Evaluation using recall results to set against a system objective of high relevant retrieved would be ends-oriented, evaluation simply capturing recall results as a matter of observation would be ends-free. For the former, the required linkage would have to connect e.g. the properties of user requests (as of the kind enabling high relevant retrieval) as environment variable, the use of full abstract texts for searching as a system parameter, high relevant retrieval as system objective, and the size and makeup of the matching document set as system output, all to one another and to the specific measure being used, namely recall (rather than simply number of relevant retrieved). The quantitative and qualitative results together would provide a worthwhile composite evaluation result, since it might well be that perceived satisfaction bore no obvious relation to the actual retrieval data. Assuming these searches are being done by end users, the obvious comparison is with professional intermediaries, but while reliable this might not be altogether valid, since the request environment variable value could be different because of differences in the way user needs are worked up as submitted requests. The analogous case of automatic versus human indexing further illustrates the need for care in such comparisons, since in early comparisons in work in the field the assumption was that human indexing was good and anything different which was automatically produced was bad; in fact human indexers differ among themselves in describing documents, and different descriptions can give similar retrieval performance.

Turning now to our database inquiry illustration, we can similarly see that evaluation criteria in the different classes would all be applicable: effectiveness in the form of correct answers or, if the content of the underlying database is not covered, in the form of appropriate answers; efficiency in the form of speedy responses for those on the workfloor; and acceptability through e.g. feedback showing question interpretations, or clarificatory dialogues when problems arise. But suppose, now, that we want more precise measures of effectiveness, which we might start by defining as percent of appropriate responses. There are different ways we could define these: we could for instance ask users which answers (i.e. data retrievals) were appropriate, or we could take user queries, independently submit formal queries deemed to represent them, and compare the pairs of answers. The former might be deemed more valid, the latter more reliable. If we proposed some measure of acceptability based on the occurrence of clarificatory dialogues (thus assuming that the more such dialogues, the less acceptable the system, an assumption itself needing justification), a measure counting the incidence of such dialogues and comparing this with the numbers of queries submitted might be reliable, but is dubiously valid. Alternatively, counting the number of exchanges in clarificatory dialogues for different user categories might be valid but not reliable. Refinements to such measures would involve decisions about whether all queries, however 'illegitimate' should be counted. The same generic notions of validity and reliability would apply in the choice of specific methods for gathering the measure data: for instance would a specific system output (e.g. "Please repeat your question") be an adequate base for the logging of clarification? How many users or sessions (assuming the former could be identified and the latter defined) be needed? Gathering data for one day would be reliable but not valid.

In the database case, comparisons with purely human means of getting required information, i.e. by phoning the warehouse, would be very difficult to make reliably, though they could be valid, and comparisons with alternative automatic means of inquiry, e.g. using a menu-based interface or even a formal query language, could be more useful. Their utility would however, be mainly for a rather narrow-bound evaluation focussed on the system, as the different means of access to the data would have wide-bound setup implications e.g. about the skills needed of those using the alternative systems.

The measures just considered also illustrate quantitative approaches: qualitative ones could involve e.g. asking people whether they still rang up the warehouse directly, as opposed to using the automatic system. Thus in investigating the database system in its immediate setup environment, or any larger setup, such a qualitative approach would have to be combined with the quantitative ones in the composite evaluation needed to get a true picture of the value of the database system: looking at the use of the system alone would not be sufficient if people were in fact bypassing it.

These illustrations also serve again to emphasise the need to make sure the linkage between all the elements relevant to evaluation is complete: for example for acceptability that all the potential system users are reasonably educated (environment variable), that the language used by the system for output (other than for the actual retrieved data perhaps) is comprehensible (system parameter), that the system gives explanations or seeks clarifications (system objective), and that it does this at appropriate times (system effects), fits with the interest in acceptability and attempt to measure it e.g. by the incidence of clarification dialogues. Note that all of these elements are still generically described: it is necessary to define 'reasonably educated', 'comprehensibility' and so forth, and especially what appropriate times to give explanations or seek clarifications are: does it mean the system has to do something whenever the user submits anything whatever which the system cannot handle? Alternatively, if the system can handle the user's input as a data query but the user then submits something which might be a paraphrase of it, should this be taken to suggest there was something wrong first time that the system should have trapped?

Our illustrations serve, finally, to emphasise the overriding requirement that evaluation be *informative*: an evaluation strategy can have every other necessary property and lack this desirable one. Informativeness is not so much a matter of establishing linkages, as of finding a useful grain level in evaluation: as noted earlier, granularity as a concomitant of experimental control was early recognised as a crucial issue in IR evaluation.

How far work on NLP evaluation has grappled with this and the other challenges of evaluation is addressed in the next chapter of this report. This first surveys evaluation research to date, and then seeks to draw together the experience gained. In the survey we start with work done on different NLP tasks, and follow with accounts of analyses and proposals dealing with NLP evaluation in general.

Chapter 2

NLP Evaluation : Work and Strategies

This chapter reviews the actual state of the art in NLP evaluation.

As already suggested, evaluation in NLP has lagged behind that in other areas of information processing, like IR. But this is not surprising given the very limited capabilities of NL processors and NLP application systems: if you know already that your system cannot do very much, or anything like as much as you want it to, there does not seem to be much point in embarking on big-time evaluation. Evaluation in these circumstances is more useful as a development aid, and given the inadequacies of most systems, it may appear that quite informal evaluation will be helpful enough, so more organised evaluation is not needed.

Until recently, therefore, evaluation has figured, both in terms of discussions of strategies to be adopted and in terms of actual performance tests, primarily in the two areas of NLP which have been of most practical, i.e. financial, operational, or commercial importance, namely machine translation (MT) and database interfaces (DBIs). MT evaluation has been a concern since the early sixties, indeed in the minimal form of demonstrations, since the fifties, and DBIs since the early seventies. But there was formerly little serious interest in evaluation outside these areas, and what was done was usually not of a very rigorous kind. For instance, an intrinsic evaluation might involve seeing whether some miscellaneous, supposedly representative, collection of sentences parsed 'correctly', an extrinsic one whether some random, supposedly typical, bunch of users found a system 'acceptable'. Even in the areas where evaluation was a concern, like database inquiry, a study like Jarke et al's of 1985 was conspicuously more rigorous than usual. At the same time, MT evaluations claimed to be of a good standard, like that connected with the ALPAC Report of 1966, could be open to criticism on many counts (cf Falkedal, 1991).

Within the last few years, however, there has been a radical change. Speech and language processing (S&LP) evaluation has become a hot topic, largely as a result of the US DARPA, now ARPA, Conferences (see especially the references to HLT, MUC, S&NLW, SLTW and TREC, and the note below), but also because attempts to bring S&LP to the market place have naturally stimulated an interest in the real utility of what is being offered (cf Engelien and McBryde, 1991, and EAGLES, 1994). The DARPA Conferences have made message processing, or understanding (MU), a major focus of attention for NLP, and thus a new task for evaluation. They are also concerned with spoken language, used for the database inquiry task, as well as with MT and IR: the concern with speech in the current DARPA initiatives is in natural succession to the ARPA SUR enterprise of the seventies (Klatt, 1977). Speech recognition narrowly construed has been an area of evaluation for some time: the DARPA evaluations in contrast have addressed speech understanding as well, and the current spoken language systems (SLS) evaluations thus place speech processing within a relatively demanding interpretive context, though also in one where speech processing per se may interact with other operations in determining system performance. At the same time, the DARPA/NIST TREC text retrieval conferences have continued and developed an older IR evaluation tradition, on a new large scale.

Collectively, the DARPA Conferences reflect DARPA's continuing ratcheting effort aimed at improving task performance by making evaluation more rigorous and thus more useful. They are, moreover, not only serious evaluation exercises in themselves: they are stimulating the wider interest in evaluation which is manifest in the growing number of meetings on it (cf Thompson in Thompson, 1992); this interest in evaluation may be deemed to date, for the community as a whole, from the ACL Annual Conference in 1987 (Bates and Weischedel, 1987; Flickinger et al, 1987), and is more recently represented by Neal and Walter (1991) and Thompson (1992), as well as by the work of the EAGLES (EAGLES, 1994) and CEC (Crouch, Gaizauskas and Netter, 1995) groups. Indeed the most ambitious current manifestation of the growth of interest in NLP evaluation as such is perhaps the work being done in Europe within the larger EAGLES project on standards for language engineering. This is a very substantial enterprise addressing both general methodological issues and three particular task areas, of writer's aids, translation aids, and knowledge management (documentation) systems. It is primarily consumer oriented, and the working group's report might be seen as a kind of *vade mecum* for knowledge engineers, providing a framework for evaluation design, illustrated by case studies. Evaluation is also discussed by King (1996) and in Cole et al's survey (in press) of human language technology.

In reviewing both actual evaluations and discussions of methodology it is convenient to start by considering evaluation under task headings, since many methodological discussions are in fact related to particular tasks. Thus this chapter of the report has two major sections. In Section 1 we review evaluation in specific task areas. In 2 we look at general developments.

Engelien and McBryde (1991) provide a usefully comprehensive review of the state of NLP systems from the point of view of systems available in the market. This identifies five task areas: database access, machine translation, content scanning, text editing, and talk writing. The first three of these are considered in detail below. We do not examine text editing: there are systems available which are well-established, with large sales, which can thus be deemed to have undergone rigours of evaluation by purhase. They are, however, so limited as NLP systems that they are not of importance here. We are also excluding talk-writing systems, like DragonDictate, since these are speech rather than language processing systems.

Engelien and McBryde's report is not directly concerned with evaluation: but as it bears on the evaluation of generic systems, we will consider it further in Section 2.6.

Evaluation in particular areas will be examined from two point of view. First, as task-specific evaluation, to see what evaluation strategies have been used in these particular contexts; and second, as a source of general lessons, or individual techniques, for evaluating NLP for other tasks. Do the particular characteristics of these three tasks restrict evaluation methodologies? Or do they, because they involve NLP as such, offer more concrete approaches to evaluation than mere calls for care and attention, for application elsewhere?

Within Section 1 we consider first machine translation (1.1), then message processing (1.2), and then database inquiry (1.3), the three main areas of NLP evaluation so far. We then review speech understanding in 1.4, i.e. spoken language understanding: we will not examine speech processing in the strict sense in any detail, and consider relevant points from this area later, in Section 2.8. There have also been a number of individual evaluations relating to other NLP tasks not previously covered, like DeJong's for summarising and Hayes' for message categorisation. These will be considered under a miscellaneous heading (1.5). We then, in 1.6, briefly consider text retrieval: though this has not involved NLP to any significant extent beyond the use of frequency and association facts, recent developments in evaluating systems for full text retrieval make some further discussion of IR evaluations appropriate. We conclude Section 1 in 1.7 with a discussion of points bearing on the transfer of evaluation methodologies from one task to another.

In all of this we cover only the essentials of what has been done. Our survey is not intended to be an exhaustive review of all the evaluations done in the past, even insofar as this could be attempted given the lack of detailed and accessible data about many evaluations. It is rather intended to summarise the salient features of major or representative evaluations, and to indicate the concepts and strategies which have been developed in these bodies of work. We will, however, attempt to present this information within the descriptive framework set up in Chapter 1, so it is easier to relate the different studies to one another.

Within Section 2, on general developments, we begin by reviewing explicit attacks on NLP (indeed S&LP) evaluation as such, as these have have been made in recent years in particular in various workshops on evaluation methodologies, the state of the art, and so forth. These examinations may refer to specific task areas, but in principle from a general point of view. In subsection 2.1 we therefore discuss, in particular, the evaluation workshop held in conjunction with the ACL Annual Meeting in 1991 (Neal and Walter, 1991) and the Workshop held in Edinburgh in 1992 (Thompson, 1992). In addition, as the DARPA Conferences are now having a significant impact on the field, and are ramifying, they are collectively reviewed here from a general rather than task-specific point of view. Evaluation has also become the subject of tutorials, as indicated in subsection 2.2. The work of the EAGLES group, which has produced what may be called a tutorial report, is examined in 2.3. We subsequently consider (in 2.4) some individual analyses of, and proposals for, evaluation methodologies for NLP in general, including in this some notes on Wizard of Oz simulation as a data-gathering and test and evaluation technique.

We then discuss some important related and embedded topics. In subsection 2.5 we examine test corpora, suites, collections and toolkits as resources for evaluation, and in 2.6 generic NLP system evaluation. The evaluation of generic and general-purpose (sub)systems and components presents special problems. Grammar and parser evaluation was a focus of interest in the first half of the eighties especially, and it is necessary to consider both what approaches have been adopted for this purpose in itself, and also how far they contribute to the evaluation of task systems as wholes. Thus while the problems of generic system evaluation are touched on in earlier sections, it is useful to consider them explicitly, in terms of their implications for the evaluation of generic NLP systems like SRI Cambridge's Core Language Engine (Alshawi, 1992) and successor Core Language and Reasoning Engine (Alshawi et al, 1992). This section naturally leads to the following one (2.7) on multi-task or 'mega-evaluations' within frameworks where processes or data may be shared. Finally, we return in 2.8 to the evaluation of speech processing in the narrow sense, as opposed to speech understanding as reviewed earlier. Speech processing work is potentially relevant in two different ways. One is how far the approaches adopted at the lowest level of speech interpretation, which we can summarily label word recognition, are of potential use for NLP evaluation in general. The other is what lessons can be learnt about the evaluation of encapsulated components from the treatment of speech components: this ties in with the earlier discussion of the DARPA SUR and SLS speech understanding evaluations.

We conclude Chapter 2, in Section 3, with a summary review of the main features and implications of NLP evaluation so far, covering both actual tests and methodology discussions, and emphasising the major issues involved.

There is a certain amount of repetition across the various subparts of Chapter 2: we regard this as unavoidable, given that we want individual subsections to be self-contained. We will also adopt the convention that where others have used a term that we have also used, but where their sense is not the same as ours, we will signal their use thus: 'term'. At the same time we mark our own terms, as *term*, both on first introduction and where particularly appropriate for special emphasis or on reintroduction after a long interval.

Information note on the DARPA Conferences

As the Conferences sponsored by DARPA, the US Defense Advanced Research Projects Agency, will figure largely in this section as whole, it is useful for reference to introduce some basic facts about them here. For convenience, as our review period covers both the DARPA and ARPA labels (the latter reviving an earlier form), we will continue to use DARPA to cover all the relevant work.

The DARPA Conferences fall into groups which subsume one or more individual Conferences, or 'rounds', consisting normally of a specific evaluation exercise and reporting meeting, as follows: the Message Understanding Conferences (MUC), subsuming MUCK-1 and MUCK-2 and MUC-3 - MUC-5, with MUC-6 underway (see references under MUC, Chinchor, and Sundheim especially, and also HLT); the Spoken Language Systems (SLS) Conferences subsuming various efforts both in spoken dialogue systems and in speech recognition narrowly interpreted, and several domains, particularly the Airline Travel Information System (ATIS) domain for dialogue (see particularly references under S&NLW and SLTW, and Pallett, also HLT); the Machine Translation Conferences, underway (see e.g. references under White); the (TIPSTER) Conferences, underway; and the Text Retrieval Conferences (TREC) (references under TREC, Harman, and Sparck Jones, in particular). There are many links between these through the use of common data, as well as through common and linked tasks. Moreover, though participation is mainly from the US, it is by no means exclusively so.

The general pattern of these Conferences is the same: they involve the specification, within the framework of the generic task, of an individual task defined by a specific given data set including system output *answers* (i.e. a test collection), a test methodology partitioning the data into a *training set* and a *test set*, and an evaluation methodology establishing performance in relation to the targets. All of these three elements are worked out in fine detail, so each evaluation exercise is designed as a laboratory-type experiment carried out under controlled conditions. Thus the Conference participants develop and run their systems, which from the Conference point of view are treated as alternative, competing black boxes to be assessed by their output performance figures. In addition, the SLS Conference in particular incorporates the notion of 'baseline' or 'benchmark' performance conditions, which appear to refer not just to the nature of the test data, but also to such constraints on the speech recognition element of processing as whether it is speaker independent. Further, as there are successive conferences for the same specific or generic task, the DARPA Conferences in any one area turn into evaluation *programmes* extended over time, with further design and conduct implications for evaluation.

The MUC and SLS groups will be examined in detail from their task point of view under text and message processing and database inquiry respectively. The MT Conferences have had to tackle problems of defining performance standards for approaches as radically different as ones engaged in machine translation and in machine-aided translation, as well as applicable across different language pairs; and as it can be described as still shaking down, is only discussed fairly briefly here. TIPSTER subsumes a retrieval task like TREC, and an extraction task like MUC, and does not call for separate treatment here. The TREC Conferences are of interest on the other hand, but primarily as an application of IR test and evaluation technology on a much larger scale than in any previous IR test, and as involving some participants who are directly applying NLP techniques in IR.

69

It should finally be noted that the numbers of teams participating in the DARPA Conferences varies, with SLS (at S&NLW 1991) less than ten, MUC at MUC-3 fifteen, and TREC-1 around twenty five, but numbers have been growing e.g. MUC-5 had twenty participating organisations and TREC-3 thirty three groups (though there may be fewer teams than sites especially for MUC and TIPSTER since there are multi-site teams). This means that even the SLS and MUC evaluations involve far more direct comparisons than any previous evaluations (since Nagao's 1989 MT comparison was both smaller and completely informal); more importantly, the TREC Conferences are in a real sense the largest strict-comparison evaluations ever conducted, and thus have a variety of implications for the design and conduct of evaluations in both IR and S&LP more generally, as well as for the lessons to be learnt from the actual task results. It is indeed the case that numerically more strict comparisons have been conducted for IR within e.g. Salton's SMART Project at Cornell (cf e.g. Salton and McGill, 1983), or in Cambridge; and it is also true that they sometimes involved comparisons between very different approaches to IR. But the scope of the TREC task, and the range of approaches being tested for it, makes TREC something grandly new.

1 Evaluation so far

1.1 Machine translation (MT)

(a) Introduction

Machine translation (MT) research of the last forty years has focussed little on evaluation methodology as such, though there have been actual evaluations. Moreover while there may be mention of different methodological approaches in the literature, primarily there is merely reference to results. This may be because such research is often carried out under contract and hence there are confidentiality agreements. Certainly there is no agreed accepted practice in terms of methodologies.

Since fully automatic, high qaulity translation is not yet possible (other than in very restricted domains), the output from an MT system is 'raw' translation which is normally taken to require post-editing. Alternatively there may be pre-editing of input. Whichever is the case, there are many different criteria which could form the basis of assessment of such 'raw' translations. There is no agreement in the field over the nature of these criteria. However the alternatives, and methods employed at some time to test them, are discussed below. The source for the following account and discussion is primarily Hutchins and Somers (1992) with a little help from Hutchins (1986). The terminology employed here and used for analysis, comparison and discussion however, is our own, as developed in Chapter 1. Hutchins and Somers suggest the proceedings of Aslib conferences as the best source of specific accounts of evaluations of particular systems. In addition, Falkedal (1991) has accounts of the ALPAC and JEIDA reports, as well as SYSTRAN and TAUM-AVIATION evaluations. A brief summary of these is given below. Finally, as a comparatively recent development there is the DARPA MT Conference, also reviewed below.

Evaluations of translations other than 'raw' translations are inevitably evaluations of the setup rather than of the system alone. The machine translation system is just one element interacting with translators, operators, technicians, as well as end users. Thus, the question of evaluating with respect to function is also variable, according to the different roles in the setup for which the MT system is being evaluated.

The overall purpose of the MT setup may be yet another factor for evaluation. In fact, as the primary focus in this context is with setups rather than systems, though we have so far considered external functions only for systems and have confined ourselves to internal purposes for setups, it may be natural in turn, since setups may be 'nested', to consider the external functions of one setup in relation to its larger encompassing one. Thus, translation occuring in the greater context of an organisation must consider, for example, the costs of installation of a (partly) automatic system versus using purely human translators. We will therefore use *function* in an extended sense to refer to external functions whether of system in relation to setup or of one setup to another encompassing one.

A consideration of the various stages of development, installation and operation of an MT system, and the evaluation issues encompassed within each, falls naturally within our view of system encompassed by setup, encompassed by larger setup. In the next section we firstly, therefore, briefly outline what these various stages are, along with associated types of criteria for evaluation at each stage. Having done that, we give a detailed account of each of these types in turn. The criteria involved are summarised for reference in Figure 1.

Stages for evaluation

1. The first stage is the development of a prototype. The criteria for evaluating prototype MT systems are primarily *linguistic*. For example, how accurate or clear the translation is, or how much post-editing would be required for an 'acceptable' translation. These refer to black box objectives of accurate and clear translation, related to the function of the whole setup as translation of a set of test sentences to the satisfaction of the researcher. There may also be some glass box testing in which the language processing is assessed for its faithfulness to particular linguistic theories.

The system parameters to be considered at this stage are such aspects as the dictionary information provided, and the grammars used. The methodology involves running various texts against the system.

N.B. It is worth pointing out that the selection of appropriate texts is an issue, and one appropriate to all areas of NL processing, not just MT. For example, should the texts cover as complete a range of linguistic phenomena as possible, or should they rather take account of the incidence of linguistic phenomena, and especially relative frequency of incidence? Should estimation refer to the resources available to the language user, or to those which are actually used, i.e. to *usage*, and for the latter, should it take account of relative usage? Thus in the MT context, should the texts reflect the structures most commonly

```
CRITERION   (1)            :  linguistic - task oriented,
                              i.e. translation
     SUB-CATEGORY          :  black box
         eg. Variables     :     setup purpose, system function
         eg. Parameters    :     dictionaries, grammars etc
         MEASURE    (a)     :        fidelity (accuracy)
             Methods        :           performance tests
                                         eg. back-translation,
                                         subjective grading,
                                         error counting
         MEASURE    (b)     :           intelligibility (clarity)
             Methods        :              readability scales
                                            eg. Flesch scales,
                                            Cloze technique,
                                            comprehension tests
                                         subjective grading
         MEASURE    (c)     :           style
             Methods        :              subjective grading
     SUB-CATEGORY          :  glass box
         eg. Variables     :     hardware/software limitations
         eg. Parameters    :     implemented linguistic theory
         MEASURE            :        syntactic parsing success
             Methods        :           observation
                                         eg. diagnostic tracing
CRITERION   (2)            :  operational
         eg. Variables     :     nature of text, intended users
         eg. Parameters    :     modularity of the system, human
                                  expertise, dictionary information
         MEASURE            :        appropriate translation
                                      for setup purpose
             Methods        :           subjective assessment of
                                         developer and purchaser
CRITERION   (3)            :  economic
         eg. Variables     :     quality of output
         eg. Parameters    :     human expertise
         MEASURE            :        cost vs efficiency and
                                      productivity
             Methods        :           balancing costs of time,
                                         equipment etc. against
                                         increased productivity
```

Fig. 1. Summary of MT criteria, measures and methods

used in the languages to be translated, and perhaps ignore obscure constructions that will be rarely met? Or should those uncommon constructions figure in the test data, but only rate according to their expected occurrences in the assessment measures?

2.   A prototype system is further developed within its intended environment. The parameters are, for example, the facilities for inputing text, compiling and updating dictionaries, and post-editing output. Variables are aspects such as the interaction of the MT system within a larger environment, including both other computational resources like those for word processing and the non-computational resources of the translators and other human operators in the setup. The criteria here are therefore linguistic and *operational*. Evaluations are of a setup, where the setup's eventual external function is to deliver adequate translations end eventual internal purpose is efficient and robust translation, but where the purpose of the setup at this stage is the slightly unobvious one of being the framework within which the system developers work.

3.   There are further operational stages in which evaluations may be necessary to determine costs of running the developed system for potential purchasers. The variables here are for example, the amount and nature of human expertise needed. The criteria therefore are linguistic, operational and *economic*. The function of this setup is cost-effective translation for purchasers.

4.   Finally, end users may become part of the larger setup within which they evaluate the translations they receive in terms of whether they are better and/or quicker and/or cheaper than the human equivalent. The criteria for users are therefore linguistic, operational and economic.

(b) Criteria for MT assessment

Linguistic assessment
A.   For black box evaluations, we can distinguish objective, quantitative measures of numbers of errors in translation, from subjective measures of quality.

(a)   'Error analysis' results in a percentage of words which have been deemed incorrect in an entire text. The method involves a post-editor counting every word addition or deletion, every word substitution, and every word transposition that he or she makes to the 'raw' output from the system. This measure is meant to be an objective measure of successful, accurate or faithful translation.

However, such error counting is not in fact a valid method for objective fidelity, unless other factors of the larger setup are kept constant. The acceptability as 'correct' or successful of the 'raw' translation (and hence need for post-editing) may vary with differing translation tasks, with for example translation for alerting versus translation for the record; in other words, the function of the MT system according to its particular setup. Again, stylistic issues are likely to be of importance in the translation of a classical novel, yet relatively less significant in the translation of descriptions of technical specifications for a manual. Error analysis of the same system in such different contexts would give quite different results, the environmental context therefore being an important variable for functional system assessment.

And there are occasions when even within the functional specifications for a setup, the nature of error counting makes it an unreliable method, and hence unreliable measure. Such occasions are when choices to change the 'raw' translation are arbitrary. For example, when the translation is accurate and clear, but not naturally fluent. Decisions about fluency and appropriate style must vary from one post-editor to another.

N.B.   For the development of prototype MT systems, it is important not only to count errors, but to be able to classify them according to types of linguistic phenomena and relative ease or difficulty of correction. There may be simply some minor solution in the form of an adjustment to various lexical entries, but alternatively the solution may require more drastic redesign of certain translation modules.

(b)   Other linguistic measures of 'quality' in MT systems can be more obviously subjective in approach. 'Fidelity' (discussed above) means accuracy, or the measure of 'sameness' of information as the original text. In addition there can be measures of 'intelligibility' or 'comprehensibility', assessing clarity or ease of a recipient understanding the translation. Finally, 'style' is the extent to which the translation uses the appropriate language given its content and setup function.

One general method to determine a score for each of these measures, is the questionnaire or investigation type of approach. Large numbers of readers are asked to assess the 'raw' translations for fidelity, intelligibility, and style, on some fixed scale ranging from 'good' through 'average' to 'bad'. Statistical analyses are carried out on the results.

For fidelity alone, there are two additional evaluation methods which have been employed. For translations which require some consequent task performance on the part of the reader, an assessment can be made as to whether the task is performed as well by those reading the translation as those reading the original text. Alternatively, back-translation is a method in which the translation is translated back to the original by the MT system, and a measure is created from the disparities with the original. For intelligibility, some methods have employed scales such as the Flesch scales, which rank on the basis of average sentence lengths, use of complex nominalizations, and so on. The Cloze technique is a method in which various words are masked and readers are asked to suggest appropriate fillers. The correlation between these and the missing words is the measure of 'readability'. Comprehension tests have also been used as a method to test whether readers have found the translation intelligible. The reliability of these methods is presumably a matter of the reader sample size. Results from readers in sufficient numbers should ensure reasonably valid measures of fidelity, intelligibility and style, by countering individual inconsistencies and recognising overall trends.

(c)   It has been suggested (but not as yet carried out) that a standardised corpus of texts be provided, covering a whole range of linguistic phenomena appropriate to MT systems, and accompanied by human translations (see further,

Section 2). This set of source texts and translation pairs could be used generally for benchmark tests within which the performance of different MT systems could be compared. Performance comparisons would be in terms of *all* the linguistic criteria mentioned above i.e. quality assessments as well as error counting. In addition, systems may be compared for production speed i.e. a measure of efficiency. These are comparative evaluations of alternative MT setups, where each MT system itself is the parameter that is changed.

The Essex MT evaluation group (Way, 1991a), which has been heavily involved with the Eurotra multilingual translation effort, advocates the use of test suites as a preliminary to testing MT systems against a corpus. They discuss the role of test suites in general, and one test suite in particular. Test suites are relevant to 'typological' evaluation, which is one of the three classes of evaluation strategy that they identify. The other two are 'declarative' evaluation, and 'operational' evaluation. Declarative evaluation seeks to specify how an MT system performs relative to various dimensions of translation quality, and operational evaluation seeks to establish how effective a particular MT system is likely to be in terms of cost effects.

Typological evaluation, on the other hand, seeks to specify the particular linguistic constructions a system can handle satisfactorily, and which it cannot, and is aimed primarily at system developers. A test suite is necessary for such investigations i.e. a set of sentences which individually represent specified constructions and hence constitute performance probes. The Essex group tried the set of sentences developed by HP (Flickinger et al, 1987), whose work is described below in Section 1.3. They found this insufficient for their purposes however, and developed their own, which is given in Way (1991b). Way (1991a) has various suggestions about the construction of test suites. Firstly, that a test suite be constructed with information concerning the relative frequency of phenomena obtained from a corpus. Secondly, the combinations of concepts need to be limited also, to prevent sentences becoming intolerably complicated. However the Essex group's main suggestion is that at least 4 test suites are needed, appropriately to the different tasks of MT systems of analysis and synthesis:

1. an initial development suite, used to test rules for coping with particular linguistic constructions in isolation;

2. an analysis suite, which is monolingual and contains purely grammatical strings;

3. a synthesis suite, which is monolingual and contains both grammatical and ungrammatical strings: this is because a primary component of the task of synthesis in MT systems is the filtering out of ungrammatical input; and

4. a transfer suite, which is constructed from the analysis suite in addition to some artificially created source language sentences, purely to test the target language.

The final stage of typological evaluation is to select input freely from a given corpus.

B.   For glass box assessments, the evaluation criteria are more straightforward. The system should perform aspects of its processing according to prescribed linguistic theory. The objective is not to produce translations, but to produce translations in the correct manner, given the system's detailed design goals as the characterisation of the theory for implementation purposes. It is essentially informal, based on the programmer's belief about what some component ought to be delivering for some specific test item. There is therefore no real sense of measure; the process is either correct or incorrect. The method involves observation by a programmer/researcher of diagnostic traces of the stages through which the MT program, or part of the program goes in order to produce the output.

N.B.   Linguistic assessment is clearly essentially effectiveness evaluation. There may, however, be an element of combined *computational* as well as linguistic assessment in both glass and black box testing. An individual component e.g. the parser, or the program as a whole, may conform to some required linguistic theory, yet do so very inefficiently in terms of computational resources. Efficiency of the program may therefore be a parameter for testing, potentially affecting the functions of the MT system in its setup.

Operational assessment

Operational measures concern setups. Evaluations to determine these concern firstly, whether the system produces translations adequately and appropriately for the purposes of the setup. Secondly, the amount of human intervention needed on the part of the translator, as well as operators and technicians. In other words, is the system in context reasonably robust and efficient? And in whose terms? In other words, the role of the user for whom the evaluation is being carried out is important. Such operational assessment is also aimed at effectiveness.

The initial task in such an evaluation must be clearly understood purposes for the setup, expressed as variable values. For example whether the intended translations are of abstracts, manuals, or reports and so on; the subject areas they are intended to cover; for whom they are intended eg. specialists or the general public; whether they are just for information or also for publication; what volume of texts is anticipated, and whether there are time constraints. Other aspects of operational evaluation concern issues such as the extendibility of the system. How modular is it in order to cope with future developments? How much additional human expertise is needed to maintain acceptable levels of performance?

Methods involve testing the setup with substantial and appropriate text corpora. The evaluation is then of a subjective qualitative nature on the part of the developer and intended purchaser. The system parameters are dictionary information, level of post-editing, software and hardware limitations, and so on.

Economic assessment

Setup evaluation for cost-effective translation for purchasers requires the initial monitoring and measurement of all direct and indirect production costs, right up to the final versions of translated texts. These are costs of transcription and transmission of texts; checking, correcting, reformatting texts; updating dictionaries; human interaction; recovering and post-editing of texts; and production and printing. A comparison can then be made with the costs of producing the same quality output with human translators. This would include costs of acquisition, preparation, transcription, preliminary reading, dictionary consultations, typing, revision, proof reading, and printing, taking into account human requirements of breaks and so on.

The benefits need also to be established and set against these costs. For example, the faster production of output and thus higher rates of productivity, greater consistency in terminology, simultaneous output in various languages, and so on.

Finally, the setup in operation should be run for a trial period such as 6 months.

All of this is efficiency evaluation. However the Essex MT evaluation group (Way, 1991; Balkan et al, 1991; Humphreys, 1990; Humphreys et al, 1991) use the terms 'declarative' and 'operational' evaluations, to cover some of what has been covered under linguistic assessment criteria in our terminology, as well as our operational and economic assessments. They are distinguished, according to the Essex group, by the 'user-orientation' of these evaluations, in contrast to the 'developer-orientation' of the typological evaluations referred to above.

Declarative evaluation is about quality assessment; scoring sentences along one or more quality dimensions appropriately to some specified scale. It has, in principle, a certain generality; a comparative, independent, evaluation for different systems. However, Humphreys (1990) and Balkan et al (1991) claim that in practice, such generality is unlikely to be obtained due to difficulties in controlling declarative evaluation procedures, and problems with result interpretation. Humphreys (1990) and Balkan et al (1991) describe the declarative evaluation carried out by Carroll in 1966 as part of the ALPAC investigation (see Hutchins, 1986; Falkedal, 1991), in which the evaluation procedure involved asking a group of English monolinguals and English native speakers with a good knowledge of Russian to evaluate human and machine translations on a 10-point scale for fidelity and intelligibility. These rater populations were controlled for factors such as scientific background, source language knowledge and training in the rating procedure.

Operational evaluation concerns individual systems with some specified, required process output performance. The assessment is then a measurement of what further resources - if any - would be required to achieve that performance given the existing use of the system. Primarily it is a comparison of human and machine translation for quality and cost.

An example of operational evaluation given by Humphreys (1990) and by Humphreys et al (1991) is a study of MT usage at the Pan American Health Organisation in 1989, reported by Vasconcellos. Two translators were hired and trained to post-edit output from a Spanish-English and English-Spanish system. The reported data included:

1. overall number of words translated by MT;

2. comparative post-edit rates (words per hour) for in-house and contracted external MT; and

3. an analysis of feedback responses from translation users. This concerned acceptability of output, which was assessed by including a user-response form with each translation. Users were asked to supply a 'yes/no' answer to the question: 'The quality of translation is satisfactory for the purpose for which it was requested'.

System costs were established by the net present value method which takes account of the value of money changing over the lifetime of a project (Humphreys, 1990). For high quality translations, the result of the overall translation process must be equivalent in quality to that produced by a competent human translator. Alternatively, in gisting, low quality machine translations may be adequate. In either case, the system should translate a 'representative' sample of texts of 'adequate' size and that may require operator intervention. Types of intervention are pre-editing, run-time intervention eg. for correct interpretation of an ambiguous attachment, and post-editing. Costs per unit time for each type of intervention is related to the employment costs of the individuals concerned. Average Intervention Costs per word translated can then be calculated. System Translation Cost per word is the sum of Intervention Costs per word and Recurrent System Costs (eg. maintenance) per word, and can be directly compared with the cost of unassisted human translation per word.

The representative sample should exhibit the anticipated heterogeneity of subject material and document type and in proportion to their relative expected frequencies. Sample corpora, as opposed to test suites, are recommended by Humphreys for this purpose.

(c) Some important MT evaluations

ALPAC

ALPAC, in 1966 (see Hutchins, 1986; Falkedal, 1991), was one of the first evaluations of machine translation. It is most notorious for having had long term and seriously damaging effects on the funding of research and development in the MT area, i.e. for the next ten years. However, it emphasised the need for practical methods of evaluation and pioneered aspects of evaluation method, e.g. Carroll's rating scale applied to measures of intelligibility and fidelity of translations.

The test material was 144 sentences randomly selected from 4 different passages of a Russian book. These provided 6 different translations, of which 3 were human and 3 were machine translations. They were organised into 6 sets, such that the different translations were merged randomly, but with each sentence only as one translation in each set. Each set was then given to 3 monolingual and 3 bilingual test persons. There were 36 test persons altogether, all of which had an hour's instruction session. They were trained using a test set of 30 sentences drawn from the same material as the test set. They were told that some of the translations were by a machine, but not which. The rating of the sentences was performed in three 90-minute sessions.

The evaluation experiment combined two measuring techniques. These were rating on scales of fidelity and intelligibility, and the use of stop watches by the test persons themselves to measure reading and rating time. The rating scale was a 9-point scale by Carroll, rating intelligibility, for example, with verbal definitions from 'perfectly clear and legible' to 'hopelessly unintelligible'. Fidelity was rated from 'extremely informative' to 'the original contains less information than the translation'. The conclusions about the methodological value of this rating system were that it had established necessary parameters, but needed refinement for relatively easy and reliable assessments of machine translation systems.

TAUM-AVIATION

TAUM-AVIATION was a machine translation pilot system based at the University of Montreal. A large scale evaluation was carried out in 1980 by the Canadian Secretary of State Department and its Translation Bureau, and as a result of the evaluation the project was discontinued (cf Falkedal, 1991).

Assessments of TAUM-AVIATION's linguistic and economic performance were made by comparison with the quality and cost of human translations. Nine versions of the test material were therefore used: the English source text, a raw translation into French, two unrevised human translations produced by the Translation Bureau, a revised version of each of the former, two post-edited versions of the raw translation by the Translation Bureau and by a private translation agency, and a human translation delivered on contract by a private translation agency. The English originals were rated for intelligibility and style, the raw machine translations and unrevised human translations were rated for intelligibility, fidelity and style, and the revised and post-edited translations were rated according to the standard quality control of the Translation Bureau and a ranked order of acceptability by a jury of potential users. Any inputs generating no translation were counted, as were corrections made by post-editors. The latter were also classified as to causes, correction-type and amount of time estimated to improve the system to deal correctly with these cases.

SYSTRAN

Wilks (1991) is initially a summary of SYSTRAN's central role in MT and a claim that it is 'the point of reference', followed by a description of an evaluation of SYSTRAN carried out for the US Air Force in 1979-80 (see also Falkedal, 1991). Wilks suggests this particular evaluation is of interest because it assumed, a priori, that SYSTRAN performed MT at a level suitable for some class of customers, whilst investigating how far revisions done to the system for a new type of text, such as political instead of scientific texts, transferred to more unseen texts of that type. In other words, the test was how 'improvable' and 'flexible' was SYSTRAN as an MT system? These are key issues in MT for Wilks. For example, what is the optimization ceiling, and when do new errors introduced by revisions to grammar or lexicon outweigh their benefits?

The testing methodology was a version of BR (from the Battelle Memorial Institute Report of SYSTRAN, 1977) in which evaluators were asked 'Is version X better than version Y in terms of quality Z?' and X and Y are two different target language translations of the same source language string, but Y was produced after the correction of errors in a body of sentences that *may* have included X. Two corpora were therefore involved: texts that were updated with corrections after the first 'run', and whose corrections were fed into the system's dictionaries and rules, and those whose improvement was only examined after the second run. The latter was the control text.

This method differs from that of Carroll's ALPAC evaluation primarily in not being a comparison with a normative or 'correct' translation. In addition, BR relies on monolingual evaluation. This is because fidelity of translation was claimed by the Battelle report to strongly correlate with monolingual judgements of output, and also because monolinguals are better able to judge overall coherence of a text as it lengthens. Three monolinguals and six bilinguals were used as evaluators in this study however, to investigate this aspect of BR. Comparisons were made between monolingual and bilingual judgements. Generally a high variance among evaluators was noted, especially monolinguals.

The results showed a 20% carry-over effect from updated to control text, with 30% of sentences improving and 10% worsening when translating a very different subject area from the one for which the system was originally developed.

Engelien and McBryde(1991) report that SYSTRAN publishes a performance rating for its language pairs based on overall quality; homograph and syntactic function errors in analysis; word order and ending errors in synthesis; unfound words; and other errors due to failures in dictionaries, in choice of prepositions, punctuation etc. These ratings are for three types of text, namely technical documentation, scientific reports, and newspaper articles. The precise way the rating is computed is not given, and Engelien and McBryde are sceptical of high reported levels of correctness. They also note, in connection with another MT system, that e.g. a text correctness rate of 80% is not so good when it means that 80sentence is correct, as this can imply a large editing effort: a similar situation holds for some standard speech recognition measures.

JEIDA and JTEC

There are many surveys of the current state of MT, of which the JEIDA Report (Nagao, 1989) and JTEC Panel Report (JTEC, 1995) can be taken as representative. They are not strictly reports on, or discussions of, evaluation, and they also focus on Japanese work. But the considerable effort being put into translation in Japan means it is fair to to take the reports as indicative of the general status of MT evaluation from the points of view both of practitioners and reviewers.

The JEIDA Report includes some general comments on evaluation, and also a quite exhaustive account of a comparative, laboratory-type test on several systems, but this was very small and there was no attempt to measure, as opposed simply to showing, performance. The JTEC Report refers to a translation exercise for patents where output was categorised as usable, requiring minor edits, etc. But otherwise, these surveys are notable for their lack of serious discussion of evaluation, whether of methodology or of actual cases. It is clear that evaluation must be critical for the many organisations, especially companies, referred to in the JTEC Report for instance, but there is no information about the extent and rigour of any evaluations they carry out. There is a manifest concern with quality, and one company reference to evaluation on a five-level scale (syntactic failure, semantic failure, needing minor edits, literal, natural), as well as notes of percentages of sentences translated 'correctly'. It is also evident from the MT utilisation case accounts in the JEIDA Report that those involved in operational translation recognise that environment factors (e.g. document type, intended output use), and the encompassing setup as opposed to the system alone, are extremely important, and that the economic perspective is (not surprisingly) critical.

N.B. As individually noted, ALPAC, TAUM-AVIATION, SYSTRAN and JEIDA are all described and critically reviewed in detail in Falkedal (1991). But Falkedal's report is not only a review of machine translation evaluations past and present: it is also an excellent general discussion of MT evaluation methodologies. It begins with a critical account of three major overviews, the Lehrberger and Borbeau book "Machine translation: linguistic characteristics of MT systems and general methodology of evaluation" published in 1988, the Battelle review undertaken as part of the SYSTRAN evaluations in 1977, and van Slype's critical study carried out for the Commission of European Communities and delivered in 1979. There is also a chapter describing the various evaluation methods. We have summarised the evaluation criteria and methods Falkedal discusses in Figure 2.

Finally, it should be noted here that the Evaluation Workshops we consider in Section 2.1 include references to MT evaluation.

DARPA MT evaluations

These compare both research teams and commercial systems, reaching nineteen participants in 1994, and ranging across systems differing in every way: languages, approach, human involvement, and user application.

White, O'Connell and Carlson (1993) note the challenge this heterogeneity presents for developing an evaluation methodology, especially if evaluation is not to be intolerably costly while the subjectivity of the human judgements that are inevitable in translation evaluation is minimised. The general style is to use concepts like those applied to human translation assessment, but to seek measures and methods that are reliable, sensitive and portable.

In an initial black box evaluation in 1992 comparing research systems against one another, external MT systems, and human translators, there were two methods of assessment: a Comprehension test for output intelligibility and and Quality test for fidelity to the input: the former was checked by SAT-type questions, the latter by professional translator ratings. However the effort involved in these led to a second phase aimed at more simplicity. Thus the 1992 evaluation had required both source and target language knowledge for judging fidelity, and made use of common Master Passages designed to ensure comparability across systems in fact operating with different language pairs: these Master Passages were 'back

A. CRITERIA AND MEASURES

a) Lehrberger: 1. Cost
                 2. Time
                 3. Quality: Fidelity, Intelligibility and Style
                 4. Improvability
                 5. Extendability: to related domains, unrelated
                                   domains, new language pairs.
                 6. Facility
b) Batelle Review: 1. Intelligibility
                     2. Comprehensibility
                     3. Readability
c) Van Slype:
I Cognitive level (effective information, knowledge communication)
 1. Intelligibility: Intelligibility, Readability, Comprehension,
                     Comprehensibility, Clarity
 2. Fidelity: Informativeness, Fidelity
 3. Coherence
 4. Usefulness: Usefulness, Quality, Applicability, Adequacy
 5. Acceptability
II Economic level (excluding costs)
 6. Reading time
 7. Correction time: Ease of post-editing, Overall performance,
                     Revision time and Post-editing time
 8. Production time
III Linguistic level (conformity with a linguistic model)
 9.   Reconstruction of semantic relationships,
         Syntactic and semantic coherence,
         Absolute translation quality,
         Lexical evaluation,
         Syntactic evaluation,
         Power of the MT system,
         Error analysis
IV Operational level (effective operation)
 10.   Automatic language identification,
         Verification of claims

B. METHODS

         Test material
         Test personnel
         Techniques: rating, performance tests, Cloze technique,
             multiple choice questionnaires, time
             measures, error analysis.

Fig. 2. Falkedal: Summary of MT criteria, measures and methods

translated' from a selected text set into the various systems' source languages, and they were used for both the Comprehension and Quality tests, along with other Original Passages in the different source languages, for the Quality test.

The 1993 MT evaluation (White and O'Connell, 1994) therefore made use of Adequacy and Fluency, together replacing Quality, and a simpler version of the Comprehension test. Adequacy was defined via the preservation of input semantic content, judged for text constituents like clauses, on a scale of 1-5; Fluency was defined by output sentence well-formedness, similarly rated; and Comprehension, regarded as giving a specially important insight, was tested using questions based on the reference human translation for each translated passage. The 1993 evaluation thus did not require Master Passages, reducing cost, but also strict comparability. At the same time, pretesting for 1993 showed Adequacy and Fluency giving the same performance picture as the original Quality, with more sensitivity. However all the evaluations reported involved rather few texts (twenty news stories in 1993), and there may be considerable variance for individual tests.

The 1993 tests moreover still called for considerable effort, and the detailed account brings out the very detailed specification of the evaluation methods that was required; as with other DARPA Conferences, there was extensive *pretesting*, for example to determine suitable rating scales.

Referring back to the earlier discussion of MT evaluation criteria, the DARPA MT tests are essentially restricted to linguistic criteria (time assessment, in 1993, was only a minor element), and are following well-trodden paths in terms of the kind of criteria and measures applied. The major new challenge is attempting to deal with systems translating between different language pairs within the scope of a single evaluation, and it is clear that as with previous MT evaluations, designing evaluations that are objective and sound remains a problem: there are many possible fine-grained choices to make, and what the detailed numerical performance figures really mean remains open to discussion. However, as with the other DARPA evaluations, the fact that the MT Conferences are a continuing enterprise makes it easier to assess and develop the evaluation methodology in a productive way.

(d) Conclusions on MT

MT is an area where research is strongly related to real systems. It is an area where there are already real systems out there working in the commercial world, and there is a good deal of activity aimed at improving existing systems and at building new and superior ones. These systems do a task which is not new; translators, in human form, have been around for some time. So it is not the case that we need to hypothesise how we might use some new automated facility. MT research is aimed at substitution for a human activity which can be costed and measured in terms of efforts and rewards. [1] So even with aspects of the evaluation such as fidelity and style, which are difficult to measure in

---

[1] MT as a purely intellectual exercise or as a test for linguistic processing is a minor irrelevance here.

themselves, there is a means of comparison. At the end of the day, do we carry on using purely human translation or, taking all the overheads into account, is automatic translation a viable proposition, given the nature of its output? As Slocum (presentation at COLING 84: see Slocum, 1984) has pointed out, and work at Hitachi is illustrating, there are many circumstances in which quite low quality translation may be perfectly adequate from the consumers' point of view, for example document title translation designed to allow human scanning of papers for potential relevance (which might then be manually translated). The US Air Force has indeed carried out large-scale MT on this basis which has been found useful (by KSJ among others). As Slocum has succinctly put it, if people will buy MT output, then that is sufficient.

Thus in summary, in MT there is

1. a clear idea what is needed, and what and whom it is needed for, and precisely what is the best performance that can be expected, for comparison; and

2. distinction of purely linguistic issues separate from the job of translation.

Given both the above aspects, can the wider field of NLP learn anything from the evaluation work in MT?

Perhaps the error-counting notion in MT, as counting any changes that need to be made for the sentence to be an acceptable translation, is more generally an interesting one. This is not aimed at precise translation of input; it is a measure of 'good enough' in measuring how many changes are needed to make 'raw' ouput acceptable.

The readability tests, comprehension tests and so on, all relate specifically to the task of translation. However, very similar if not identical strategies can be used to evaluate summary production and report generation systems, and also as a development aid for those working on language generation generally, especially for multi-sentence output. Obviously the methodology of subjective assessment and grading on a large scale with a large number of readers could be employed in other areas of NLP.

Finally, an evaluation methodology in one area will generally influence attitudes to evaluation in related areas, and helps generate ideas and experience for NLP as a whole.

(e) Translation aids

While the evaluation of translation aids is on the edge of our concern with NLP *system* evaluation, some recent work in this area is worth noting because of the sophistication and detail involved in treating evaluation.

Thus the (interim) report on the EAGLES group's work (EAGLES, 1994) includes a detailed discussion of evaluation for Translators' Aids, treated partly as an illustration of the EAGLES approach to evaluation, partly as of interest in its own right in relation to the present NLP system marketplace. We consider the EAGLES Report as a contribution to NLP evaluation methodology in general in Section 2.3; for the present, in the MT context and using the Report's own terminology, it is sufficient to note that it adopts the Consumer Report (CR) paradigm, seeking to apply notions drawn from international standards, notably ISO 9126 for software (ISO, 1991) which refers to desired *quality characteristics* (e.g. functionality, usability, reliability), their specialisation for an NLP task as a set of system (or setup) *attributes*, and the provision of measures and methods to determine, combine etc attribute values. Thus following the CR style, evaluation is seen as a customer-oriented comparative tabulation of task attributes against different systems, where a technical task analysis is presented in terms of customer-meaningful *reportable attributes*. One major motivation in the EAGLES work is standardisation of evaluation for NLP tasks.

The detailed treatment of translators' aids is a valuable illustration of what is involved in doing a proper evaluation. Thus the Report discussion is supplemented by appendices with extensive concrete detail. We can consider only the main points here, with an indicative illustration in Figure 3 below.

According to the Report, evaluation is ideally based on a formalisation of evaluation in terms of functional relations between the objects (O) of evaluation (evaluation subjects for us), users (U) and utility values (V) which may be either O − > (U − > V), i.e. object oriented, or U − > (O − > V), user oriented. These functions depend on feature descriptions of of the objects, i.e. the specification of pertinent attributes, so *featurisation* is the foundation of the entire evaluation process. As a practical mechanism, featurisation can be approached via *checklists*. The checklist mechanism can indeed be taken as a general-purpose one for 'working up' an evaluation, but its primary manifestation is the feature characterisation for evaluation with attributes whose values are supplied by the evaluation measures and methods, and where subsets of these attributes refer to the quality characteristics of interest in a particular evaluation situation.

Then, applying ISO ideas about the stages of the *evaluation procedure*, in the *preparatory phase* of the evaluation the translators' aid checklist is approached via *user profiling*, itself given the checklist treatment. This covers, for example (as users are really user organisations), the type of material to be translated, the form of the translation activity and the embedding organisational role (e.g. international status), leading to profiles for users as e.g. freelance translator, or multilingual organisation, say.

In reviewing the translators' aids themselves, the Report considers multilingual dictionaries, multilingual thesauri, terminology management systems, and translation memories, and illustrates the business of featurisation for the objects of evaluation via an analysis of translation memories (TMs), i.e. systems for recording and accessing translation pairs to see whether a new text item has a previous translation.

For TMs, the featurisation checklist is built up using a characterisation of the functional properties of TMs as such, which can be taken as *facts*. The TM property characterisation covers first import formats, types of offline prior processing e.g. name markup, parse tagging, segmentation, alignment, term extraction etc, and export formats; TM online functions then cover the facilities required to match an input item against against a source language file so as to locate the corresponding stored target language equivalent, which subsumes operations like evaluate source candidates, display, extract selected target equivalent etc.

For the final, critical step of evaluation-oriented featurisation, relations have to be established between user profiles and TM property descriptions by reference to chosen quality characteristics. This can be seen as 'customising' the *catalogue* represented by the fact description of the object of the evaluation, i.e. for market-led evaluation the description of the product type, in this case TMs. The catalogue reviews the product under a very broad notion of user needs. It is therefore necessary to to consider the specific user profiles that have been developed and to relate the TM functional properties to these through appropriate particular interpretations of the general evaluation quality characteristics. Thus given users of a certain professional type, say, and the general requirements for functionality and usability, for TMs with their online input-file match operation featurisation could refine the feature 'range of match definitions' with the possible values 'large', 'medium', 'small', 'none' and the feature 'choice of definition' with the values 'complicated' and 'easy', say. (The EAGLES emphasis on standardisation leads to the suggestion that standard catalogues for types of product can be developed which could be relatively easilty customised.)

The preparatory stage of the evaluation thus also requires, as part of the customisation with its specialisation of quality characteristics, the definition of quality metrics, of rating levels, and of derived assessment by summarisation over the ratings. For the example above, for instance, a higher score may be given to a TM system offering a large range of match definitions. The *evaluation proper* is then the actual measurement and assessment. The Report considers general desiderata for evaluation tests including reliability and validity (and also efficiency) and different types of test, namely simple *specification/inspection*, i.e, checklisting alone, *scenario testing*, and *benchmarking*. These serve different purposes, and require different degrees of effort. Benchmarking addresses the quality characteristics of functionality, accuracy and efficiency, but it is onerous. For TMs, benchmarking has to be related (under the CR paradigm) to properties that serve customer choice, i.e. has to address usefulness, as well as attributes that can be satisfactorily measured, i.e. has to be feasible. Thus for TMs usefulness may refer to e.g. memory size, speed (as online properties), to segmentation scope and reliability (offline import properties). Benchmarking measures can involve e.g. keystroke counting, time, errors etc. Benchmarking also requires test data, and procedures for conducting the benchmark. The Report offers some specific examples for TM benchmarking, for example using primitive (i.e. mouse) actions to align two texts.

As mentioned, the Report appendices provide extensive elaboration if this approach to translators' aids, aimed at widely-applicable, standard catalogues or foundation checklists. They include more detail on user profiles, leading to some 'typical' profiles, which can be correlated with types of aid, and examples of feature checklists, clearly demonstrating the fine-grained analysis required to support product evaluation: part of the TM checklist is shown, slightly summarised, in Figure 3.

Overall, the EAGLES approach as exemplified in the translators' aids case shows a very strong concern with regular and explicit evaluation procedures facilitated, especially in the interests of standardisation, by checklist formation and use. Applying checklists to featurisation, to determine attribute/value sets pertinent to evaluation, is appropriate for product assessment, but is also a useful strategy for evaluation in general, though building helpful checklists may be much harder with (relatively speaking) less 'straightforward' task systems than translators' aids. The emphasis on featurisation, characterising evaluation objects (systems) in the context of user profiles is valuable, and so is the reference, well suited to market products, to the generic ISO quality characteristics even if these have to be specialised for any particular evaluation. At the same time it should be noted that in the EAGLES view of the Consumer Report evaluation 'grid' as attributes against systems, the attributes are primarily (at least as illustrated for TMs) what we have called system parameters, and reference to our environment variables is only indirect, through the choice of attributes and their value sets, and not direct and explicit. The relation between individual system performance and characteristics of the environment is not clearly visible. (It should also be noted that what on some accounts might be taken as environment variables, e.g. the nature of the input material for a translators' aid, are here treated as a system constraint, i.e. parameter.

1.2 Message understanding (MU)

(a) Introduction

A major series of message understanding (MU) system evaluations began in 1987, the MU Conferences sponsored by DARPA, initially under the label MUCK but subseqently MUC. The intention in setting these up was "to advance the understanding of the merits of current text interpretation techniques, as applied to the performance of a realistic information extraction task" (Sundheim, 1990). The extraction task was to provide material for a structured information base.

As noted in the Introduction to Chapter 2, five conferences have now taken place, with a successor in progress at the time of writing (see in particular the references under MUC, Chinchor, and Sundheim). We will focus here on the third, MUC-3, which illustrates the general pattern for the whole series from MUCK-1 to MUC-5, and for which there is now a large amount of descriptive and review literature: see especially MUC-3 (1991), Lehnert and Sundheim (1991), Sundheim (1991) and Chinchor, Sundheim and Lewis (1993). The last paper, by Chinchor, Sundheim and Lewis, is particularly important as it attempts a more thorough and detached analysis of the whole effort than the participants could make at the time: thus it addresses the important issue of determining the statistical significance of the test results, and proposes methods applicable to other data. We subsequently comment more briefly on MUC-4 and MUC-5, and consider the innovative proposals for MUC-6 and its actual design.

```
TM updating/maintenance :

  Alignment :

    Is segmentation automatic ? Y/N
      If so  :
          Units of segmentation by selection ? Y/N
            If so  : how many, what kinds of unit ?
            If not : what kind of standard unit ?
          Is it possible to check/correct output ? Y/N
          What is average speed of procedure ?
      If not : (same questions)

    Is alignment automatic ? Y/N
      If so  :
          Are the user-defined regions ?
            If so  : how many, what kinds of region ?
            If not : what kind of standard region ?
          Is it possible to check.correct output ? Y/N
          What is average speed of procedure ?
      If not : (same questions)

    What is average percent correct aligments ?

    Does segmenting plus aligning impose conditions on
    input text :
      Character sets ? Y/N
      Format ? Y/N
      Markup ? Y/N
      Other ? Y/N
    If so  :  Which/Number/Seriousness ?

    Do these features appear unchanged in segment, align :
      Format ? Y/N
      Markup ? Y/N

    What is the minimum number of primitive actions for
    aligning (with automatic segmenting) on two texts ?
```

Fig. 3. EAGLES Translation Memory (TM) feature checklist example

From the point of view of test and evaluation methodology, as well as in meeting the challenge of the MU task as represented by the increasingly difficult conference specifications, the MUC conferences have made continuing progress even if, as Hirschman (1991) point out, changing both method and task definitions makes comparisons between results and hence their generating NLP techniques over the long term much more difficult. At the same time, though improvements may be being made in the MU evaluation specification, and this is continuing to raise evaluation consciousness, it is sufficient for our purposes to take MUC-3, of 1991, as representative of the general MU evaluation state of the art. We comment later, in Section 2.1, on the MUC evaluations within the framework of the DARPA evaluations as a whole, setting aside MUC-6, which has some new evaluation concepts but at the time of writing had not yet taken place.

(Some tasks which are clearly closely related to MU, like summarising, are considered separately in 1.5 below: this division is justified here on the purely pragmatic grounds that MU is treated specifically in the DARPA efforts as extraction without any regard for coverage of whole documents, which is normally required in summarising.)

(b) MUC-3

The conference preceding MUC-3, MUCK-II, was held in June 1989, following a three-month black box evaluation by the developers of nine NLP systems. This entailed the generation of a simulated database in the form of templates, the information for these being gathered from short, free-form texts describing naval tactical events.

MUC-3 was held in February 1991. The scope of the investigation was much broader, and fifteen sites participated in the evaluation. The evaluation methodology was also much improved, in particular in using bigger data and test samples and better scoring techniques. The basic test strategy was to use one body of materials as a development and training set to define the kind of material to be dealt with and the desired outputs from processing this, and then to comparatively evaluate the systems built using this information with a second test set of articles. An overview is given in Figure 4.

The MUC evaluations are not explicitly of setup, as MT ones often are, though assumptions about the kind of information required, which are embodied in the (human) template designs, draw attention to the relevance of setup in this case too. The MUC tests themselves, however, are system tests, and evaluation is concerned with system effectiveness. Thus an extraction task is specified, and the different systems are compared, in black box style, for their performance as wholes. The criterion is a linguistic one: eliciting essential information of the specified kind. The measure is the number of template slots of information correctly filled in each case. The results are therefore quantitative in nature, but when analysed in relation to the particular system's text analysis techniques, can yield qualitative insights into some 'glass box' characteristics. MUC-3 used a corpus of articles about half a page long, of varying text types i.e. newspaper

```
CRITERION              :  linguistic - task oriented,
                          i.e. eliciting relevant
                          information

    SUB-CATEGORY       :  black box
       eg. Variables   :      possible nos of slot fillers,
                              slots filled by simple extraction
                              or not
       eg. Parameters  :      domain coverage,
                              degree of robustness,
                              ability to make use of novel input
       MEASURES        :          completeness (recall),
                                  accuracy (precision),
                                  overgeneration (spurious),
                                  fallout (spurious and
                                      incorrect)
          Methods      :          performance tests i.e.
                                      counting slots filled in
                                      templates

    SUB-CATEGORY       :  glass box
       eg. Variables   :      message type,
                              template specification
       eg. Parameters  :      implemented linguistic theory
       MEASURES        :          (as above)
          Methods      :          performance tests i.e.
                                      counting slots filled in
                                      templates relating to
                                      marked sentences in
                                      test data
```

Fig. 4. Summary of MUC-3 criteria, measures and methods

articles, TV and radio news, speech and interview transcripts, etc. These covered a range of linguistic phenomena (both well and ill-formed), and were taken as using an open-ended vocabulary, especially with respect to proper nouns. 1300 texts were used as training data, with 300 additional texts used for the test data.

The fifteen test systems can be grouped into three broad classes (Chinchor, Hirschman and Lewis, 1993):

1. 'Pattern-matching systems', in which there was fairly direct mapping from text to fillers, without the construction of elaborate intermediate structures.

Only five systems used pattern-matching exclusively.

2. 'Syntax-driven systems', in which a traditional syntactic representation of sentences was produced from the text. This was input to subsequent processing.

3. 'Semantics-driven systems', guided by semantic predictions and evolving semantic structures, but using also some degree of syntactic information as well as pattern-matching with a close coupling to the domain model.

The specific task was to extract information on terrorist incidents, such as incident type, date, location, perpetrator, target, instrument, outcome, etc. in a blind test on 100 previously unseen texts. Many articles of the test set were irrelevant to the task, and relevant articles did not necessarily consist only of relevant information. Some had germane words used in irrelevant senses, such as 'social explosion'. Others concerned other forms of criminality or military conflict.

The technical requirements of the systems demanded the following abilities, most frequently as separate modules (Chinchor, Hirschman and Lewis, 1993):

1. 'Preprocessing' e.g. segmentation of the message into fixed field information and free text, and identification of 'interesting' segments of text.

2. 'Lexical processing' including morphological processing, assignment of syntactic classes, semantic analysis, special form processing e.g. for times or dates or names, spelling correction, and categorization of unknown words.

3. 'Linguistic processing' including syntactic, semantic and discourse processing.

4. 'Template generation'.

The initial phase of the evaluation provided an extensive and carefully-developed set of relevance criteria and rules, defining relevance both for articles and for information to be extracted. 'Relevance' was the all important base for measuring performance. How well would the systems being tested discriminate relevant from irrelevant articles, pick up the relevant information in relevant articles, and assign it to the correct template slots? All members of the evaluation study manually generated an agreed set of filled templates from the training set which further established these rules and criteria.

The environmental variables in the system tests were such things as the number of possible slot fillers, namely small, finite or open-ended, and whether the slot could be filled by straightforward extraction. System parameters across the systems were such things as amount of domain coverage, degree of robustness, and ability to make use of information in novel input.

Performance for systems on the test set of messages was evaluated by reference to an independently-provided set of 'answer templates' for the articles and information that ought to have been selected. A semi-automated scoring program was developed to calculate the various measures of performance. The overall notion of relevance was divided into two primary measures. These were 'completeness' ('recall') and 'accuracy' ('precision') Recall was calculated as ratio of number of correct fills generated ('correct' earning a score of 1 and being exactly the same as in the key; those judged by humans to be a good partial match scored .5) over the total number of fills in the key. Precision was the ratio of correct fills generated but in relation to the total number of fills generated.

The other two measures were 'overgeneration' as a measure of spurious data generated, and 'fallout' as a measure of tendency for incorrect generation. Overgeneration was a count of the spurious fills generated over total fills generated, and fallout was both incorrect and spurious fills generated over the number of possible incorrect fills. (This can obviously only be calculated for those slots whose fillers form a closed set). All but overgeneration have a correlate in the IR field and were borrowed from IR, where they have an analogous but not identical meaning.

In the training, the systems were normally designed to generate templates which produced a 'maximum tradeoff' between recall and precision. i.e. templates which scored as high as possible and as similar as possible on both recall and precision, though in some cases other tradeoffs could be applied. Scores were also obtained of system performance on a particular linguistic phenomenon, in this case, of apposition (N. Chinchor, referenced in Sundheim, 1991). Sentences exemplifying this phenomenon were marked for separate scoring. Obviously, such an approach is extensible to other phenomena.

Chinchor, Hirschman and Lewis (1993) have developed a method to calculate the statistical significance of the results of MUC-3, that they hope can also be adapted more generally to other evaluation results. They claim that one of the problems with evaluations is that the statistical significance of the results is unknown. In the case of MUC-3, the questions they were asking concerned the *relative* ability of different systems to perform a data extraction task. Recall and precision measure absolute ability, but relative ability requires a measure of effectiveness which can also be distinguished as 'meaningful', as opposed to an inconsequential difference in effectiveness. Inconsequential differences in data extraction effectiveness may occur if there is a significant probability that the difference resulted from chance. This can be determined by statistical hypothesis testing

Statistical hypothesis testing begins with the posing of a null hypothesis. This is stated in terms of a single statistic e.g. System X and System Y do not differ in recall. (To be null, the hypothesis says that a relationship of interest is not present.) To test this means finding the probability that the difference in overall recall score observed on the 100 MUC-3 test messages could have arisen randomly, given the null hypothesis. For this Chinchor et al used a computerized significance testing technique called approximate randomization.

The lessons learned from MUC-3 relate to questions such as the state-of-the-art in message understanding, specific techniques that might provide significant performance gain, particular linguistic phenomena and the nature of evaluation methodologies themselves (Chinchor, Hirschman and Lewis, 1993). (Though actual results are not our concern, we note them here to illustrate the kind of outcome given by such evaluations: of course later MUCs produced new results.)

1. *The state-of-the-art in message understanding:* In general the results here were encouraging. Systems were able to handle a large volume of text in a realistic domain and achieve reasonable precision with fairly low overgeneration. However, all systems performed more poorly in recall than precision. And the linguistically-based systems could not adjust by increasing recall at the expense of precision. Therefore high recall (over 60%) is a problem for current text understanding systems. Another major problem is *transportability*, specifically the cost of porting the systems to new applications.

2. *Specific techniques:* The syntax-driven systems needed robust parsing techniques, and there were two successful aproaches to this i.e. use of partial parsing and use of heuristics added to a standard full-sentence parser for recovery of parsed substrings.

Acquisition of domain knowledge was a big problem for all systems. Techniques here ranged widely. One approach which seemed to work well was the use of a handcrafted but domain-independent semantically rich lexicon. Other systems 'learned' the lexicon and semantics from a training corpus.

Discourse was another area identified as needing more work. Most systems had difficulty, for example in distinguishing the elaboration of previously mentioned events from the introduction of new events.

And finally, although preprocessing is not generally considered as part of NLP, techniques for relevance filtering in order to reduce processing load, proved very helpful.

3. *Testing linguistic phenomena:* Specific linguistic phenomena were isolated and system performance on these was measured. However, no conclusions were drawn about the relative effectiveness of the various linguistic techniques used by the participant systems.

4. *Evaluation methodologies:* The participants in MUC-3 all felt that the evaluation was successful. Their conclusions were that this kind of evaluation is costly, but provides worthwhile insights into each individual system and comparatively against others. However, whereas black box evaluations such as these provide a good snap-shot of the field, they are not necessarily a good predictor of future performance, or of which techniques are responsible for good performance across systems. Some glass box measures are needed for this. In addition, it was suggested that effectiveness measures should go beyond recall and precision to take the structured nature of the extracted information into account.

(c) MUC-4, MUC-5 and MUC-6

As Sundheim and Chinchor (1993), reviewing the development of the MU programme up to 1992 as a whole, make clear, MUC-3 and MUC-4 together represent a new phase in the MU evaluation enterprise including, for example, the use of a new domain, new (and varied) text types, and more refined scoring. The main difference between MUC-3 and MUC-4 (see also Sundheim (1993a) and Chinchor, Hirschman and Lewis (1993)), was an increase in the number of template slots and the addition of a new, single-number performance measure, the F-measure (familiar from IR, combining recall and precision), along with the characterisation of areas of performance in the recall/precision graph, and significance tests. Some 'adjunct' tests were also carried out for MUC-4, on the one hand exploring a variant of the task, namely filtering, and on the other meta-questions, for example the effect of discourse complexity.

In their review, using King's categorisation of evaluations as for 'progress', 'adequacy', or 'diagnosis', Sundheim and Chinchor note that the MUC evaluations have been primarily progress ones, relative both to previous system performance (individually and collectively) and to human performance (on which a study was carried out within TIPSTER). The introduction of significance tests, retrospectively for MUC-3 and in MUC-4, was a major advance in putting the system comparisons on a sound footing, though changes in the test details mean that they are are primarily applicable to different systems at a single time point, rather than to the same system over time. At the same time, while the main measures focus on cross-system comparisons, but require heavy abstraction to allow this, the detailed scoring data allow finer-grained views of system differences that provide a disgnostic lever.

Sundheim and Chinchor further argue that the MUC programme also involves some adequacy evaluation, not directly since the tests are laboratory ones, but indirectly through the choice of metrics that are of interest to (and are understood by) the eventual system consumers, even if they may still be more meaningful to researchers than others. Of course the MUC tests remain divorced from an actual setup. In relation to diagnostic evaluation, there had been very little by MUC-4, apart from the few adjunct tests.

While MUC-5 (cf Sundheim, 1993b; Chinchor and Sundheim, 1993) was in the same general spirit as previous MU evaluations, conjunction with TIPSTER introduced some new elements, namely two languages (Japanese as well as English) and two domains, as well as a change in the nature of the templates used from flat formats to objects. These changes meant that direct, detailed progress comparisons with earlier MUC performance were not practicable. However studies were done, following the approach first tried for MUC-3, to establish task difficulty and hence allow some indirect comparisons. These showed that at least for one domain language pair the task was overall harder than the MUC-4 one; nevertheless, while some system performance for MUC-5 was impressive, especially given the challenging data, these studies emphasise the extremely task-specific nature of these evaluations and the difficulty of achieving more than a rather coarse and simplistic comparison between individual applications even of the same general type. Thus the aessessment of task difficulty was based on test corpus complexity measures (e.g. vocabulary size, sentence length), corpus dimensions (e.e. number of texts, of sentences), template fill characterstics (e.g. number of slots and object types, number of fills per slot), and nature of the task (e.g. number of pages of relevance rules).

The other important changes marking MUC-5 as representing a significant new step within the broad MUC conventions lay in the introduction of new metrics. These error-based metrics were taken as the primary ones, but the older recall/precision ones were retained, giving a range of measures at different grain levels and suited to different needs. The overall error measure, Error Per Response Fill (EPRF), defined as the ratio of wrong template slot fills to total fills based on a fill categorisation as correct, partial, incorrect, spurious, or missing, gives a single number metric for ranking systems, but was supplemented by secondary metrics for undergeneration and overgeneration (first tried for MUC-4), and substitution. The ERPF was itself computed at both template and test set levels, and could be applied 'naked' or normalised, while the secondary measures provided detailed diagnostic information: substitution, in particular, was designed to reveal performance features not isolated with the earlier recall and precision. The error-based metrics thus complemented the older single number F measure and supporting specific recall and precision figures, and can be viewed as more consumer-, and less developer-, oriented (cf Sundheim and Chinchor, 1993); however the move to error metrics was also justified as offering system developers more detailed information of value to remedying their systems' errors. The two single-number measures (not altogether surprisingly given their source data overlap) in fact behave consitently in ranking, but EPRF appears more discriminating than the F measure.

The research community's dissatisfaction with the lack of diagnostic, glass-box evaluation in MUC, and its interest in developing general-purpose rather than special-purpose NLP systems, led to proposals for new evaluation components in MUC (Grishman, 1994). Sundheim and Chinchor had already acknowledged the problem that the form of the MUC evaluations stimulated not just task-, but application-specific *tuning*, and also that the level and kind of information extracted could only be a partial test of general-purpose NLU capabilities, as shown by the fact that shallow techniques performed almost as well as deeper ones.

The proposals for evaluation components for MUC-6 thus sought to address systems assessment via their ability to capture a range of entities and relationships of indubitable semantic import and interpretive importance, and hence relevance for any putative general-purpose NLP system. Thus Grishman's list covers the ability to determine named entities (e.g. organisations); syntactic structures (in Parseval style); basic predicate-argument structures; word senses; and coreferences. Some of these, like the first, could be claimed to be directly pertinent to MU needs as well as to NLP generally, along with a 'mini-MUC' component (defining entities and events in much simpler style than previous MUC templates) and document cross references, even if others in explicit form, like predicate-argument structures, might not be manifestly necessary. These proposals had the additional advantage of overlapping with concurrent proposals, with similar intentions, put forward for the SLS evaluation under the designation SemEval (Moore, 1994): here identifying predicate-arguments, co-references, and senses would similarly address the development and assessment of general NLP capabilities.

In the event, however, the MUC-6 Call (Sundheim, 1995), though it preserves many of these ideas, is much more modest, presumably largely for practical reasons. Thus it contains only named entity and co-reference. along with mini-MUC. The MUC-6 specification nevertheless represents a significant break with the previous tradition, not only because the actual extraction task is less aggressively specified (the mini-MUC notion), but because its two components, namely template element identification and scenario template determination, are separated as domain-independent and domain-dependent respectively and, further, because neither component is compulsory and MUC-6 participants may choose which of the four components they will tackle. Evaluation in MUC-6 will (as far as appropriate for the different components) involve recall and precision, the F measure, and error metrics, again using the familiar scoring categories.

The MUC-6 design thus clearly represents a shift towards more general NLP concerns, even if ties with the past remain and consumer interests are represented not only by continued use of previous measures but also by interest in portability and resource minimisation for the scenario template component. It could also be claimed that the long previous MUC programme, along with TIP-STER, demonstrated that there was a proven range of technologies available for deployment in individual applications, where particular tuning rather than competitive evaluations would be most helpful. It will be interesting to see how MUC-6 turns out.

(d) Conclusions on MU

As with MT, the evaluation here has been task-driven and primarily black box in style. Before MUC-6 there was no distinction of purely linguistic issues separate from the job of slot filling. Sundheim (1991) suggested that in future evaluations the task should be modified to focus on language processing capabilities as separate from information extraction capabilities, calling for new ideas for test design related to specific linguistic phenomena. MUC-6 represents a very significant move in this direction. Sundheim also suggested that further study was needed on *human* performance of the task, in order to ascertain concrete performance goals for comparison. This point was made about MT systems earlier, but MT has the advantage that such data is readily available, which is not the case here.

Again, a major role of this evaluation has been to put NLP evaluation 'on the map' as an important issue. It is not only about evaluating message understanding; it is also about evaluation methodologies themselves. In particular, it is a start at benchmark-type tests for NLP, where performance measures for different theoretical approaches and techniques can be compared using the same tests and data. The results concerning what approaches or techniques fared better with particular contexts or for what particular aspects of which task, can then feed back to the wider research community, and hence relatively rapidly affect development of both linguistic and computational understanding. In other words, these issues are effectively separated out from the intricacies of particular systems and particular methodologies for all researching in that area.

The sheer length of time the MUC series has continued, and the successive Conference cycles, have mattered not only because they have emphasised the importance of evaluation, but because they have shown how the business of evaluation itself can be improved through better motivated and more clearly worked out remit and design. From this point of view the MUC use of *dry runs* within the cycles is noteworthy.

The implications of having such extended programmes, along with the open design for MUC-6, raise questions for the nature of 'mega-evaluations' that are taken up later in this chapter and in Chapter 3.

Rau and Krupka (1992) discuss in detail some of the consequences of the MUC-3 evaluation metrics for the text extraction task. Their analysis is highly specific to this case, but nevertheless illustrates the problems of devising appropriate and informative measures with respect to e.g. different aspects of performance and to determining system component contributions to it in a way which avoids confusion and interference effects, as well as of devising measures which can be reliably applied automatically for scoring results. These concerns are reflected in the introduction of new measures in successive MUCs, even if they all ultimately depend on the fill data. Thus it is not at all clear how extraction tasks defined without templates (which is perfectly plausible) would be evaluated.

For the record, it may be noted that Anderson et al (1992) report a message extraction evaluation for a non-MUC application. However their actual performance measures, for the message selection and the fact extraction subtasks, were analogous to those used in MUCK-II, the former quite closely related but the latter only more roughly corresponding. This illustrates how what may be described as generic or *abstract measures* may be given different precise forms for individual tests. It is clear, for instance, that the abstract measures Recall and Precision, which may be taken as embodying notions of completeness and correctness together representing accuracy, subsume a whole family of individual recall and precision measures. This point is indeed well illustrated not only by the variant forms used within the MU area, as just mentioned, but by the difference between the interpretations for Recall and Precision when applied to fact extraction within MU and when applied in IR (see Chinchor, Hirschman and Lewis, 1993). It is thus of some interest to establish what the range and utility of such abstract measures is, as general-purpose resources for evaluation. Lewis (1991) considers some of these points in the context both of the evaluation of categorisation by analogy with IR, and of the implications of the operational link between categorisation and extraction for evaluating either.

1.3 Database query (DBQ)

(a) Introduction

Like machine translation, database query has been a long established area of NLP work. In particular it seemed much more tractable than machine translation, and attempts were soon made to build practical, and subsequently commercial, systems. It then became necessary, from both the suppliers' and the consumers' points of view, to demonstrate utility. The LUNAR investigation

(Woods, 1973) is of interest as an early evaluation, and those done by IBM (Damerau, 1980) and HP (Flickinger et al, 1987) are important because they reflect the concerns of potential commercial market suppliers. Bates and Weischedel's (1987) tutorial on interface evaluation also reflects these concerns. Jarke et al (1985) and Whittaker and Walker (1989) describe comparatively recent *field evaluations*: these naturally reflect the fact that in the database area, as in machine translation, commercial products have been available for some time. Jarke et al's study is noteworthy, from a methodological point of view, for the care taken in it, especially when compared with other earlier or contemporaneous investigations. The most rigorous current evaluation in the database area, though it does not include field studies, is that being carried out within the DARPA SLS programme. As mentioned earlier, this has involved successive evaluations of speech-driven database inquiry systems using the Airline Travel Information System ATIS domain. It is considered in this section primarily from the database query, rather than speech technology, point of view. The systems involved in the SLS evaluations are regarded by their developers as generic DBQ systems, though the tests tend to emphasise the specific application. Commercial suppliers are of course interested in generic systems, and the HP study was explicitly focussed on generic system evaluation (see also Nerbonne in Thompson, 1992).

The relevant features of all the evaluations we are considering here are given in Figure 5.

(b) Two early DBQ evaluations

LUNAR

Woods (1973) describes the informal testing of the LUNAR system with a community of geologists in 1971. LUNAR was developed as a research prototype for a system which would assist lunar geologists in accessing, comparing and evaluating the chemical analysis data on lunar rock and soil composition which had been gathered on various Apollo moon missions. The NLP facility was aimed at easing the geologists' task by not requiring complex or unnatural input. The informal evaluation consisted of running a demonstration of the system twice a day for three days at the Second Annual Lunar Science Conference, at which time lunar geologists attending the conference were invited to ask the system questions. 110 requests were processed which were freely expressed, without any prior instructions on phrasing. The restriction of content was the database of the system, and poeple were asked not to give it comparatives.

The objectives of the system were to process the English input in order to query the database and to obtain a reply. [2] The system function was to provide replies to geologists' questions about lunar rocks. The purpose of the whole 'conference test' setup was to provide feedback as to whether the system was

---

[2] As we use "answer" specifically to refer to correct task processing outputs, we use "reply" here in the ordinary sense of reply to a question. Only some actual replies will be answers in the evaluation sense.

```
CRITERION              :  linguistic,
                          computational

    SUB-CATEGORY       :  black box and glass box
      eg. Variables    :     style and linguistic components
                             of input sentences
      eg. Parameters   :     implemented linguistic theory,
                             nature of database
      MEASURES         :        habitability,
                                accuracy of lexical analysis,
                                accuracy of parsing,
                                accuracy of domain-
                                   independent semantics,
                                correctness of dbase query,
                                correctness and
                                appropriateness of reply.
      Methods          :        task performance tests,
                                observation

CRITERION              :        operational

      eg. Variables    :  nature of user
      eg. Parameters   :  regular, irregular
      MEASURES         :     processing time,
                             numbers of user messages,
                             numbers of operator messages
      Methods          :        observation,
                                comparative analysis of
                                   results
```

Fig. 5. Summary of database query criteria, measures and methods

able to deal with the way in which geologists naturally refer to the objects and concepts in the database.

The results of the informal investigation indicated 10% parsing or semantic interpretation problems. Another 12% of inputs failed due to clerical errors such as dictionary coding errors. Overall, Woods claimed that after correction of trivial errors, 90% of the questions asked fell within the range of English understood by the system.

Obviously, this does not constitute a thorough evaluation as it involved only small amounts of data, and relatively informal assessment of results: there is no indication of precise measures and methods for obtaining those measures.

However, in essence the LUNAR evaluation had something which much of the other work described in this section as a whole has not had. It was evaluated by those members of the community for whom it was intended, i.e. expert geologists, the real end users. The main measure, however informal, was of habitability to lunar geologists.

TQA

The TQA (Transformational Answer System) project (Damerau, 1980) was practically motivated, like LUNAR, but can be seen as having more concern with the commercial potential for database query systems. It too was evaluated by testing the system in operation with its intended end users. This is also an example, similar to the MT case, where there was an existing operational data query setup with which an alternative setup using NLP could be compared. There was already a town planning database, more complex than the LUNAR one, which was accessed by planning department employees via a conventional retrieval language. TQA was an experimental NL query system which took this existing data as its database, and was placed in operation in the planning department offices to answer queries from late 1977 through 1979.

The TQA included two logging facilities, one of which was a verbatim record of all output that appeared on the user terminal. The other was a comprehensive trace of the system flow whilst it processed each question. The results from these for a whole year were statistically analysed to produce measures per month of numbers of queries, queries completed, queries aborted, user comment, user message, operator message, program error, user cancelled, lookup failures, lexical choice, parsing failure, nothing in database. In other words, this was both a black box evaluation and glass box one based on linguistic criteria.

Operational considerations were in the form of statistics concerning user messages (no message implied user satisfied) and operator messages. There were computational and linguistic and operational considerations altogether in the statistics denoting numbers of queries taking longer than 1,2,3,4, or 5 seconds to process to logical form stage and so on. It was found, for example, that the greatest processing time was taken in surface structure parsing and not database lookup or printing.

One methodological point to note is that the system was constantly being changed in order to make queries that failed, and hence future ones like them, run successfully. Evaluation and modification were therefore going on simultaneously.

One result which generally has implications for NLP systems concerns the issue of linguistic coverage. For example, the evaluators found that there were a number of constructions TQA permitted that the human planners using the system never used. On the other hand, there were many constructions involving personal pronouns, three-argument comparisons and so on, which were never used because the users knew the system could not deal with them.

In other words, the TQA evaluation showed, as Waltz's earlier design analysis for PLANES did (Waltz, 1978), that the role of a NLP system, and what and who it is being developed for, can usefully direct and constrain the capabilities of the system. Such results have obvious relevance to considerations of generic NLP systems. This point will be discussed further in Section 2.6.

(c) Generic DBQ system evaluation

HP Laboratories study

This study was grounded in a review of the problems of evaluating NLP systems in general, and on a view of what is feasible in NLP evaluations. Thus Flickinger and his colleagues (Flickinger et al, 1987) outline what they do and do not see as 'doable' in NLP evaluation. For example, they say that they do not imagine it will ever be possible to plug a random NLP system into an evaluation tool and read out grades for correctness in lexical analysis, or in conversational cooperativeness etc. Their two main reasons for this are the lack of common assumptions that are brought to NLP efforts, and the wide range of uses to which NLP is put. However, in order to make some progress, they set up an evaluation in a context in which assumptions are shared and similar applications sought i.e. that of a database query interface.

Their evaluation suite consists of a large number of sentences annotated by a construction type and code which asks the NLP system to evaluates these sentences against a database. The style of sentences is informal typewritten communication and includes intersentential dependencies. The aim with these is to cover a wide range of syntactic and semantic phenomena as well as the discourse phenomenon of anaphora. Ungrammatical examples are included; the vocabulary is limited.

The criteria here are linguistic and computational. The objectives of the system are to process a set of English sentences, the results of which are used to query a database, and provide replies. The function of the system is then to provide feedback to the researchers about bugs, potential modifications and general progress monitoring. The purpose of the whole setup is to provide data and experience about evaluation in an NLP application.

The measures used were: accuracy of lexical analysis; accuracy of parsing; accuracy of domain-independent semantics; correctness of database query generated; and correctness and appropriateness of reply. Flickinger et al do not describe their methods for obtaining these measures. They do say, however, that each is dependent upon the theory incorporated in the system in the first place. For example, you can only get a measure of accuracy of parsing which reflects the particular theory of parsing implemented in your system.

Their conclusions reflect the intention of the enterprise. They point out that not every measure is applicable to every NLP system, for example, their 'accuracy of domain-independent semantics' measure. They also suggest further mneasurements of system performance outside range and accuracy of linguistic coverage. For example, compatability, modifiability, good software 'citizenship', and size, speed and installation costs. These were the kinds of measures discussed in the earlier section on machine translation with respect to operational and economic criteria.

Flickinger et al also express the desire that this work be the beginning of a larger experiment of the benchmark kind that was described in previous sections. This would compare a variety of NLP systems. It requires the continued development of the test sentences to cover as many linguistic phenomena as possible, and also the establishment of a standard database. Some progress has since been made in this area, but it is a major task and presents many problems: these are indicated in Section 2.

(d) Recent DBQ field evaluations

Jarke et al's study

Jarke et al (1985) describe an evaluation program based at New York University comprising both laboratory and field evaluations of a restricted general-purpose natural language front end, NLS, to a relational database system. The objectives of the NLS system were to process the English input into a database query, using a parser, an English grammar comprising some 800 rules, an application -specific lexicon, a set of interpretation rules for semantic analysis and the database management system. The system function was to provide replies to queries. The purpose of the whole setup was to perform tasks related (in this instance) to fund raising activities, which required information about grants and alumni available from the database. For the researchers involved, the purpose of the experimental setup was a comparative evaluation between natural language and an artificial query language, SQL, as to the practical usefulness of natural language in such a context, and also as part of the development of a methodology for studying computer languages in real work settings.

The emphasis of the paper is on issues of field evaluation, specifically for evaluating natural language for database retrieval application, in contrast to an artificial query language. Initially, the conditions for the field evaluation were outlined as follows:

1.   The human 'subjects' [3] had to be performing real work. This required a nontrivial application system for a work situation. The application selected was a question-answering system about alumni of the Graduate School of Business Administration at NYU. Data for loading the NLS database was extracted from the university's record keeping system.

2.   Subjects were designed to be a group with sufficient application domain knowledge and analytic skills to be likely to use the NL database interface. They were paid as subjects to be users acting as intermediary advisors on behalf of the Deans and Development Officers that normally made enquiries about alumni. Subjects were selected on the basis of their similarity, other than their gender, in which there was an equal distribution of men and women. They were of similar ages, with a familiarity with computing but without being experts.

3.   There were as many controls as possible for unexpected factors. The performance of subjects using the natural language interface was compared with

---

[3] This social science use of "subject" overlaps but is not identical with our larger use to refer to what is being evaluated as a whole.

another group of subjects using a reference artificial language, SQL. Thus, the measures were relative as opposed to absolute, with other factors as constant as possible i.e. both groups were working with the same application, with the same type of users, and in a similar system environment.

Both groups of subjects were trained in the application domain, and in either NLS or SQL. At the end of a six week period they were retrained in the other language, and the testing repeated. Finally, they were given an additional practice session and then asked to use whichever language they preferred to accomplish selected tasks. The research design was intended to reflect infrequent use of an application, as may be the case by a novice or specialist professional user.

4. There was a formal evaluation scheme within which to interpret results.

A set of hypotheses was firstly formulated for the field evaluation based on the results of the laboratory trials. These were:

H1. There will be no difference in performance between subjects using NLS and SQL.

H2. Subjects using NLS will be more efficient than those using SQL.

H3. The performance of subjects will be negatively related to the difficulty of the task.

H4. The performance of subjects will be negatively related to their perceptions of task difficulty and positively related to their understanding of a solution strategy.

The results of the field evaluation showed that H1 was to be rejected; SQL outperformed NSL. This was a quite different result from the laboratory trials. H2, H3 and H4 were confirmed however.

In the field experiment, subjects were given tasks to perform, which required a number of queries to be made to the database. The analysis of results was both at the task and at the query level. Evaluations comprised:

1. a measure of 'success' in terms of the syntactic correctness of queries and the contribution of the answer to accomplishing the task i.e. whether the likely objective of the query was accomplished.

2. a measure of 'effort' in accomplishing the task, obtained by measuring the number of sessions, length of time taken and number of queries used.

3. the factors likely to influence success or effort eg. complexity and uniqueness of the task, as control parameters. 'Task difficulty' was measured with several different factors eg. the number of concepts such as entities and relationships, referred to in a request.

4. likely reasons blocking task accomplishment were also identified; reasons for 'failure'. For example, at the query level, a query may be syntactically incorrect due to a typing, spelling or interface error, or it may be syntactically correct but have an incorrect reference such as a file number or index, or it may be the wrong question to ask, or there may be a system bug or feature of the application which does not work, and so on.

5. the subjects 'perceptions' of the clarity of their task, certainty of their solution strategy, adequacy and preference for a particular methodology.

The evaluation was thus primarily oriented towards effectiveness, with some indirect reference to efficiency and some elements of acceptability.

Distribution-free statistical tests were used on the results. At the task level, SQL outperformed NLS in terms of essentially correct task completion by more than 2:1. Also, in terms of effort, NLS subjects used about 50% more queries than SQL subjects. The major reasons for failure to complete a task were a lack of language functionality and interface problems for NLS, but subject errors in using the language in SQL. At the query level, SQL also outperformed NLS in producing partially correct output from a query by more than 3:1. In NLS, the major problem was a lack of feedback when errors occured. In SQL, it was the complexity of the query structure that introduced the most errors.

It is obviously the case that general conclusions cannot be widely drawn from these experiments about natural language systems versus query languages for database retrieval. Another language system or a different application system might have produced very different results. However, some implications that confirm previous studies are for example, that natural language queries are more concise and require less formulation time. In terms of experimental design, one important issue was feedback to subjects about the nature of errors, given that the task is one in which there is correction and learning. Most significantly however, the importance of the entire operating environment on the performance of subjects is underlined in an experiment such as this. Especially given that the results of the field experiment varied from those in the laboratory, a crucial component of evaluation tests must be that they include those performed in realistic operational settings.

Whittaker and Walker's comparative study

Whittaker and Walker (1989) describes the evaluation of a restricted natural language as an interface for database access in comparison with a menu database interface system. Both options were available to the users in their study, the natural language interface and the menu system, and so it could be observed when the natural language interface was used in preference to the menu system. Importantly, this was also a field study and so users were examined whilst carrying out real tasks which were part of their everyday jobs. The purpose of field studies, the authors claim, is to avoid the problem of representativity of experimental tasks in laboratory studies; different tasks elicit different language features. Whittaker and Walker point out that other investigations involving real users in real settings, such as the Jarke field study described above, used only limited numbers of users, whereas their own involved 50 real users.

Whittaker and Walker contrast their approach in terms of the interpretation of results with studies such as Jarke et al's, in which natural language is compared with a formal language such as SQL. The latter tend towards global measures such as time-to-solution or the number of queries required to complete a task. The suggestion is that such measures do not allow the disentanglement of costs involved in using a language, such as errors made, from benefits such as greater expressivity. It is also impossible to determine precisely which language features contribute to the successful completion of a task. This study, on the other hand, began with a set of communicative features provided by the natural language interface that were not supported by the menu interface (Walker, 1985), for example sorting, meta-level information about data, discourse reference, negation, comparison, coordination, ellipsis, quantification, and format. The authors then evaluated which of these features, if any, better supported information access requirements. Meta-level information, negation, comparatives, coordination and quantifiers concern the 'selectivity' of language i.e. the availability of operators that allow users to specify as precisely as possible what data they wish to retrieve. Ellipsis and discourse reference concern the 'flexibility' of language i.e. the number of available ways for expressing a given operation and the support for shorthand means of expression. Sorting and format allow manipulation of the 'output presentation', and hence represent the control users have over presentation of retrieved information. Thus this study, like Jarke et al's, addressed all of effectiveness, efficiency and acceptability.

The users were in two groups. There were persistent users and non-persistent users. The use of features were compared between the two groups to determine the features persistent users found useful, as well as the features elicited by the tasks themselves. The costs of using the natural language system were evaluated by an investigation of errors. Errors of the persistent users indicated which aspects of the system were opaque; errors only found in the non-persistent group were those that can be overcome by learning.

Both the menu system and the natural language system accessed the same database. This supported the information needs of managers and was large and complex. The main functions of the interface were to support querying and report generation. The menu system was tailored to the needs of the user group and produced results about three times faster than the natural language system when the same query was put to both. However, the observed usage of the language system, despite a high percentage of errors, indicates that there was some added value to managers in the persistent group in using the language system. The results showed that persistent users exploited the additional selectivity of natural language through their use of coordination. They constructed ad-hoc sets of objects and constructed complex queries out of simpler ones. They also exploited the output presentation possibilities of natural language. Flexibility was exploited with elliptical inputs. The features that all users failed to exploit were discourse reference, negation, comparatives and quantification. Whittaker and Walker suggest that users may need to be explicitly taught the benefits provided by a feature over those of alternative interfaces. Users may also have been using the system in the way they had been accustomed to using the menu system. Many users repeated queries rather than use discourse representations or ellipsis, for example. And the error rates were high, particularly for lexical errors. Consequently, out of the 50 potential users, only 9 used the system in more than 30 sessions. It is unclear whether the lack of persistence on the part of most users for the language system could be improved with a more adequate lexicon and less restrictive syntax.

(e) The ATIS evaluations

The ATIS evaluations are relevant both to the database query task and to speech understanding evaluation. We concentrate on the former here.

ATIS is a DARPA Spoken Language Systems (SLS) application: Airline Travel Information System. It uses a database of flights and information on aircraft, stops, connections, meals and so on, which has been taken as a common test and evaluation base by teams participating in the SLS conferences (S&NLW, 1991; S&NLW, 1992) and also also, now, by others working on S&LP. The RM (Resource Management) corpus has been similarly used for speech recognition.

The ATIS evaluations are of interest here both as major, multi-site evaluations of DBQ systems, from the point of view of the particular task problems involved, and as following the pattern of IR evaluation in promoting serious comparative evaluation through the use of a common test collection, in the same way for NLP as the MUC conferences. The initial development and form of the ATIS evaluations, and the experience of and lessons for evaluation methodology gained from them are described in detail in Boisen and Bates (1992) and Bates (in Thompson, 1992).

The methodology was black box and has been implemented using an automatic evaluation system. It is performance related, addressing effectiveness in a simple way; only the content of a reply retrieved from the database is evaluated. If the reply is correct, it is assumed that the system understood the query correctly. Queries were collected initially as raw data in both spoken and transcribed text forms, using 'Wizard scenarios'. The advantages of this are firstly that it produces queries and draft answers at the same time, but additionally it provides evidence that the language obtained is strongly influenced by the particular task, domain and database being used, and by the amount and form of data returned to the user. The disadvantages are the time and effort involved in setting up Wizard of Oz data collection exercises. Also, the technique is very sensitive to the precise protocols under which the data is collected; small deviations can often lead to significant effects on the linguistic data collected.

Once answers to the queries are provided and expressed in a common standard format, some portion of the queries and answers need to be set aside as evaluation data, the remainder functioning as training material. One of the hardest tasks is agreeing the meaning of queries. Without some consensus, it could easily be the case that systems produce very different replies to the same query, and each is right according to their own system's definition of terms. Similarly, it has to be agreed what constitutes an acceptable answer. For the sake of automatic evaluation, a canonical reference answer (or minimum 'right' answer) is developed for each evaluable query in the training set, determined by both domain-independent linguistic principles and domain-specific stipulation.

The results are presented as : number right, number wrong, and number not answered, with a weighted error percentage (so wrong replies are twice as bad as no reply at all). The overall score is right - wrong. There is some flexibility in accepting additional information in replies not explicitly requested. This is because ATIS has an interactive setting. However, such tolerance could conceal the system's inability to determine exactly what the user requested. Overall, therefore, the ATIS evaluation is effectiveness oriented, addressing a system's ability to meet its objective rather than serve its function, and to a considerable extent treating system development as setup.

As well as the actual ATIS evaluation results (cf S&NLW 1991, S&NLW 1992), the enterprise provided a body of evaluation resources now available from NIST for any research group that wishes to purchase them, and with which they can evaluate their own NLP system. This comprises the ATIS relational database, a corpus of paired queries and answers, protocols for data collection, software for automatic comparison of replies, the 'Principles of Interpretation' specifying domain-specific meanings of queries, and the CAS (Common Answer Specification) format.

ATIS and dialogue evaluation

Bates and Ayuso present a slightly different evaluation methodology for using ATIS, for evaluating *dialogues* (Bates and Ayuso, 1991). They argue that in dialogue evaluation, it is wrong to measure whether systems produce the same answers as the wizard, or ones agreed upon by the Principles of Interpretation. The goal should be for systems to respond reasonably to each input, and allow the user to reach her goal. They suggest two ways of possibly doing this. The first deals with the aspect of breadth in the dialogue tree, and the second deals with reasonable responses to partially understood input.

Breadth in the dialogue tree concerns an ability to handle diverse utterances in context. In other words, at a particular point in a dialogue, how many possible alternative utterances, from a given set, can each system handle? The set is obtained by asking at least 10 people to add a next possible utterance at that point in the dialogue. For evaluating responses as reasonable or otherwise in the case of partially understood input, a new class of response is suggested called 'qualified answer', this being a response based on the partially understood input, but indicating that it may not be quite what was required. Two new categories should then also be added to the current set of possible results as Right, Wrong and No Answer; Qualified Answer Reasonable, and Qualified Answer Not Reasonable.

In fact, the manifest limitations of the narrow, answer-based method of evaluation initially used for ATIS led to new evaluation proposals with approaches based on the use of dialogue session log files: these allow for assessment determining whether over the whole session a scenario problem had been solved, and in what time, etc, as well as many more specific measures addressing particular aspects of the system's interactive operation.

Hirschman et al (1993) describe the first such end-to-end evaluation, designed to overcome some of the perceived limitations of the earlier tests focussed on question-reply pairs, i.e. to consider system function as well as objective, though still with some abstraction or approximation on setup. The intention in particular was to broaden assessment to allow for utility as well as correctness in a strict sense; to cover two important features of real extended dialogues, namely mixed initiative and the user's responses to system deficiencies; and also to consider timing as relevant to entire tasks and to the whole dialogues, involving more than one exchange, normally required to carry these out. The experiment therefore gathered complete dialogue information (primarily in the form of log files) as the basis of both task-level and utterance-level metrics, where the latter were more richly characterised than in the earlier standard tests. The task-level metrics covered correctness of task solution (and indeed whether the task was completed), and time to solution; and there was a user satisfaction questionnaire. This more elaborate style of evaluation therefore to some extent addresses efficiency and acceptability as well as effectiveness At the utterance level user inputs where characterised as new information, repeat, rephrase, or unevaluable; and system outputs as answer, system-initiated directive, diagnostic message, or failure to understand, with further categorisation of the first three of these output types: answers could be correct, incorrect, partially correct, or can't decide, while directives and diagnostics could be appropriate, inappropriate, or can't decide. Timing information was also gathered for the utterance-level transactions. The earlier ATIS Principles of Interpretation were applied as far as possible; however a separate study showed, not surprisingly and in line with many other similar studies, a lack of complete agreement between judges and a decline in agreement with an increase in the number of judges.

The evaluation was immensely more effort than the previous ones, since human judgements of the log files were needed, but it must be deemed more suited to the general nature of information-seeking inquiry where the user's needs are very often not fully specifable in advance. However human variability in the experimental subjects, i.e. notional system users, was high, and to control for it properly a much larger test than the trial would be required; it would also be necessary, for future, serious end-to-end assessment, to make careful choices of task scenario, to extend the Principles of Interpretation to cover utility, and to derive reliable log file scores from multiple evaluators. More generally, Hirschman et al's discussion of the trial and of such issues as dealing with variability e.g. across the different sites at which the trial was conducted, shows the permanent tension in evaluation between the control required for informative and sound tests, the large range of environment variables and values, and the expense of evaluation.

As noted in the earlier discussion of recent developments in the ATIS MU evaluations, there have also been glass-box oriented proposals for SLS evaluation under the heading SemEval (Moore, 1994). The intention here would be to allow strictly NLP-motivated system comparisons at the technical level through assessment of a system's ability to deliver predicate-argument structures for inputs, to identify word senses (as defined by, for example, Wordnet) and semantic roles, and to determine co-reference relations. Clearly for this type of evaluation there is (as Moore notes) an intellectual as well as practical challenge in defining reference answers in a sufficiently detailed but theory-neutral way (albeit for the task domain), and a considerable effort to provide the stock of answers.

In fact, partly because of the costs of these approaches to evaluation, especially end-to-end, and partly for independent DARPA administrative reasons, these has been not official follow-up of the evaluation experiments and proposals just described. The main stream of ATIS evaluation, subsuming the three specific lines of spontaneous speech recognition, natural language evaluation, and spoken language evaluation, has continued much as before with a primary focus on a larger domain database and extended training and test data (cf Dahl et al, 1994; Pallett et al, 1994; also SLTW, 1994, 1995): points about the data collection are considered in Section 2.5.

(f) Conclusions on DBQ

Overall comments to be made from this section concern the evaluation of systems in situ, being used by the intended end users, with a concrete understanding of what the system is intended to do and for whom; in other words the system's function within the setup, given the purpose of the entire setup. The objectives in all three cases considered were the same i.e. to process English sentences, the results of which are used to query a database, and obtain replies. In the field evaluations, the end user community was a 'real' one, and within TQA , the database was also 'real'; its content had previously been available for query in the planning department used in the test. The functions of these systems were to provide users with answers to queries.

The good intent and relative success, in evaluation terms, of this area of NLP-related work, as in the MT case, is inevitably bound up with both areas having a clear understanding of function, purpose, role and standards for comparison. However, just as those engaged in NLP have found even the supposedly simple database query task much harder than was expected, it is also the case that, especially where query systems are intended to be robust and cooperative, evaluation is more complex than it may seem. In the database case too, because there is a necessary non-linguistic complement to the language subsystem, namely the data retrieval system, which does not apply in the translation or message processing case, it is essential to be clear, from the point of view of performance and evaluation, about what constraints this imposes on the language subsystem and what can properly be expected of this (Copestake and Sparck Jones, 1990; Androutsopoulos, Ritchie and Thanisch, 1995).

1.4 Speech understanding (SU)

(a) Introduction

Evaluation in the speech area is relevant for two different reasons. One is where speech is being viewed as spoken language. Here, though dealing with the acoustic signal presents a large and distinctive challenge of its own, evaluation is clearly relevant to (written) NLP. The other reason is that even where speech processing is approached simply as a signal processing task, the methods used to evaluate these systems may be of use for NLP.

As the account of the DARPA SLS evaluations in the previous section makes clear, having speech input adds an extra dimension of complexity to language processing. It is important in particular to be quite clear about just what is being evaluated: speech components or speech understanding systems. One of the problems with the ARPA SUR evaluation (Klatt, 1977) was that the design focussed on speech-relevant factors, like vocabulary size, or speaker properties, without sufficient regard to how these interacted with the global task, which was not itself constrained for the participating teams beyond being a generic inquiry task. Thus the impact of the nature of a user's question, in relation to language and meaning predictability, or branching factor, in input interpretation was not controlled. The ATIS design, in contrast, explicitly addresses this point.

Within the overall remit, the evaluation of the narrowly speech elements of a speech understanding system is (or is taken as) relatively straightforward, and is much the same as for a speech recognition task where either no language interpretation is needed, as in speech dictation, or simply a mapping onto fixed codes or messages. These speech elements may be taken as comprising the acoustic and lexical processors, without reference to higher language and knowledge levels from syntax upwards, though they may exploit statistical data including e.g. data on word pairs. In this situation evaluation can be by recognition error rate, definable for single words, or for sentences, in terms of the system's substitutions, deletions and insertions compared with the actual input word string. This method of evaluation thus presupposes that the 'real' input string is known, e.g. because the system has been read from a prepared text, or because an accurate, independent transcription of the input speech is available. It further presupposes that whatever the further system task is will benefit from lower error rates up front. It is of course possible to allow for feedback to or control of the speech processing using higher-level information. But this in turn presents two problems: one is that it may be difficult to separate out the contributions of the speech processors proper, and the other is that it does not allow for the fact that many tasks can be adequately performed without correct identification of all the words in the spoken input (see e.g. Boisen and Bates, 1992; Bates in Thompson, 1992). The DARPA results reported in Pallett (1991) and Pallett et al (1992) illustrate both speech recognition performance evaluation using the RM and ATIS data, and the closely related speech understanding evaluation. The material is also of interest in providing separate results for written and spoken input for the same application.

It is particularly difficult to engage in speech evaluation where the entire system design assumes a high degree of interaction between user and system, and makes explicit allowance for clarification and recovery, as in the VODIS telephone train inquiry case (Young, 1989). A field evaluation for this (Cookson, 1988) was essentially forced to address successful performance of the test inquiry tasks as wholes, since whether or not a particular word, or even whole input utterance, was correctly recognised at its particular time, or at some dialogue state, was not particularly relevant to system performance, even if it was intuitively apparent that some dialogues collapsed primarily because the speech processor could not cope: failures could equally occur because the dialogue design was not flexible enough or the system's model of the application was not comprehensive enough.

The VODIS task was intrinsically much less constrained than the ATIS one, which is database inquiry in a relatively strict sense, treating input questions apart from local anaphoric references and ellipsis as self-contained: in VODIS the specification of a user's need might be built up over a long series of exchanges. It thus illustrates how much more difficult it is to achieve any kind of control on testing and evaluation for dialogue systems. One way of doing this within the ATIS framework is suggested by Bates and Ayuso (1991), where a system's dialogue capabilities would be evaluated by its ability to handle any of a set of follow-up inputs at fixed points.

For speech recognition per se, therefore, the major concern is not so much evaluation design (the criteria used, specific way of measuring error e.g. weighting some types more than others), as test design: what sort of test data should be used. This covers vocabulary and utterance (sentence) specifications, speaker numbers and categories, speech style (running or with pauses etc), recording conditions, and so forth; and also how detailed and stringent the data collection conditions should be. Underlying this there has of course to be a view of the representativeness of the data, whether for the language in question or the task. The application of criteria like error rates is closely associated with the idea of benchmarks, and the DARPA evaluations make heavy use of this notion, embodying a de facto level of fair performance for a specific task (cf Pallett, 1991). These aspects of data provision and the invocation of benchmarks are considered in more detail in connection with the Evaluation Workshops discussed in Section 2.1.

As the ATIS experiments have already been considered in detail, and we are primarily concerned with systems using language, the material in this section will be relatively limited. We will consider two evaluations where speech processing is explicitly subsumed within language understanding. One of these is the ARPA SUR evaluations, taken here as making the first serious attempt to deal with the complex questions involved in evaluating speech understanding systems, and thus defining a starting point for the development of evaluation methodologies for these. The other is the VODIS field study, which explicitly addressed the question of evaluating a complex system with real, unprepared users. However we will as a preface indicate briefly the particular mode of evaluation used for continuous speech recognition (CSR) under DARPA, for instance with the RM material, with the aim of determining whether, and how far, the particular criteria, measures and methods used for the narrow speech case have any potential utility for NLP evaluation.

(b) DARPA speech recognition evaluation

The DARPA CSR evaluation used first the so-called Resource Management (RM) data, and then Wall Street Journal (WSJ) material, but in both cases read speech, so the prompt has been taken as transcript for comparison in evaluation. Relevant details for earlier work are given e.g. by Pallett (1992), and see S&NLW

(1991, 1992) gernerally. The material covered two broad categories with (a) a few speakers, allowing speaker-dependent recognition, and (b) many speakers, for speaker-independent recognition. The tests were also done without and with a fixed, common word-pair grammar. Evaluation tests were done with standard software, with scoring by Word Error and Sentence Error Rates. The former is defined as the ratio of errors (insertions, deletions and substitutions) to total words over the corpus; the latter as the ratio of sentences with one or more errors to total sentences. Significance tests for each measure are also applied. Examples of the results are given in e.g. Pallett (1991) and Pallett et al (1992).

The continued later development of the ARPA CSR evaluation (SLTW 1994, 1995) has been along the lines already laid down, with on the one hand increased challenge in the task and on the other with more sophistication in the evaluation methodology. Thus the RM data has been succeeded by the WSJ data, and tests have involved a much larger (20K) vocabulary and more emphasis on speaker independence. In relation to methodology, Pallett et al (1993) notes the introduction of further significance tests (while also noting a need to determine performance measure uncertainty), and of 'stress' tests designed to assess how systems perform without prior training on the relevant kind of data. The work reported in Pallett et al (1994) and in Kubala et al (1994) have exploited the idea of the 'Hub and Spokes' paradigm for a set of tests, making it possible to address a wide range of issues while imposing some common tests, but at not overwhelming cost, on all participants. Interestingly, the latter (the hub), while tackling a challenging task, imposed constraints on the training data and grammar models used, in order to maximise performance comparability. The optional spoke tests pursued trials relating to adaptation and to channel noise.

These CSR evaluations, while not directly concerned with NLP, are relevant in several ways. Thus while the tasks set are by no means simple, they are more restricted than SU or NLU and therefore serve as a convenient testbed for exploring evaluation methodologies and bringing them to a point where it is possible to consider the tools developed and lessons learnt for their positive or negative bearing on NLP system evaluation. In particular, there is a great deal to be learnt from the many finer points of evaluation that require attention, and the many tests called for, even where there is such a relatively unproblematic performance measure as word error rate. However these evaluations also concentrate on system objectives, and within a developer-oriented research setup.

(c) ARPA SUR

The ARPA SUR evaluation, summarised in Figure 6, was carried out in the seventies but has lessons for evaluation now. We have used Klatt's (1977) review of the evaluation, when the Harpy system developed at Carnegie-Mellon University was considered to have the 'best performance' (Klatt, 1977).

The criterion upon which these systems were compared was again linguistic. And also, as in the last section, the system's function in the setup was understanding in order to do a task. Harpy, for example, had the task of document retrieval. There was no interest in operational or economic considerations; this

```
CRITERION              : linguistic - task oriented,
                         eg. document retrieval

   SUB-CATEGORY        : black box
      eg. Variables    :    1000 word lexicon,
                            quiet room,
                            good close microphone,
                            cooperative speakers,
                            artificial syntax,
                            100 MIPS machines,
                            several runs
      eg. Parameters   :    average branching factor
      MEASURE          :       semantic error as % of
                                  sentences correctly
                                  responded to
      Methods          :          task performance tests i.e.
                                     accuracy of response
```

Fig. 6. Summary of ARPA speech understanding criteria, measures and methods

was a scientific evaluation where the task did not need to be relevant to real-world problems, nor the languages habitable, nor the systems cost-effective.

The systems' objectives were to be able to accept connected speech, from many speakers, in a few times real time. The variables were the size of the lexicon (1000 words); external conditions, such as the room being quiet, the microphone being close and good, and the speakers being cooperative; speakers having been trained and using an artificial syntax; the systems being run on a machine capable of executing 100 million machine instruction per second (100 MIPS), and the results were taken over a number of runs. The internal system parameters were such things as average branching factor, in other words, numbers of words to be considered at any point in processing, which was also used as a means of quantifying task difficulty.

The performance measure was semantic error as a percentage of sentences correctly understood, but the method for obtaining this measure involved determining performance or accuracy of task-related response, not checking whether all the words in a sentence were correctly recognised or not.

The SUR project was thus a study where systems were compared in their performance of a task as a means of drawing conclusions about their specifically language (in this case speech) understanding ability. It is also comparable with the MUC study described earlier in being a comparison of systems with the same environment variables. There was no attempt at realistic comparison with humans; the evaluation was against the set of ARPA goals, expressed here as system objectives given specific environment variable values i.e. accepting connected speech in a few times real time from many cooperative speakers, using a good microphone in a quiet room, with an artificial syntax and a constraining task, a 100 MIPS machine, and yielding less than 10% semantic error.

Is this a good model for NLP evaluation methodology? Most of the points about this kind of constrained laboratory evaluation have already been made about the MUC tests, though the constraints were more arbitrarily selective then in the MUC case. The main difference is that a seemingly arbitrary performance rating was set i.e. no more than 10% error, where instead of this ad hoc approach to effectiveness it would have been better to relate effectiveness to some analysis of human performance and the nature of the task itself, and thus perhaps to consider acceptability and not only effectiveness. However a much more important failing was that the systems under comparison were not engaged in the same task other than in the broadest sense, and certainly not the same application. Two were doing document retrieval but the other two were respectively doing travel budget management and answering questions for facts about ships. It was recognised too late that differences in the individual tasks meant that how successful the systems were in meeting the general, application-independent goals that were set could not be attributed only to differences between the systems themselves. It could also be attributed to the properties of the tasks which led to inputs which were more or less difficult to handle, as reflected in average branching factor. This was an important lesson which has clearly been learned and applied in the MUC evaluation, where the systems are all engaged with the same specific application.

(d) VODIS

VODIS (Voice Operated Database Inquiry System) was evaluated in a field trial, reported in Cookson (1988). VODIS was a prototype for a system for use over the telephone by the general public, in the domain of train timetable information inquiries. The field trial was to evaluate how untrained users interacted with the system during realistic tasks. The methodology was that of task performance for given travel 'scenarios' with analysis of results via the answering of questionnaires. One important variable was the gender of the subject. Results were compared between twelve males and twelve females. Another variable was the complexity of the task, in terms of whether the subject was inquiring about one or more than one journey.

The criteria considered were firstly, completion of the task, measured with times as well as rates, supported by an analysis of the number of occurrences of five different reasons why the task was not completed eg. frustration, too many subject pauses, too many misrecognitions, or system errors. Secondly, apparently applying a user effort criterion, the evaluation measured response length in number of words uttered by the subjects; the overwhelming majority of responses were one-word. The evaluation also considered isolated word recognition, and recognition of silences.

The results indicated primarily a difference in completion rate according

114

to task complexity, but males had a higher completion rate for all tasks. This was to a considerable extent a function-oriented evaluation within a 'semi-real' operational setup; however it also contentrated on performance effectiveness, albeit with some indirect concern with acceptability and even efficiency.

(e) Conclusion on SU

The main lessons of the speech work for evaluation are first, the fact that while being able to isolate a system component operationally and consequently test it independently is very useful, as with an acoustic/lexical processor, this is likely to be a suitable design and evaluation strategy for NLP systems only whose global task is relatively limited. All of the speech evaluations so far have been confined to narrow or undemanding tasks or setups. The second lesson is the requirement for proper coverage of environment factors: speech evaluation calls for considerable sampling effort to cover the many variables involved.

1.5   Miscellaneous NLP task evaluations

Some non-trivial evaluations have been carried out in other task areas than those considered so far. One of these is summarising, which though obviously related to message understanding both in terms of general goals and processes, is sufficiently different in detail, especially from message understanding as interpreted in the MU conferences, to deserve separate treatment. It is also obviously related to indexing but, as noted earlier, because indexing has not in general involved heavy NLP, we are not considering indexing evaluation in detail in this report. Another area where there has been some evaluation work is in message categorisation. Categorisation (sometimes called classification or assignment in IR) may be intended simply to sort material for future retrieval, or may be designed explicitly for immediate routing (conventionally called 'selective dissemination of information' in IR). Both categorisation and routing may be based on quite refined content or topic classes (as in the current TREC evaluation (Harman 1991)), though work on this within an NLP framework has hitherto been based on rather broad content or user interest classes. Thus while categorisation and routing may appear to be related to ordinary IR, when the purpose and probably also classification grain are different it is not clear that normal approaches to IR evaluation simply carry over. In this section we consider first DeJong's evaluation of his summarising system, and second one account of an experiment in categorisation.

(a)   Summarising: FRUMP

FRUMP (DeJong 1979, 1982) was a text skimming program developed as an AI effort at Yale. It summarised news articles, and was based on the use of a data structure called a sketchy script. Altogether, FRUMP had some sixty scripts, covering a large range of topics, but the set was not viewed as exhaustive.

Evaluation in FRUMP took place initially over a 24-hour period in 1979, and there was a second evaluation on a different basis over a 6-day period in 1980.

```
CRITERION                :  linguistic - task oriented.
                            i.e. eliciting relevant information

    SUB-CATEGORY         :  black box and glass box
       eg. Variables     :      story types
       eg. Parameters    :      sketchy scripts,
                                 vocabulary,
                                 syntactic knowledge
    MEASURES             :          completeness,
                                    accuracy (precision)
       Methods           :              task performance tests i.e.
                                        comparison with 'correct'
                                        results
```

Fig. 7. Summary of FRUMP criteria, measures and methods

During these times, FRUMP was run continuously in real time on United Press International news stories. On both occasions there were some 120 stories that FRUMP could have possibly understood: there were some articles with topics outside FRUMP's stock of scripts; others were not news articles, or not scripty news articles. In the second evaluation, summarised in Figure 7, processing was classified as correct (understood everything), nearly correct (missed a fact or incorrect script variable binding), missed (correct script available but not identified), or wrong (incorrect script used with either correct script missing or correct script present).

In other words there were two measures here for a linguistic criterion assessed on a task-oriented basis. The main question was: does the program understand the linguistic input, but this was evaluated according to whether it understood sufficiently to access an appropriate script and fill in the appropriate details. The measures for this were accuracy or precision, and completeness. The method was comparison against stories as they would have been summarised correctly within the constraints of FRUMP's sketchy scripts. Causes of errors were ascertained, so the investigation was 'glass box' as well as 'black box'. These were primarily missing vocabulary, and secondly missing scripts. Some errors were caused by insufficient knowledge of syntax.

FRUMP's objectives were to process linguistic input, correctly predict the appropriate sketchy script, substantiate it, and fill slots. Its function was again within a research setup, namely summarising news stories for the purpose of investigating a particular method and theory of text analysis.

The FRUMP study can naturally be compared with the MU evaluations described in Section 1.2. The systems in both cases have similar objectives: processing news stories as linguistic input to identify key content, though in

FRUMP's case this notionally refers to 'covering' concepts where MUC allows for very selective concept extraction. The appropriate type of evaluation is thus also similar, since it has to determine whether key content in the source text has been correctly captured and (re)presented. However the evaluations themselves have important differences. MUC is about the comparison of different systems in order to draw some conclusions about these different methods for attaining their objectives. A major issue in MUC is standardisation of evaluation methodology and data to establish benchmark tests for systems of this sort. FRUMP was too early a contender for such an analysis, and its evaluation methodology was thus less rigorous. However, the measures and issues are not altogether different. It is also worth noting that, as DeJong has pointed out, the evaluations of FRUMP were more substantial and more demanding because they involved raw external data, than many conducted in academic NLP research.

Similar problems arise, for example, in considering how expert system performance can be measured in relation to explanation quality. Swartout (1990) lists a number of desiderata, namely fidelity, understandability (which subsumes factors like terminology, abstraction, viewpoints, coherency etc), sufficiency (of knowledge to support explanation), low construction cost, and operating efficiency. Swartout claims these desiderata lead to some metrics for evaluating expert systems, though this is not too obvious and he does not elaborate. Thus it is not clear how precisely a system's ability to give explanations from different viewpoints, at different levels of abstraction, or of detail, is to be measured. More importantly, from the NLP point of view, while it may be possible in some cases, like terminology, to separate the NLP contribution from the non-NLP one determining explanation content, it may be much more difficult in others, e.g. composability or explanation flow. It is true that Swartout's examples from the medical domain suggest that in such a domain the NL/non-NL distinction could be made. But this does not mean that the practical evaluation business of showing whether and how far an NLP subsystem succeeds in using terms familar to its users, or in defining unfamilar ones through familiar ones, is a straightforward matter. And overall, Swartout's desiderata illustrate the real problems of NLP evaluation when NLP is used as an integral and necessary part of a task which is itself not primarily an NLP task, and is also an intrinsically open one.

(b) Categorisation and routing: CONSTRUE

Though as noted (and cf Lewis, 1991), is not obvious that standard IR performance measures should be applied without qualification to evaluate text categorisation, Hayes, Knecht and Cellio (1988) report an evaluation doing this in a simple way. Thus they measured the performance of their system (later called CONSTRUE, and designed to support both routing and retrieval of news stories) against human categorisation, taking the human results as the base to measure recall and precision for the system. The study illustrates the care needed to interpret performance figures very well, since high figures may be obtained with coarse categories.

1.6 Text retrieval

As mentioned in Chapter 1, information retrieval has a well-established test and evaluation tradition providing, in particular, a methodology for laboratory experiments. It is not appropriate to discuss work done in this field in detail here, as language processing other than that exploiting statistical facts does not figure largely in conventional automatic indexing and retrieval. However, though text retrieval is not defined here as an NLP task, of the fine-grained kind with which we are primarily concerned, [4] recent developments make some points pertinent.

First, the DARPA/NIST Text Retrieval Conferences (TREC) now underway (cf Harman, 1995a,b; IP&M, 1995; TREC-1, 1993; TREC-2, 1994; TREC-3, 1995), are very large comparative evaluations in terms of the amounts of data involved, the number of participating teams, and the range of approaches tested. The sheer scale of the TREC evaluations, significantly larger than the other DARPA ones, is noteworthy in itself. More specifically, from the data point of view, the TREC tests have involved both files with very large numbers of items and retrieval on full text as opposed to shorter document surrogates like titles and/or abstracts. However, as is evident from Sparck Jones (1995), TREC-1, -2 and -3 have been evaluations entirely within the classical paradigm with automatic offline processing delivering ranked output assessed using recall and precision for both retrospective, one-off searches and (very artificially) for incoming document routing; and as Saracevic (1995) in particular emphasises, it is necessary to take a much wider view of retrieval, especially in relation to users, i.e. to allow for much richer and more varied setups and hence system environments than these remote, laboratory-type tests do.

This is related to the second point, namely the spread of interactive searching, especially by end users, and the challenge to evaluation design of conducting proper and informative tests for interactive searching: these are, in particular, the sheer variety and complexity of the users' activities, and the lack of replicability for individual searches.

In general, following the pattern of other DARPA community evaluations, the trend in successive conferences was first to try new, though not radically different data, and to make the task harder, primarily by using less well-formulated requests. But again, as with the other evaluations, TREC has started to move on the one hand towards more genuinely different specifications of the task (e.g. as interactive, as filtering), and on the other towards glass box tests on system factors that are intended to identify the performance contributions made by individual components of the large and complex systems hitherto evaluated as wholes (e.g. (sub)database discrimination, interactive search resources). The interest with the latter is not so much at the finest level of alternative parameter settings within individual systems, but at the coarser grain where parameter settings can apply across systems: for instance for the linguistically-relevant topic of the value of phrasal index terms this is the distinction between, say, whether indexing phrases of the type used by an individual system are or are not defined

---

[4] and it must be emphasised this is only a matter of present definition

to include conjunctive phrases, and whether phrases as defined by two different systems are of distinct types based, say, on linguistic or statistical criteria. TREC-4, underway at the time of writing (Harman, 1995b), thus has a less monolithic design than the previous TRECs, covering both mainstream tests of the same type as previous conferences and other tests defined by 'tracks' e.g. an interactive track.

As a natural consequence, new evaluation measures are being introduced, like 'utility' for the filtering task and elapsed search time for the interactive track. Other, finer measures more appropriate to interactive searching are also envisaged for the latter, like 'effort' and 'complexity', which however not only require a rich reporting format for the search protocols but also raise considerable difficulties for inter-system comparison, however useful they may be for intra-system diagnosis. Significance tests are also a problem. Some tests were explored for the TREC-3 results, but there was controversy over their suitability.

The evolution of TREC has therefore resembled that of the other DARPA evaluations, with an initial stage of design and performance consolidation on a 'main' task followed by branching out on the one hand into variant tasks (whether determined by change of data or function), and on the other into system 'deconstruction'. But there are serious difficulties, as with the analogous written and spoken language proposals for MU and SLS (Grishman, 1994; Moore, 1994), with the deconstruction strategy, since this requires either the ability to isolate individual components and define their roles, so that one can in principle and even in practice conduct cross-system tests by 'plugging in' alternatives; or the ability to define data-derived 'objects' like predications or word senses that are deemed necessary intermediates for successful task performance. However in the retrieval case there may be a necessary interdependence between parameters, for example in the definition of phrasal index terms and the form of scoring in request-document matches, so the former alone cannot be changed; and past research testing assumptions about natural or proper index terms has precisely shown that objects may be much less autonomously solid than the MU/SLS ones. We return to these issues for the structure of mega-evaluations later and in Chapter 3.

The broader view of IR evaluation than TREC has so far been able to compass is reflected not only in Saracevic's emphasis on retrieval as a 'living' task with human users, but also in IP&M 1992, a successor to Sparck Jones (1981) in addressing a range of retrieval evaluation issues that are equally of general relevance to NLP system evaluation in recognising the effects of environment and task or function complexity on evaluation. The growth of automated retrieval systems in terms of larger files, more varied materials, and world-wide networks increases the difficulty of evaluation, and this is further exacerbated, as Saracevic points out, when retrieval is just one embedded task in a user's heterogeneous working situation.

The design for the interactive track of TREC-4 is a first attempt in this direction for full-text searching, but is still relatively modest; and it illustrates the problems very well because, since it is basically an evaluation of a setup, namely interactive searching, as a whole and thus is only indirectly and weakly a comparative test of the system resources that the searchers use.

1.7 Cross-task issues

The aim of this section is to consider implications for NLP evaluation from the evaluation studies in particular NLP task areas discussed so far. What are the commonalities, the differences? How application dependent are they? How successful or useful are their evaluations, and for what or whom? Section 2.6 then leads on from this to consider the implications specifically for the evaluation of generic NLP systems such as CLARE.

Two things are clear from the preceding descriptions. Firstly, although there is much NLP research which is academic in motivation and style, and is evaluated (though this is perhaps too strong a description) in an informal way ("This suggests theory T is computable."), we are not concerned here with this kind of evaluation. Even though as with much of AI in general (Cohen, 1991), raising the scientific standard implies addressing evaluation more seriously, we have concerned ourselves here with what may be described as 'working system' evaluation. This subsumes investigations and experiments both with existing 'in-service' systems and with systems, subsystems and components designed for future practical use or envisaged as potentially applicable. And as the evaluation of FRUMP suggests, this approach to evaluation is also relevant to what may be primarily viewed as academic research. Secondly, system-oriented evaluations in NLP to date have been scattered, with patchy coverage and of uneven quality. It may be argued that this is mainly because the systems themselves are so inadequate. But as MT shows, some areas are quite well developed and so justify evaluation; and both here and elsewhere there is both scope and a need for more evaluation, if only because it is important for monitoring research design.

However as a good deal has been done in the practically most advanced areas, the important question is: what can we learn from this about NLP evaluation?

First, it is evident that we have a great deal to learn about both the goals and the methods of evaluation. In the MT and database cases, the goals were clear. Systems intended for the commercial world, especially those designed to replace some existing system, must show themselves to be worth replacing the existing system with. They must either perform better, or faster, or more economically than the existing system. They should certainly 'fit in' operationally with the other components of the setups, both human and computational. So, in this sense, the criteria are obvious, and the important measures follow naturally i.e. accuracy and completeness of task performance versus cost-effectiveness, *and* in comparison with existing alternative ratings of accuracy and cost. In addition, the natural users to test the system with are those who currently interact with the existing means of translation or query, and who would therefore be interacting with the replacement system if operational. Issues such as habitability follow naturally then, within the calculations of gains versus costs. However, as the MT case shows, the setup can be as important as, or more important than, the system proper as the focus of evaluation, since the nature and scope of the system may imply considerable change in the structure and working of the setup as a whole, and in particular in the activities of the immediate system users, for instance when they become post-editors rather than translators.

In a non-commercial environment, with a task that has no, or at any rate manifest specific, existing, counterpart, such as in the MUC case or the ARPA SUR speech evaluation, or more generally in NLP, what are the possible goals of evaluation? It could be aimed at testing the linguistic theory implemented within a system. Alternatively, it could test the implementation of the linguistic theory. Both these goals require glass box evaluations, and the methodology would therefore be primarily observation and diagnostic tracing. But even with so straightforward a goal, the eventual function of the system and the purpose of the setup in which it finds itself still play a part in evaluating behaviour in the black box sense. For example, it may be unnecessary to deal with particular English constructions in some contexts and yet very important in others. This point was discovered in TQA's evaluation. Certain constructions that the system could handle were never used by the users. Should such constructions appear in the test set and hence be part of the evaluation? And what about those constructions that users rapidly and easily learn never to use? Should they be represented in the test data?

MUC's answer to this is to set up an artificial exemplar context i.e. the extraction of information about terrorism from news articles. This is (we infer) deemed either to represent the kind of information extraction that is currently done, albeit more informally, by humans, or to embody a new, machine task specification. The constructions common to such contexts are included in the test data. The system function becomes one of linguistic processing for message understanding and about terrorism, and the evaluation goal that of establishing whether linguistic processing is adequate for this, so systems are compared as to how accurately and completely they can perform this particularly defined task. Thus in MUC-3 there was no comparison of time and costs to offset against accuracy and completeness, though these two measures were compared with the collective performance of a set of humans. Later MUCs, though more complex and using new data, shared these characteristics, though the use of new data implied a a new goal of establishing system generality, and the extra measures moved slightly towards consumer interests. Secondary goals in the MUC case were about evaluation and methodologies for evaluation, but leaving such motivations aside for the moment, what has been gained from MUC? Initially it demonstated that one system performed better than another (or not) with respect to an 'understanding' of terrorism and being able to extract such information from texts. But generalising these message understanding capabilities, as sought and to some extent shown by later MUC results, has still been decoupled from the full demands of operational environments and reference to qorking setups; and there seems to be no escape from the fact that the precise capabilities required of such working systems will have to be laid down, and then the systems evaluated against these, just as in the MT and database cases.

It could be claimed that the ARPA SUR evaluations did have such precise requirements, albeit without being about working systems in real environments. But this is just where these evaluations were somewhat meaningless. Of what value was it to discover that one system could perform some toy task 'better' (according to a set of arbitrary requirements) than another system performing a different task? In other words, clarity of goals are essential to an evaluation, but unless those goals conform to something 'real' in the world, this can only be a first stage evaluation. At some point the *utility* of a system, has to be a consideration, and for that one must know what it is to be used for and for whom, and testing must be with these considerations in mind.

So what are the possibilities for application- and task-independent NLP evaluation *strategies*, as opposed to just independent evaluation *principles*, even NLP-oriented as opposed to quite generic ones? Is Flickinger's view that general evaluation tools are a chimera, correct? Can we find evaluation criteria and strategies that are independent of task and setup types, given two problems:

(a)   that of distinguishing NLP from a larger task (as in medical consultation) as far as the system itself is concerned; and

(b)   that of distinguishing the system from its setup, especially in relation to the activities of its human users.

These questions are discussed in the next section. For now we only comment that the linguistic evaluations discussed in this review were all closely and dependently associated with task performance, with system indistinguishable, or at any rate not properly distinguished, from setup.

From a different tack, it is possible to view the evaluation efforts discussed so far as contributing to the advancement of evaluation methodology in NLP as a whole. They all provide important lessons for the future with regard to what is involved in setting up an evaluation, even if the NLP evaluations done so far have been limited and inadequate in many respects. We shall attempt to summarise here what those lessons are, noting that Figures 1 to 7 can be referred to again for examples:

(a)   clarity of the system's *objectives* for testing, in the light of the system's *function* and the setup's *purpose*. (See Figure 3 of Chapter 1 for examples which indicate clearly the distinctions and boundaries between these terms). The performance *criteria* and *measures* used should accurately reflect these objectives.

(b)   clearly understood environment *variables* and system *parameters*. Each should only be altered whilst keeping all other factors constant, implying a correct perception of the nature of a system *run* and of the limited informativeness of the performance measure obtained for that run alone. A set of runs in *grid* formation will therefore generally be required for a useful evaluation.

(c)   an understanding of the role and nature of possible *qualitative* and *quantitative* measures, and in particular of the limitations even of quantitative measures grounded in ultimately subjective judgements about, for example, correct concept representation or information extraction.

(d)   the importance of numerous, and more specifically, statistically sound, *test data* samples with clarity as to precisely which of the objectives they are designed to test, and about the environment variable values they embody.

(e)   clarity of *rationale* for comparisons, both comparisons with human performance of a task, or competitive comparison with other systems performing the same task. Proper comparison also requires correct *granularity* in evaluation, because of the redistribution of tasks and functions within and between systems and setups.

(f)   awareness of the depth to which particular strategies can be pushed downwards from *black box* to *glass box* evaluations. In other words, what conclusions can be drawn about implemented theory, from observed behaviours? It is worth pointing out, that generally any such conclusions would require further testing as the focus of different evaluations.

(g)   the potential utility of a general purpose *test suite* with wide coverage of linguistic phenomena, and which could be generally available for testing (possibly however, only within specific areas of NLP evaluation, such as database query, where the notion of general-purpose (i.e. 'typical') *test collections* is perhaps more appropriate).

The only common system objective for the evaluations examined so far, is a general one of processing some natural language input in order to produce some output. In the MT case, this was input in one language to be converted to output in another; the function of the systems was translation for a variety of purposes depending on context, and users. In the database query case, the input was converted to a form in which the database could be queried and an answer obtained; the function was to provide answers within a setup purpose again varying according to the nature of the task and users. In the MUC case, the input was processed to determine whether it was relevant and to elicit only what was relevant to the system's function of filling information slots.

There was a linguistic criterion therefore in all cases, but only in terms of language FOR something. The point has already been made that the NLP-related evaluations discussed have been task-oriented. The common measure is that of task performance i.e. accuracy or precision of translation or of eliciting appropriate information for example, and recall or completeness in terms of not missing anything. Common methods for obtaining these measures were such things as error counting, subjective grading, and observation. None of these are purely objective, or purely quantitative. How 'good' as in faithful or accurate a translation is, or how 'good' as in 'relevant' a piece of information is are difficult things to quantify. This is why it is important to know what one's measure is in comparison with. In the ARPA SUR evaluation and in MUC, there was a notion of the 'perfect' or 100% performance rating. In MT, there is a human translation comparison. Operational and economic criteria were only relevant in the MT and database cases which involved some comparison with an existing, commercially viable system.

In general, there are four aspects of evaluation to be considered:

(a)   what is involved in evaluation in itself?

(b)   what is involved in comparative evaluation, especially in relation to human performance?

(c)   what is involved in competitive evaluation, where different systems are used for the same task in the same setup?

(d)   what is involved in evaluation with benchmarks?

What characteristics do these all have in the NLP area, and what constraints do they therefore place on the conclusions to be drawn from evaluations?

It may be the case that attempting to determine commonalities across the evaluation studies of these different areas, and trying to generalise and to consider the possibility of NLP evaluation methodologies as general tools is, as Flickinger et al (1987) suggest, an impossibility anyway. If task performance is crucial to evaluation, then the fact that language has so many diverse uses surely presents an insurmountable problem for a uniform approach. Flickinger et al (1987) also refer to the lack of common assumptions brought to NLP efforts. They illustrate this point by suggesting how problematic it would be to rate the syntactic accuracy of a semantically driven parser, whose main purpose is to avoid many anomalous, but syntactically correct, parses. Maybe this is simply a realistic viewpoint; evaluation studies must inevitably be related only to systems and setups grounded in common assumptions about such things as the boundaries between syntax and semantics, between domain-independent semantics and application interpretations, and how such aspects might therefore be separately evaluated. Maybe the development of benchmark testing within particular sub-areas, such as within MT, or within database query and so on, is as 'general' as we can aim to get with NLP evaluation.

2   General developments

In this section of Part 2 we review material and topics bearing on NLP evaluation but independent of specific NLP tasks. We consider first some workshops devoted to evaluation, and then tutorials (2.1 and 2.2). These sections are followed by a discussion of the EAGLES Report in Section 2.3, and then in 2.4 of some other individual proposals for general methodologies. After this we examine data and tool issues (2.5), generic and then 'mega' evaluation (2.6 and 2.7 respectively) and, very briefly, speech processing as a task-independent requirement. In Section 3 we draw our overall conclusions on evaluation to date. These discussions range widely over such concerns as the goals of NLP system evaluation, different angles on it, types of evaluation, prerequisites for evaluation, etc.

2.1   Evaluation workshops

One indicator of the significance that is now being attached to S&LP evaluation has been the occurrence of workshops devoted to evaluation, covering the issues involved, current practice, desirable practice, necessary resources, and so forth. This section considers three such major workshops held respectively in Pennsylvania in 1988 (Palmer, Finin and Walter, 1988), at Berkeley in 1991 (Neal and Walter, 1991), and at Edinburgh in 1992 (Thompson, 1992). We also consider separately, and briefly, two parsing evaluation workshops. Finally, as the various DARPA conferences can be seen from one point of view as evaluation conferences, we consider them together, for the light they collectively throw on S&LP evaluation methodology and its present state, in the last part of this subsection.

a)   Workshop for the evaluation of NLP systems, Pennsylvania, 1988

The two basic premises of the Workshop (Palmer, Finin and Walter, 1988) were firstly that it should be possible to discuss NLP system evaluation separately from the application task, and secondly that there are two types of evaluation i.e. glass box and black box. The Workshop then set out to define the notions of glass box and black box, and define criteria for each of these.

'Black box' evaluations focus on what a system does. Performance should then be measured according to the accuracy of the output, given a particular input. But, since such performance is in terms of the particular application task, it can be difficult to comparatively evaluate systems using language when they have different functions in their setups.

'Glass box' evaluation focusses on how well a system does something, rather than just whether it does it or not. It is an consideration of internal concerns such as linguistic theories and their implementations. For example, the coverage of particular linguistic phenomena and the efficiency of algorithms designed to deal with these.

(It will be evident that these are subset definitions of our notions of black box and glass box evaluation.)

The Workshop comprised some presentations and also working groups. The results of the black box working group were that useful black box evaluations can be done for message understanding and database question-answering domains, but more general text and dialogue understanding systems were not good candidates. Individual components from these latter types of systems could perhaps benefit from black box evaluations, however. This working party had divided into subgroups according to task application i.e. message understanding, database question answering, text understanding, dialogue understanding, and generation. The glass box working group focussed primarily on Marcus's proposals for the University of Pennsylvania on collection of data and automatic testing of parsers i.e. Treebank (see Section 2.5). Glass box methodologies for the areas of syntax, semantics, pragmatics and discourse and knowledge representation were also discussed in subgroups.

MUCK-11 (see 1.2) and Treebank (see 2.5) followed on closely from this Workshop, which was evidently the first indication of growing interest in the problems of evaluation amongst the American NLP community.

b) ACL systems evaluation workshop, Berkeley, 1991

Introduction

This section is an overview of the papers presented at the ACL Workshop on systems evaluation held at the University of California, Berkeley, 1991 (Neal and Walter, 1991). It is intended as an indicator of the state of NLP evaluation methodology at a key stage in the growth of interest in NLP evaluation, after some DARPA evaluations had become established and evaluation was becoming a matter of wide concern: what the most pressing concerns then were, the general levels of sophistication, the balance between generic and task-oriented methodology, and so on.

Both the ATIS and MUC evaluation initiatives described in earlier sections are represented, and there is also a comparison of these as two prominent, task-specific and domain-dependent evaluations. Neal et al contrast these with a proposal for a general methodology for evaluation across task types, domains and for different types of NLP systems. Automated syntax evaluation is represented, as is evaluation of semantic analysis and dialogue performance, although in the case of the latter two, only as discussion of issues and suggested criteria for evaluation. There is no associated actual evaluation program. Two papers address evaluations of on-going developments of particular systems. Two papers also discuss the issues hindering evaluation programs for natural language generation (NLG) technology. Again two papers then concern themselves with MT evaluations. And finally, a report is given of the NL Software Registry sponsored by ACL. Its aim is to facilitate exchange and evaluation of NLP software.

Evaluation of NLP systems via MUC and ATIS

(Though MUC and ATIS have already been considered in their own right, the material for this Workshop is summarised here, for completeness.)

126

The MUC and ATIS evaluation programs were then both concerned with comparing the performance of multiple systems on a common black box task, MUC for information extraction systems, and ATIS for spoken (and written) inquiry processing. Both enterprises have involved the development of evaluation procedures, and a comparison is made by Dahl, Appelt and Weir. Their considerations are of the issues arising from large-scale, multi-site evaluations, as well as any general insights into evaluation methodologies.

MUC and ATIS tasks are both simplified versions of real world applications. The simplification exists in order to reduce a hardware and software infrastructure which is peripheral to the evaluation, whilst avoiding oversimplification. As large scale enterprises involving many independent researchers they both have a formal process for decision making and administration. Issues related to data collection and scoring vary, but this is because of the different applications involved. For example, large volumes of data were easy to obtain for MUC, whereas for ATIS data collection required running Wizard of Oz experiments, and this is labour intensive. Also data collected at multiple sites needs standardising and coordinating. ATIS involves interactive question answering and so the ability to provide correct answers is of paramount importance. MUC, however, is about data extraction. Here the ability to recover certain types of information is all important. This focus on particular objectives was emphasised by Dahl et al; thus they claim it is most important not to lose sight of other important aspects of NLP systems. In particular, they refer to system 'usability' and '(trans)portability' i.e. the need to evaluate system setups and the role of operational as well as purely linguistic criteria. It was noted that neither MUC nor ATIS had yet used statistical significance tests on scores.

A non task-oriented evaluation procedure for all NLP systems

The Benchmark Investigation/Identification (I/I) Program (Neal, Feit and Montgomery) comprises the development of an 'evaluation procedure', intended to assist an evaluator in producing comprehensive, descriptive, evaluative 'profiles' for NLP systems. Such profiles should provide hierarchically organised, quantitative, objective descriptions of an NLP system's capabilities, interpreted in terms of the application for which the system is to be used. The procedure is appropriate for any type of NLP system, in any application domain and without modification for a particular test corpus or domain. This last aspect separates Benchmark I/I from other evaluation efforts, such as MUC. It is an attempt at designing an objective and general evaluation 'assistant' to an evaluator (who does not need to be a trained linguist). The procedure helps the evaluator create, modify or tailor test sentences for the particular NLP system, and score its performance. The scoring method quantitatively registers either success, failure or indeterminacy in processing a natural language test sentence, or an inability to compose a natural language test item at all for a certain procedure item.

Supporting the development of the evaluation procedure is the development of a database of non-subjective descriptive terminology for describing NLP capabilities (outside the context of their application to target software), and a classification scheme for NLP capabilities and issues that provides for the hierarchical organisation required. The procedure involves ensuring that each NLP capability is tested one at a time, without any other 'intruding' NLP capability to obscure the system's performance on the focal capability for the particular test item. The procedure is evaluated itself in an assessment program applied to three different NLP systems by three different evaluators at the end of three, six month periods. Assessment is by statistical analysis of variation of results, error analysis, informal critique of use and questionnaires for evaluators.

This Benchmark I/I Program is now also known as The Neal-Montgomery System Evaluation Methodology, described in Section2.4.

Evaluating the syntactic performance of NLP systems

The Workshop also reported on the automated syntax evaluation program developed as part of a collaboration between Boeing Computer Services, Bellcore, IBM, Hewlett Packard, University of Pennsylvania and others, to assist the evaluation of syntax performance of different broad-coverage parser/grammars of English. Parses are assessed in comparison to a hand-parse of the same sentence from the University of Pennsylvania Treebank, and this yields two measures of 'goodness': 'crossing parentheses' and 'recall'. The crossing parentheses score is the number of times that the candidate parse has the structure (A B)C for example, when the Treebank (reference) parse has one or more structures such as (A (B C)) which 'cross' with the test parse structure. The recall score is the number of parentheses pairs in the intersection of the candidate and Treebank reference parses (T intersection C) divided by the number of parentheses pairs in the Treebank parse T i.e. (T intersection C)/T. This is an additional measure of the degree of fit between candidate and reference parses.

The other paper from the Workshop proceedings related to syntax evaluations, by Nerbonne et al from the University of Saarlandes relates an attempt to develop a catalogue of syntactic data exemplifying the major syntactic patterns of the German language, i.e. to construct a test suite. The objective of the enterprise is primarily to obtain an empirical basis for diagnosing errors in NLP systems analysing German syntax. Such an exercise is comparable to the Sourcebook research program as described in Section 2.5, although more constrained in relating only to syntax. Also the Treebank project at the University of Pennsylvania is similar in being a large scale construction of test data, although Treebank concerns naturally occuring text and speech and the scope includes phonetics, semantics and pragmatics.

Nerbonne et al chose to construct their test sentences artificially, as opposed to collecting them from naturally occuring text. They justify this as follows:

1. in order to control systematically the range of phenomena and combinations of phenomena covered,

2. to include ill-formed data,

3. to maintain a small vocabulary, and

4. to exploit existing collections of data in descriptive and theoretical linguistics.

Evaluating semantic and pragmatic aspects of NLP systems

The two papers relevant to this subsection of the workshop indicate that semantics and pragmatics are relatively unexplored areas in terms of NLP system evaluation. Neither paper refers to any existing evaluation program; they are suggestions for preliminaries to eventual evaluation methodologies.

Hoard's paper, from Boeing Computer Services, is a suggestion about the development of test suites and evaluation metrics in which the resolution of ambiguity is primary. Resolving ambiguities is a fundamental task for any NLP system. He claims, however, that even for glass box evaluations it is not necessary to know precisely about all alternative interpretations, merely that all possible interpretations are recovered and the correct one is selected. Ambiguities may be word ambiguity, structural ambiguity, anaphora and definite reference resolution, and quantifier and negation ambiguity (scoping). In addition, evaluation criteria should consider how well a system establishes discourse relations, draws inferences and how fast it does all of this.

The focus of the paper is a proposed set of considerations with which to categorize NLP systems according to their capabilities. This would instruct researchers on the types of test suite to construct for the above evaluations, relative to the objectives of the system. These would additionally provide a means of comparative evaluation of systems in terms of their inherent coverage and extensibility, but not tied to specific domains or application areas. The evaluations would be at a high functional level. The considerations are:

1. the intended meaning of the semantic representation;

2. the closed- or open- world assumptions that are made and the values that the logic is capable of supporting;

3. what kinds of valid conclusions can be drawn using the logic and reasoning system;

4. what finitary assumptions are made;

5. what semantic primitives are assumed;

6. whether the semantic representations are intended to be partial or complete descriptions of sentences, and whether the representations support both full and elliptical constructions;

7. what kind of well-formedness conditions apply to the semantic representations;

8. whether an arbitrary or non-arbitrary mapping is assumed between syntactic and semantic representations;

9. the kind(s) of knowledge on which pragmatic interpretations are based;

10. the types of inferencing that are supported;

11. whether reasoning about classes (or higher-order rules) is available; and

12. whether the full range of natural language quantification is handled.

Fraser's paper on evaluating the dialogue management performance of SUN-DIAL (a large, collaborative, European speech understanding and dialogue system) also merely makes recommendations. In general in the SUNDIAL project, 'abstract' descriptions of a test corpus (or, more strictly, test collection), are what is modelled, where these descriptions are made at a number of different levels. For example, at the word recognition level, the corpus provides an abstract description of the words to be recognised which are then collected elsewhere and used in training. At a higher level, the corpus is tagged for word classes, syntax and semantics. Up another level, the largest phrases such as sentences are assigned a dialogue act label, and there is a dialogue grammar. At yet another level, the unfolding goal structure of each dialogue is described. Dependencies between descriptions at different levels result in the production of equivalence classses. In this way, generalisations over the corpus are produced.

Fraser suggests evaluating SUNDIAL using such a corpus annotated at different levels, including annotations for a range of dialogue phenomena. The capacity of the system to generate annotations which conform to a generalisation of those found in the corpus should be measured. He suggests developing an abstract, multi-level description of a corpus of simulation dialogues to define (i) a set of correspondences between different levels of analysis for a given string, and (ii) a set of well formed progression paths through dialogues, expressed at the levels of dialogue acts and goals. The primary criterion for evaluation of a dialogue system should then be its ability to reach the end of its progression paths consistently. A second criterion is that there should be no more insertion sequences than are required, for clarification, confirmation or repair of dialogue failures.

N.B. It is worth noting from the introductory section of the Workshop proceedings that amongst the MUC-3 participants at the Workshop, the prevailing view was that energies would be focussed on discourse analysis over the next year, and that issues of evaluation of pragmatic aspects of NLP urgently need addressing.

Two ongoing NLP system evaluations
The first of the papers in this subsection concerns natural language understanding within a data extraction system, by Flank et al, from Systems Research and Applications (SRA) Corp. Their claim is that it is better to separate out the NLP capabilities from the data extraction process. This contrasts their approach with ATIS and MUC, for example. They also do black box testing on individual 'modules' of the system, in order to get quantitative measures for each aspect individually. SRA's NLP system has separate modules for preprocessing such as morphological analysis, lexicon lookup, multiword phrase handling, and syntactic analysis, semantic interpretation and discourse analysis.

Cullingford and Graves then describe LMF (Lexicon Maintenance Facility) which they propose as a first pass at the kind of technology needed to both create and evaluate NLP systems. It comprises three subsystems; lexicon control testing and maintenance, a menu selection system and a Lisp reporter-interface. Lexicon control informs the user of the contents of the lexicon on demand, defines the corpora to test the English lexicon (each corpus being a collection of sentences designed to exercise the functionality of one lexical entry, i.e. a test suite), maintains the corpora and keeps track of changes to them, and assigns unique system-wide identifiers to query sentences. LMF has been used for the last two years, to extend EasyTalk, which is a commercial English language DBMS access tool. It documents the interrelationships between words and phrases 'understood' by EasyTalk, and controls its testing.

Evaluation and natural language generation

Evaluation for natural language generation remains at the discussion stage. Evaluating generation is difficult; it is hard to define what the input to a generator should be and it is hard to objectively judge the output. There are various reasons for this. Firstly, as an application becomes more complex, the more possible inputs the generator has to deal with and the more structurally complex these will be. Related to this is how closely the generator is tied in with the underlying program. The application may or may not be customised to the needs of the generator. Fluency as an aspect of the output may be better from generators using template selection, and so on. One answer may be to evaluate generation systems in the context of their application, by evaluating task performance. This does introduce the problem, however, of designing the task so that the better generators perform the task better, as opposed to the ones with the best interfaces, for example. Moore suggests a task-oriented evaluation of generation by assessing the impact of the generated utterances on users' behaviour and/or satisfaction with the system. This can be done directly via interviews with users or indirectly by measuring user performance.

Evaluation and MT

Alshawi, Carter and Rayner propose a simple method for evaluating the compositionality of a transfer-based MT system. Transfer-based systems can be seen as selecting word translations and then using rules to adjust the word replacements to form a sentence in the target language. Good compositionality means fewer adjustment rules. The emphasis here therefore is on linguistic coverage as opposed to system or setup behaviour, the latter being more usual for MT evaluations. There is also only the one evaluation criterion i.e. compositionality of transfer rules. The proposed evaluation method uses compositionality tables, claimed as a "good method for objectively evaluating one aspect of MT systems."

Church and Hovy offer a more extensive discussion of evaluation issues and MT, in which they argue strongly for task-dependent evaluation criteria. In particular, the task or target application should be well chosen for a satisfying evaluation paradigm, and they propose six desiderata for a good niche application. These are as follows:

1. it should set reasonable expectations; it should make sense economically;

2. it should be attractive to intended users;

3. it should exploit the strengths of the machine and not compete with the strengths of humans;

4. it should be clear to users what the system can and cannot do; and

5. it should encourage the field to move forward towards a sensible long-term goal.

The suggestion is that with a high payoff niche application, an MT system can stand up well to evaluation, even though the system may produce "crummy translations".

The Software Registry

The National Language Software Registry was established at the University of Chicago's Center for Information and Language Studies not long before the Workshop. Its purpose is to facilitate the exchange and evaluation of non-commercial and commercial software, and it is sponsored by the Assoctaion for Computational Linguistics. At the time of the Workshop, a summary had been produced of software sources and capabilities via reports from software developers. This was offered as a guide for researchers in terms of where to direct their efforts, and also as an index of the state-of-the-art in NLP. Large-grain metrics and parameters are employed to enable comparisons between systems, and this is complemented by extensive testing and review of selected software. For the latter, a pilot study was carried out on 33 items, each being tested, reviewed, and compared.

The survey information breaks down into:

basic administrative parameters, such as developers' address;
conditions on availability, such as fees, licenses and support provided;
description of system goals and underlying principles;
basic technical parameters, such as language of implementation; and
design features and test set size.

The software categories are: speech signal processing systems, morphological analysis programs, syntactic parsers, knowledge representation systems, multi-component systems, and applications such as interlinear text, dialect analysis etc.

Conclusions on the 1988 and 1991 workshops

The most obvious statement to make about the status of the whole area of NLP evaluation at the time of these two Workshops is that it had finally become accepted in the community at large as an important and serious issue. The 1991 ACL Workshop illustrates this by comparison with the previous one in 1988. The ACL Workshop reports on the evolution and development of real evaluation programs, some of which like MUC and ATIS were multi-site and involved many companies and universities. Test data were becoming available, including test suites and large collections of texts and other resources, in some cases involving rigorous or exhaustive treatment of linguistic phenomena. There was a Software Registry for NLP systems, and the Linguistic Data Consortium (LDC) was being established to develop and distribute speech and text corpora, lexicons and grammars. The Treebank project at the University of Pennsylvania provided linguistic analyses of quantities of spoken and written text.

Another important role of the 1991 Workshop was in the evolution of evaluation *standards*. These have to be accepted by the NLP community, and the Workshop was a focus and forum for discussion and feedback, as well as an indicator to the rest of the world of the current state of play.

In terms of the issues being dealt with and yet to be dealt with (in 1991):

1. In relation to the development of test corpora and other resources, there was some discussion at the ACL of the pros and cons regarding naturally occurring and artificially generated data for various testing purposes.

2. The papers concentrate almost exclusively on linguistic evaluation criteria, as opposed to operational, computational or economic aspects of NLP systems, with the exception of one of the papers on MT. This reflects a perceived need for evaluation at the research and 'pure' system level, prior to evaluations out in the market place.

3. As to applications, MT and database enquiry were taken as primary, but there is an indication of interest in general evaluation procedures, such as the Benchmark I/I program, and those used to compare systems for the Software Registry. On an individual basis, there is also the issue of testing the linguistic component of a system separately from its task. The SRA system for database enquiry did this, and similarly the MT system of Alshawi, Carter, and Rayner. However, the other paper on MT strongly advocates the alternative, task-oriented option, and this was clearly an open issue.

4. There seemed to be a consensus that the next major concentration of evaluation effort should be in the direction of the semantic and pragmatic aspects of NLP systems. It also seemed that evaluation for natural language generation systems would probably get off the ground soon.

c) Workshop on the strategic role of evaluation, Edinburgh, 1992

The Edinburgh evaluation Workshop (Thompson, 1992) was designed to focus specifically on the state of the art in S&LP evaluation with the aim of determining the strategic role of evaluation in S&LP research. This role was formally within the context of European funding programmes, but was in practice interpreted as relevant to S&LP research in general. The contributions also covered a wide range of topics, drawing in all aspects of evaluation. At the same time, the European context meant that the implications for evaluation of multilingual need and provision in NLP, so far neglected outside MT, were explicitly addressed.

Thompson's introduction, placing the Workshop in its strategic context, noted the rapid growth of interest in evaluation of all kinds, and listed the many recent meetings, initiatives and policies bearing on the principles and practice of evaluation. At the very least this interest implies more concern with evaluation at the individual project level; it also covers attempts to develop evaluation methodologies for language-using processes like generation in which little had (and has) been done so far, and to improve methodologies for areas long subject to evaluation, like MT; and it is more thoroughly embodied in the major controlled and competitive DARPA evaluations, which are complemented by the increasing range of enterprises intended to provide test data. The technical context for the Workshop could be taken as on the one hand the need to determine proper evaluation methodologies, and on the other to supply evaluation data. The challenge was thus on the one hand how far detailed as opposed to generic evaluation methodologies can be established for 'pure' NLP systems (or components) in themselves, and how far specific methodologies can be established for NLP tasks and applications; and on the other how far evaluation data can be provided which is relevant to and hence should be exploited by different NLP enterprises, partly for the information comparative evaluation supplies, and partly for cost-sharing reasons. If S&LP evaluation has been both inadequate and parochial, can it at least be made more adequate even if not, for good reasons, more metropolitan? The European interest in different languages, in porting systems across languages and, more specifically, in multi-lingual applications serves to emphasise both the direct value of multi-lingual test data in all senses, including translational 'equivalents', and that of any test and evaluation methodologies which can be applied across individual systems.

The Workshop presentations fell into a number of groups, but with overlaps and significant cross connections. The groups were those reporting on actual NLP evaluations and examining their general implications; considering challenging problems of evaluation; discussing speech processing evaluation; and analysing and presenting tools for evaluation; there was also an account of the lessons to be learnt from the related IR field.

The first group covered Bates's report on and analysis of the DARPA ATIS and MUC evaluations, and Gamback's account of a diagnostic study for MT. Bates's presentation made and suggested many relevant points, but for convenience in this report these are treated separately in our subsection (e) below on the DARPA evaluations. Gamback described in detail the development and application of a 'grid' design test for translation coverage and propriety for a compositional analyser/generator, showing how the methodology was applied in different domains.

The second group covered problems of evaluation, especially for individual components and subsystems, namely syntactic modules, semantic components and generation systems, and for particular tasks. Taking database access as the system task context, Nerbonne examined the problem of capturing and characterising individual component performance given its dependencies on other components within the system as well as on the system's functional task: he thus elaborated on the challenges also encountered in the ATIS evaluation. Dale drew attention to the substantial difficulties of evaluating language generators in the absence of anchors, i.e. of of clear specifications of starting points in the shape of intended message content expressed in some (common) meaning representation language, and in consequence of any means of determining whether linguistic output is 'correct'. Netter emphasised the value of systematic data for diagnostic testing as a response to the difficulties of establishing the performance of a syntactic component in isolation. Humphreys surveyed all aspects of MT evaluation, acknowledging its general intractability but also suggesting that for strictly linguistically-based translation, evaluation along rather narrow lines relating to the 'transformational' work done between source and target language sentences might be of use to system developers.

In relation to speech evaluation, Hieronymous reviewed assessment[5] goals, requirements, resources and methods, illustrating these by reference to e.g. the DARPA resource management task. Gibbon described the aims, approaches and products of the very comprehensive SAM project, designed to provide community speech assessment resources including both standards and methods specifications for data provision and recogniser/synthesiser assessment, along with definitions for support tools like a phonetic alphabet and lexicons, and actual data (for more than one language) and hardware and software. Much speech evaluation is addressed to recognition capability: Isard in contrast described a particular illustrative experiment in speech synthesis evaluation. Bates's report on the DARPA tests also covered strictly speech evaluation issues.

The treatment of tools included a discussion by King of the nature of tools that *customers* in particular may find helpful as aids in deciding whether to buy or install systems, especially when supplied with proper guidelines for their use. These guidelines could cover data collection for representative task corpora and test suite construction; instructions about how data and programs (or indeed evaluation programmes) should be combined to maximise information about individual phenomena; how simple quantitative measures should be designed, applied and interpreted, with the care needed here illustrated by the problems of translation error analysis given error ambiguity and overlap; and so forth. Netter reported on the provision of a catalogue of controlled sentence data, i.e. a test suite, for syntax analysis, and Gamback's investigations involved the use of a systematic test suite. The speech presentations by Gibbons and Hieronymous contributed to this topic as well, showing in particular how comparatively well developed the understanding of methods and tools is for speech work, though this is primarily where the needs to be met are rather narrowly defined, as often in speech recognition work.

Finally, Sparck Jones reported on the IR community's experience of evaluation, particularly emphasising the role of test collections; the need for grid designs to meet the requirements of extensive testing to allow for the ranges of environment variable values and system parameter settings; and the cost and effort of serious evaluation, a point which Bates's account of DARPA and Gibbons's and Hieronymous's speech presentations also made plain.

Workshop themes

The major themes running across the Workshop as a whole, the nature of

---

[5] "assessment" is the standard term used by the speech community

evaluation itself, of appropriate methodologies, and of relevant data, can be seen as naturally following from the Workshop remit. But they can equally be seen as major issues emerging from the various presentations and discussions, since though the Workshop was very constructive in contributing to a better understanding of evualation, it cannot in any way be taken as conclusive. The relevant general points and lessons to be drawn from the Workshop for our purposes are therefore as follows.

Theme 1: the nature of evaluation

First, on the nature of evaluation itself, the Workshop discussions were taken as suggesting a need, in considering evaluation, to maintain some key distinctions (see Thompson's introduction). The first is between evaluation for system developers, and evaluation for potential buyers or users, as this can involve not only the use of quite different criteria, but also can be associated with quite different perspectives. This distinction is typically, though not necessarily, associated with a second distinction between an examination of whole system performance with reference to some norm or exemplar (or through comparison between systems), and the examination of a whole system in relation to its fitness for some function or vis-a-vis some setup purpose, i.e. in some application context. This distinction is between intrinsic and extrinsic views of a system, and the two types of examination in question might be labelled "assessment" and "evaluation" respectively. These uses of these terms were not, however, universally accepted, and we believe it is preferable to use "evaluation", as we have hitherto, as a general cover term, decomposing it more specifically to characterise both these and other relevant distinctions in a finer-grained way. Thus, for example, we consider that assessment can refer legitimately to the extrinsic as well as intrinsic cases, as this recognises the role of performance criteria, measures and so forth in the extrinsic case. At the same time, it is not clear whether it is useful to envisage evaluation as an explicitly customer-oriented notion. One major danger of labelling only the extrinsic case "assessment" is that developers focussing on it may make unexamined, and in fact unsound, assumptions about what constitutes a system's fitness for function. But the main relevant point is that it was recognised that in general evaluation becomes more straightforward as the nature of a comparison is restricted, e.g. to alternative technologies, while evaluation that is more informative because broader in bound is harder to do.

Evaluation from either of the points of view just mentioned was further distinguished at the Workshop from 'diagnosis' ("finding where it hurts"), which was seen as being a glass box rather than black box operation, and one naturally of importance primarily for developers. However as diagnosis in this sense can refer to performance measurement as, for example, in investigating parsing correctness for a syntactic component, it is still a form of evaluation, and we prefer to refer to it as such both to emphasise the need here, in common with that for other types of evaluation, for proper procedures and to avoid 'portmanteau' effects like that of implying that glass box evaluation is only of interest to system developers. Glass box evaluation tends to be confined to the actual system (or subsystem); but it can cover human factors either explicitly by considering setup rather than system, or implicitly via environment variables. At the same time, as black box evaluation can be done for components at any level of system decomposition (though it may sometimes then have to be done indirectly), and as glass box evaluations may be handled more as comparative than as diagnostic enterprises, the claim that there is a real difference between evaluation and diagnosis may appear suspect.

However the consequences which flow from the attempt to determine the how and why of what happens, which may be taken as distinguishing diagnosis from evaluation, are important for S&LP evaluation. Thus while diagnosis may involve no more than seeking to account for outputs, the main motivation for diagnosis is when outputs are defective, whether by comparison with the performance of some other system or relative to some norm. Glass box evaluation is these respects just like black box evaluation, which may also be comparative or relative, but the particular danger which arises with diagnostic evaluation is that the attempt to attribute responsibility for performance by ever sharper decomposition and focussing can lead to artificiality and distortion. This point is well illustrated by Grishman, Macleod and Stirling (1992) where the attempt to evaluate parser performance against an external reference norm leads to quite radical modification of what the parser is intended, in its own terms, to produce. Evaluation of this sort, which is typically diagnostically motivated, clearly raises questions of legitimacy or at any rate, if it is very narrowly constrained, of real utility in relation to system behaviour and performance as a whole. Log data on the other hand, for example from interactive dialogue, is a good example of information which is useful for diagnostic purposes, if only informally, though it can also be used directly for evaluation, say as the base for measuring user effort, as in IR searching.

Thus though there may be differences of emphasis according to whether evaluation is just one part of well-conducted research with its own 'intellectual' goal or is the prime objective of a project, e.g. in seeking to determine whether System X is better than System Y, the evaluation principles should be the same, though the detailed procedures involved may quite properly not be. Again, though not merely perspectives on evaluation (e.g. cost versus quality) may differ, but also parties involved fall into distinct prompting *interest* or result *consumer* groups (users, buyers, developers, funders), this does not imply necessary differences in the qualitative or quantitative way that evaluation itself is done, even if the specific criteria and so forth applied may be different. The important point is to determine what the right criteria etc for perspective and punter are.

Theme 2: proper methodology

However in relation to its second recurring theme, developing proper and, ideally, common evaluation techniques, the Workshop's individual topics and examples served rather to emphasise the complexity and heterogeneity of S&LP, and also specifically NLP, evaluation. For instance just for grammars, what does it mean to say that one grammar has more 'coverage' than another? One has to look at how grammars handle phenomena as well as at what phenomena they handle. Similarly, how does one take account of the influence of the user's knowledge and of context in evaluating the effectiveness of language processing for a dialogue interface? The many elements involved in evaluation, perspectives, criteria classes and levels on the one hand and system structures and applications on the other, mean that it is quite unreasonable to look for common, or simple, evaluation techniques. The Workshop instead emphasised the need for very careful analysis of what is involved in and required for any individual evaluation, and the limited extent to which evaluation techniques and resources can be effortlessly, routinely, or even legitimately transferred from one case to another. It is essential to determine comparability before such transfers can be made, and as in many situations true comparability will be very restricted, what can be common to the field is rather a set of methodologies and an attitude of mind. Thus evaluation in NLP is best modelled by analogy with training the cook and supplying her with a good batterie de cuisine.

The well-trained cook, drawing on the DARPA experience reported by Bates for example, has to be quite clear first, about what all the relevant environmental factors are, especially in relation to what optimal performance levels can be attained and what kinds of predictions can be made about future performance; and second, about what the goals of an evaluation are, notably in recognising the distinction between levels of performance attained on some intrinsic basis and how those levels may be perceived by external users. The complexities here are well illustrated by 'quality' versus 'utility' for speech synthesis (cf Isard), but are also manifest in the fact that 'correct output' is a relative and unreliable notion, obviously in machine translation but even in database query, and that subjective and objective right answers may be different. This difficulty in specifying correct outputs is related to the fact that individual outputs on the sentence scale normally cannot in practice, and therefore should not in principle, be divorced from their context and especially their immediate linguistic context. The is obvious for many generation cases (cf Dale) but also applies to translation where the propriety of an output sentence has to be explicitly considered in relation to the surrounding output sentences, and it cannot be assumed that if each sentence is 'well-enough' translated by itself, whatever contextual effects applied to it as input will be taken care of in its corresponding output. The same point applies in a broader way in dialogue where compensating devices may be brought into play so that, for instance, failures to interpret a single input may be perfectly adequately dealt with, from the user point of view, by the system's clarification mechanisms. (To say that systems would be better if they never failed does not take account of the fact that dialogue in general involves interactive interpretation.) Thus measures of success in processing single utterances, though clearly useful in system development, have to be recognised as limited measures. This point is also related to the general one of recognising the role of deliberate tradeoffs in system design, whether between system components or between system and user.

The Workshop presentations and discussions thus served to emphasise the fact that evaluation confined to 'purely' linguistic matters is problematic both because, as Nerbonne, Netter and Date pointed out, linguistic components and subsystems are in a fundamental sense incomplete with respect to what language is for, and because of the fact that performance *targets* cannot be adequately specified, so surrogates or approximations have to be used or assumptions about what is reasonable be made. As noted for IR, it is not rational to take perfect recall and precision as performance goals, and evaluation relies primarily on relative performance, either in comparing any two systems or, in a widely accepted approach, by comparing performance for a system of interest with that for a *baseline* system of a certain type. The baseline is accepted because it is defined by a simple, cheap strategy and has been shown to be sufficiently competitive over a range of comparisons with more elaborate approaches.

One problem for NLP evaluation is not having minimum baselines of this sort. A baseline in this sense is not necessarily a *benchmark* in the sense of par at golf, i.e. a normative standard. The benchmarks which are a conspicuous feature of the DARPA speech evaluations (cf S&NLW, 1991) are not properly benchmarks in this sense either. The SLS benchmarks are task definitions, with associated data, but they do not have explicit, concrete target performance specifications such that for instance for speech recognition, where the task might be isolated word recognition for certain speaker and vocabulary conditions, the performance target is some stated low error rate, measured in some way. There is an implicit, if unrealistic, speech processing target, namely perfect performance, but it appears that the SLS benchmarks are in reality informally defined as the collective levels of performance reached for the various task and data specifications. In the IR case some statement of retrieval conditions and a test collection meeting them, along with stated recall and precision goals, could constitute a benchmark. A baseline could therefore be adopted as a benchmark. The DARPA benchmark tasks and data embody increasing levels of challenge, and they are individually and collectively respectably motivated in terms of their relevant generic task, namely speech recognition or, for MUC, message processing. So from this point of view, the benchmarks defined post hoc as the results for one cycle can be taken as setting a baseline for the next.

Both baselines and benchmarks can be seen as *exemplars* setting minimal, typical (or even high) performance standards, whether or not the standards set by exemplars are viewed as absolute. So the problem with e.g. MT, is not so much that this is impossible for MT setups but rather that for narrowly linguistic evaluation it is extremely difficult to provide the actual *answer* data i.e. output translations analogous to IR's relevant documents on which detailed evaluation depends, as well as to define how this data is to be used for performance measurement. For many evaluations, reference data (or *references* for short) extending beyond answers in the obvious sense may be required which may also be similarly troublesome to provide: for example amount of attention or effort or time put into translation or relevance assessment. The MUC evaluations represent a determined effort to provide references where task, performance criteria, and performance targets are much more complex than in the basic speech recognition case where all of these are clear cut. For internal evaluations of components like parsers it need not be difficult to provide references for what ought to be delivered: the problem is rather in comparisons between very different approaches, where external, 'theory-neutral' references are required.

Thus the second group of issues the Workshop raised concerned the nature of targets and the roles of the associated elements of evaluation, namely baselines, benchmarks, exemplars and references, while the Workshop contributions showed how complicated they are to apply in specific evaluation situations.

Theme 3: test data

The third major theme was the provision of test data. This is clearly related to evaluation targets, but has its own complexities.

Thus "test data" can refer to materials of rather different kinds which are not interchangeable for evaluation purposes. Several presentations, like Netter's, Nerbonne's and Gamback's, referred to *test suites* in a strict sense, i.e. test material, in this case sentence sets, deliberately designed to cover all the phenomena defined at some linguistic level and in as explicit, unambiguous and decompositional style as possible, so system behaviour and outputs can be firmly correlated with the features of input data. These may also usefully include negative examples, e.g. sentences a parser should properly reject (or at least query). Test suites of this sort are primarily intended for diagnostic purposes, and as they are system inputs rather than outputs can in principle be common resources for different projects (cf also Flickinger et al, 1987) even if their relevance for any specific project has to be clearly shown. The distinction between test suites and test collections is precisely that the latter has references, i.e. outputs as well as inputs, e.g. parse trees for the sentences, translational equivalents.

However even though test suites may be for only relatively restricted purposes and need to be treated with caution for the kinds of reason mentioned earlier in interpreting single-sentence processing results, they may still be hard to design, even if they consist only of sets of independent sentences. The Workshop drew attention to the problems of test sentence design and in particular to the problems of trying to apply the 'one phenomenon at a time' scheme given that whole sentences are necessarily multi-facetted. Decompositions designed to separate phenomena and distribute them across the sentences in a test suite are hard to formulate, and their utility for diagnostic purposes is in any case counterbalanced by their artificiality, since the interaction effects of multiple phenomena, which may well be what affects perceived system behaviour for the end user, are lost. Certainly applying such a scheme requires a clear and consistent characterisation of all the relevant phenomena, and as the examples in Sourcebook (Read et al, 1988; and see Section 2.5) suggest, many phenomena are not readily pinned down. The syntactic case may appear relatively unproblematic in this respect, but is far from being so, and definitions of semantic and pragmatic phenomena sufficiently rigorous to support controlled 'decompositions' are much more problematic. It may also not be easy in practice to relate application specifications to phenomena definitions, as required to establish what phenomena can be expected to occur in some particular situation, either to design a test suite or to exploit one which is already available.

The SAM enterprise as described by Gibbons illustrates the complexities of data provision in this connection very clearly, in particular not only the need to discriminate carefully between test suites and other kinds of data, but also the danger of uncritical adherence to the 'inclusion fallacy'. Multi-purpose or hospitable data designed to serve a range of needs by representing a range of sources (e.g. many speaker types) may appear to have sufficiently broad coverage that it can not only in some cases be properly used as it is, but also have subsets drawn from it for limited purposes. But quite apart from the point that its coverage may not in fact be adequate since some relevant data types are not included, it does not follow that categorised subsets drawn from it will be well-founded in their own right in terms of other properties either specifically correlated with, or indifferent to, the discriminating category definition (eg male speakers and long sentences, or any length of sentence). (There are separate issues about random subsets.) The SAM material is designed to cover a range of speech-relevant factors: in terms of our view of factors these are environment rather than system factors, and thus it does not follow that the SAM environment factors are necessarily relevant to specific applications, either collectively or individually, though as the SAM range is broad some are likely to be. The general implication is therefore that it is necessary to look extremely carefully at the specification of the embedding data to ensure that inferences about the properties of embedded subsets are justified, especially in terms of attribute value combinations.

The Workshop presentations and discussions made it clear that it is essential, in relation to form and legitimate uses, to distinguish test suites from at least two kinds of *corpus*, as well as from test collections. Test suites are, as noted in a strong sense, designed, i.e. are constructed in a controlled way which combines coverage with decomposability, for some types of linguistic or linguistically-relevant phenomena. Test suites in this strongest sense do not consist of naturally occurring data, however much they are designed to display features of natural data. Corpora are drawn from naturally occurring materials, with more or less control on the selection process. As Gibbon noted, a strongly controlled 'reference corpus' of the kind of interest to speech communities may well be properly labelled a test suite.

However for evaluation purposes as much as discovery purposes it is normally essential to work with a corpus, and it is then necessary at least to recognise the broad distinction between *coverage corpora* and *distribution corpora*, i.e. between corpora aimed at capturing examples of all phenomena (e.g. all major word senses) or combinations of phenomena, and corpora having the same patterns of relative frequency of occurrence of phenomena (e.g. of senses) and combinations as the underlying 'universe' of data from which the corpus sample is drawn. This is a familiar distinction for lexicographers, and though it to some extent embodies ideal rather than attainable goals, leads to data sets with different characteristics and therefore different implications for evaluation, for instance for the significance of performance failures, say when parsing. As will be clear, these types of corpus are distinguished from test collections which additionally include references for performance evaluation, though corpora in practice may be used as minimalist test collections on the basis that systems should not breakdown or notify failure of some sort when processing them. For many purposes, though not necessarily, test collections are more usefully built from distribution corpora.

These various distinctions, and their implications for evaluation, are more fully considered in Section 2.5. The point here is that the Edinburgh Workshop referred to and illustrated quite distinct types of test data but also, in doing so, drew attention to the fact that the relationships between data types and evaluation types are not simple: thus while at the limit diagnosis calls for test suites and operational setup evaluation calls for test collections, there are many intermediate cases where it is the precise individual goal of an evaluation, not its general character, that determines the appropriate form of data (see, for instance, the examples in Part 3 below). It is therefore essential to be clear, and more clear than it often is in S&LP evaluation, about what the conditions and purpose of an evaluation are, and what consequences follow from these for the kind of test data required and for its detailed specification in terms both of material legitimacy and statistical propriety. This is particularly important where, as in the DARPA cases, evaluation is not done only with a general predictive intent, but is explicitly based on separate *training set* and *test set*, where the relation between these two test collections has to be sound.

As noted, the various types of test data may be part of an evaluation *toolkit*. The implication of relevant Workshop presentations is however that the provision of useful *tools* in the strict sense - hammers rather than bags of assorted nails - is a more difficult enterprise. This is particularly true for general-purpose tools other than very low-level support ones (like text editors), but also applies to tools intended for some specific task like translation. The SAM project covers tools for carrying out speech assessment but, as indicated, this is a restricted area where agreed approaches are at least to some extent established. Similar comparatively general-purpose tools are illustrated by the UK Alvey NL Tools (Briscoe, 1992) which include e.g. a parser for grammars of a broadly-defined type, and software for developing such grammars.

However King's presentation raised questions about what exactly an evaluation toolkit is. Thus she emphasised the point that while data and software may be desirable, because much evaluation has to be not just task but application specific and, further, is driven by the interests of particular customers with particular perspectives, it is as important for toolkits to include *guidelines* and to amplify these with examples. While some tools, like medium-weight hammers, have very many uses, the real question is what a toolkit is for, so the choice of tools is determined, in evaluating an NLP system, by what the system itself is for. Thus the starting point is the specification of the application, along with the perspective and any constraints stemming from the consumer category, as these lead into what is needed for and in evaluation. Much of a toolkit then becomes a 'manual' showing how to characterise an application from the viewpoint of evaluation, and how to size choose and apply suitable evaluation strategies, whether quantitative or qualitative. A toolkit is therefore a compendium with a mix of metalevel and object level elements, the former recommendations on e.g. how to design questionnaires, what kind of mistakes to avoid in assembling test data, how to be sensitive in counting system errors (because of error ambiguity), the latter at least concrete examples e.g. of proven questionnaires for types of need, or actual software, say concordance programs to support input or output data assembly and analysis. An analogue in many ways of such a toolkit would be a combination of a statistical analysis cookbook like Everitt (1986) with some matching programs like the CLUSTAN package. Clearly a toolkit can be more or less comprehensive in terms of the types of applications for which it is useful, and also more or less specialised in terms of the refinement of the tools it provides for a particular type of application (spanners and planes, or lots of different planes). There is apparently more challenge for NLP evaluation in providing the former especially via a few universal tools, but as King's presentation showed, the set of tools needed for various sorts of MT evaluation is no small business. (This topic line is further developed in the EAGLES Report discussed below in Section 2.3.)

Conclusion on the Edinburgh Workshop

The Workshop gives a very useful picture of the state of the art in, and perception of, S&LP evaluation in 1992. It confirms that, while there was rapidly increasing awareness of the need to evaluate, of the difficulties of doing this and of the investment of effort it requires, and also some progress in actually conducting evaluations, NLP evaluation has not in general been well developed, so the DARPA evaluations or Gamback's laboratory tests were relatively uncommon. Speech evaluation offers lessons in the area of test suite and corpus design and of data standards, and IR lessons in the area of test collections and grid designs to ensure systematic testing. The latter is particularly important because individual evaluation runs provide only very limited information, so that for evaluation as a general enterprise relating to some system it is necessary, for informativeness, to cycle round cutting the cake in finer or different ways.

In his concluding remarks Thompson noted not only the different stages of development in different task areas (or subdisciplines) of S&LP, and also, given that tasks have their proper differences, the challenge of whether generally-applicable but concrete test and evaluation techniques (as opposed to mere nostrums) can be devised. There is an unresolved conflict between the desire to have good concrete strategies for NLP evaluation relevant to different applications and valuable not only for purely economic reasons but through being broadly-based rather than ad hoc, and the implications of genuine differences between tasks: how relevant are any means of evaluation for database query to evaluation for MT? There is an explicit or implicit assumption that it is possible to ring fence the purely linguistic parts of NLP, and that common evaluation techniques can be developed for these. But the difficulties of conducting 'purely' linguistic evaluations described by different Workshop participants suggested that this is not a well-founded assumption, or at least that a great deal of care is needed in evaluating purported general-purpose processors, given that these are only partial and we do not have the encompassing comprehensive language understanding systems they presuppose. (We return to this in considering mega-evaluation in Section 2.7.)

Some of the area differences relating to evaluation that Thompson noted are natural consequences of their different stages of research development, and it is therefore very reasonable to consider different approaches to evaluation for, say, interpretation as opposed to generation. Equally, of course, different approaches within any one area may be appropriate according to whether e.g. basic or applied research is in question. However the important point that emerges from the Workshop is that a good, if not the only proper way to approach evaluation is to look at the task and application first, to see what they imply for language processing and hence NLP evaluation, rather than to start with some notion of what a language processor per se ought to be able to do and then attempt to derive one's evaluation techniques from this: there's too much danger in this of the anchor failing to grip, or dragging. From this point of view, the DARPA experience is very valuable, in showing what is involved in the design and conduct of evaluations though, as Bates observed, this does not imply that the DARPA approach is the best in every respect, and it is not clear what guidance it offers either for evaluation for multi-lingual tasks or evaluation techniques suited to processing different languages. But the cycling round on successive linked evaluations characteristic of the DARPA projects, and also of early IR evaluation work, is particularly helpful in developing evaluation techniques.

The Workshop's own fairly upbeat conclusion was that evaluation promotes community synergy and community synergy gets more research results. But the Workshop also showed how much need there is to further develop key notions like *test methodology* and *evaluation methodology*, test collection, and so forth, to ensure both that NLP evaluations are well designed and that their results can be properly understood. It also showed that whether or not evaluation in the end always boils down to cost/benefit in money terms, a point which was not explicitly addressed though it is recognised in e.g. MT evaluation, NLP evaluation in general has barely begun to apply notions like cost/benefit analysis, however defined, in any systematic way. There is also clearly a problem, both practical and intellectual, in handling multi-lingual evaluation: data has to be collected for different languages, and the data has to be comparable: however if data is functionally comparable it is not necessarily descriptively comparable (or vice versa), since languages are intrinsically different. Thus, for instance, functionally comparable data intended to test a transportable NL front end might be descriptively different, while descriptive data specifications for speech assessment for one language might not carry across to, or have the same functional representativeness for, another.

d) Parser/grammar evaluation workshops

It is convenient to comment separately on two small workshops concerned specifically with parser and grammar evaluation, covering the design of metrics, use of Parseval (a parser evaluation system), and experience with a common test set of sentences (Harrison et al, 1991; Harrison, 1992; Thompson, 1992a).

These workshops were part of an ongoing enterprise, ultimately stemming from the 1987 ACL session (Flickinger et al, 1987), and the reports on them are instructive for the problems of fine-grained comparative evaluation. For example, the first meeting showed very little consensus on sentence structure across candidate analyses for the same sentence. More importantly, in order to allow 'unbiassed' comparison with a reference parse (taken as that given by the Pennsylvania Treebank), individual system structures are diluted and re-formed, and comparisons are in fact confined to constituent boundaries, without regard to their labels. (Further, reference as well as candidate analyses may be modified to make comparison possible.) The metrics, all referring to parenthesis pairs, are 'recall' (percent reference pairs in system output), 'precision' (percent system pairs that are reference ones), and number of 'bracket crossings'.

At the second workshop it was evident that evaluation on this basis is of only limited value: in particular, though useful for intrinsic evaluation purposes, extrinsic evaluation relating parser/grammar output to some encompassing NLP system requirement would need to refer to more descriptive information in the output, and hence require that this also be available for comparison with the reference parse. One possibility would be deeper syntax, another predicate/argument structure, though both are clearly more problematic to provide, especially in an uncontroversial form. Thus one conclusion was that several metrics allowing for different degrees of structure 'distortion' should be allowed.

Thompson comments on the progress the meetings represent, albeit facilitated by a narrow focus and strong community of interest: the development of methodological consciousness is well illustrated by the fact that it was recognised that goals for the metric(s) are needed. However there seems to have been little perception of the need to address the properties of test data needed for evaluation, and the compromises needed to allow the application of the metrics show how hard it is to carry out task-independent, but meaningful, NLP component evaluations.

e) The DARPA Conferences overall

The discussion which immediately follows is our assessment of the DARPA Conferences for the evaluation experience they had provided by 1993, the time of our original report. Our observations still apply, but since the Conferences have continued apace and expanded, we conclude this subsection with remarks reflecting the further growth of the DARPA effort.

Taking the DARPA Conferences up to 1993 together, there are a number of points to be made, particularly in relation to the longest-running groups, MUC and SLS, and concentrating on the ATIS task for SLS. As noted earlier, it is not appropriate for our purposes to describe or analyse the Conferences in full detail, but it is necessary to emphasise that the detailed accounts of all aspects of the evaluations - the design and implementation of the test and evaluation methodologies, and of their development over time, as well as of the performance findings themselves - are of the greatest value in showing how much care, and how much effort, is involved in serious evaluation, and in illustrating many specific matters relevant to S&LP evaluation. For the earlier DARPA period, the proceedings of the Conference meetings (e.g. MUC-3, 1991; S&NLW,

1991); the overviews in Bates (in Thompson, 1992), Boisen and Bates (1992), Lehnert and Sundheim (1991), Pallett (1991), Sundheim (1991) and Chinchor, Hirschman and Lewis (in press); the various Conference evaluation specifications and guidelines (e.g. Appendices A and B in MUC-3, 1991); and the discussions of generic matters in e.g. Chinchor (1991) and Hirschberg (1991) provide this very relevant, detailed information. The initial aim of this section is rather to summarise the salient features of the earlier Conferences in relation to the state of the art in S&LP, and thus NLP, evaluation: we have made use in this, in particular, of the overview of both MUC and SLS in Bates (in Thompson, 1992).

General impact

One set of points refers to the general impact of the Conferences up to 1993: for while this is not directly relevant to our theme, namely how to do NLP evaluation, it is indirectly relevant in emphasising the importance of evaluation. The Conferences have served not only to the NLP community that evaluation matters, and certainly matters more than was generally accepted in the past: they have also served to get results. Thus as Bates (1992) observed, although very frequent evaluations may inhibit innovative research, this is outweighed by the positive gains for the field from the community synergy generated by the mixture of competition, cooperation, and openness the Conferences have involved, since this synergy in turn has led directly to improvements in system capabilities as well as a more general gain of knowledge and experience, for instance in how to characterise applications so they are amenable to S&LP technology. In MUC and SLS the NLP community has engaged with the kind of evaluation the IR community has long been familiar with, and taking on board the notion of fine-grained and rigorous evaluation the DARPA Conferences have involved is a significant advance for the NLP community. The care with which the detailed test and evaluation methodologies and their implementations were worked out is important in itself, and though there have been failings, for instance in the control of ATIS test data gathering for SLS, the analysis required to establish test materials and to determine the correct targets for intrinsically complex tasks is an object lesson for the IR as well as NLP communities. The evaluations thus have scientific as well as practical utility.

It is true that as the detailed S&LP test and evaluation methodologies have been developed by the system communities involved, rather than by their 'end customers', i.e. customers or users, there is a danger that the evaluations may not merely be 'misdirected' from the end-customer point of view, but be positively self-interested and lacking in objectivity. This applies in particular to MUC and SLS, as opposed to TREC which is exploiting a more broadly-based tradition, But the evaluations have been fairly well linked to end-customer interests though, as described below, in varying degrees implying varying degrees of 'realism', and the system community involvement has served to make the evaluations credible to the participants in the way that scenarios imposed by external bodies like funding agencies might not. At the same time, the care with which they have been carried out makes them credible, especially as the first serious tests for some tasks like message processing, to others.

The test materials, and specifically in the present context the MUC and SLS materials, are also a major gain from the Conferences. These are indeed, as they include output reference answers - the MUC templates and SLS replies, test collections in the sense defined earlier. As such, and despite the limitations considered further below, they are of great value, particularly since they are more solid than would typically be produced by any individual S&LP group. Quite apart from their direct utility within the framework of the Conferences themselves, these collections provide a longer-term training and development resource for research: they allow both internal comparisons for individual projects experimenting with system variants and external comparisons between projects, and they also supply goals for wholly new approaches. They can thus meet for the NLP community at least some of the needs met for the IR community by their test collections, though the very specific character of the MUC and SLS materials may limit their utility in various ways. In particular, these collections can serve not only the direct practical end of earnest and comparative system testing: they can, by allowing this, raise the research standards in the field. (The TREC collection (set) is not a novelty in this respect, since it is an IR collection in the usual sense, but is much larger than any systematically constructed ones hitherto (see Harman, 1991); and it is, moreover, linked to the MUC collections within the framework of the TIPSTER project.)

Evaluation character

The other set of points relates directly to the evaluations from our point of view in this book. Again referring initially to the period up to 1993, one feature of the Conferences was that the specific tasks within a group became harder over time: thus SLS progressed over successively more challenging benchmarks and MUC-3 was significantly harder than MUCK-II (Hirschman, 1991), and the communities involved were also evolving their test and evaluation methodologies. At the same time, the Conferences clearly show that to stimulate research effectively, their evaluation methodology has to be broadly based as well as well founded. Thus while quantitative measures may be handy (especially for the funding agencies), and single numbers appear preferable to multiple ones where the wood is liable to be lost in the trees, single numbers themselves may be over-selective, biased, or opaque. More seriously, as illustrated by the use of error rate reduction for speech recognition, it is not just necessary to show that there is no incestuous link between test methodology and performance measure; it is necessary in evaluating S&LP systems to ensure that the methodology and measure used have an appropriate justification in the entire task functionality required and are not geared exclusively to just one part of it.

From this point of view, the DARPA evaluations up to 1993 (or certainly MUC and SLS as longest running) were limited by their essentially laboratory character. There was no real attempt to capture relevant wider aspects of the task including setup ones. For instance in SLS's ATIS there was no provision for dialogue to compensate for first pass inadequacies in input question processing, or in MUC to explore what level of template filling would actually be quite good enough for all or even most practical purposes. There is also no check at all

147

on costs. It is thus not possible to explore the effects, for system design and performance, of context-dependent tradeoffs for the system task specification.

Finally, the evaluations were based on agreed, and fully specific performance targets (as implied by the question answers, the template fillings): this is a dangerous strategy without some solid notion of what level of performance it is rational to expect. Thus as the IR case has shown, to judge system performance by assuming that perfect performance is achievable is a fairly serious mistake. Human performance may alternatively be taken as a standard of comparison, but while this may be legitimate if the aim is to automate a hitherto human activity, it should not be assumed that this human model either is, or could, be perfect; whatever the human level is has to be properly established, and under real rather than ideal conditions of time, effort, expertise etc. However as the IR community has also learnt, there is not necessarily any good reason to accept that the human level is the best attainable, even if it is not perfect performance.

It may sometimes be possible, as has been shown for particular classes of case in IR, to establish what the optimal level of performance for given environment data actually is (see e.g. Robertson and Sparck Jones, 1976), to obtain a well-founded goal for associated system design. It is not obvious how feasible it would be to establish such performance optima in a strict sense for NLP tasks, though attempting to do this could well be instructive; however the implication of the way the DARPA reference answers were devised, namely as the finely-honed products of human argument, is that while these may be proper and useful for laboratory tests, they need to be treated with great caution as bases for defining attainable target performance. In MUC and SLS, moreover, the particular character of the tasks involved made it possible, albeit with manifest effort, to reach agreement on the answers and to allow, where appropriate in this, for some flexibility in their specification: but there are other tasks, like summarising where this would be much more difficult. It is also the case with MUC, though not significantly with SLS, that the answers are taken as functionally satisfactory; but this has not been demonstrated and is just assumed to be established by reference to their antecedent human models. However the lesson of IR has been that reference data when in the form of index descriptions are not objectively justified by any such means, but only by their ability to retrieve documents. The experience of the MT community is setting targets for evaluating translations illustrates the general difficulty of agreeing on answers and hence on 'operable' targets, and of knowing how these targets match real functional requirements, and points up the nature of the rather ruthless assumptions made in MUC especially.

These points are one aspect of a more general question about the reality and representativeness of the DARPA evaluations. *Reality* refers in a quite straightforward sense to the extent to which the test data and conditions are taken from, or are legitimate surrogates for, independently existing operational task contexts. *Representativeness* refers to the extent to which such selected material is characteristic of its source, which can be taken here as synonymous with using statistically valid samples. Thus in the strongest sense realism requires that the test material and conditions should be drawn from some individual application, as by analogy in the IR case documents, requests, and assessments would be taken from a real library and its users. However some dilution may be acceptable, for instance in the IR case by using requests that might have been, but were not actually, submitted, having assessments by librarians instead of end users, and so forth.

All laboratory tests imply some loss of realism, but this has not been limited in the DARPA evaluations to unavoidable abstractions and compromises imposed in the interests of laboratory control. The MUC messages were real, though the set was not necessarily statistically representative; neither the generic template nor its specific instantiations were taken over, and while they could be deemed to be in principle like those actually used, the answer templates were more carefully formed than would in reality be the case. From a statistical point of view, it is not clear what degree of representativeness should be assigned to a test with just one generic template, though with some subordinate variants, and with a very high proportion of relevant messages in the complete message file. The ATIS data, on the other hand, was essentially constructed in all its aspects, under a notion of plausible surrogacy embodied in the Wizard of Oz simulations etc (Hemphill, 1990) pitched at a level of task complexity in principle within the reach of current S&LP technology. Requirements for statistical representativeness thus do not really apply. The TREC data, on the other hand, includes real documents in a sufficiently large set to be to be taken informally, if not formally, as reasonably representative, and requests and assessments like those of the relevant background operational service, though not actually taken from them and hence not obviously formally representative.

Limitations

The limitations of the DARPA MUC and SLS evaluations (up to 1993) are in most cases complementary to their strengths. The whole-system black box approach, assessing system outputs against answer data, makes it hard to make cross-system comparisons to determine the relative merits of alternative treatments of system components or functions, or even to throw light on the relative contributions made by different elements of the same system; and it also makes it hard to establish the functional roles and importance of different linguistic phenomena in relation to the task requirements and a system's capabilities and performance. It equally makes it difficult to see how strategies from different systems or approaches might be combined for more effective hybrid systems. Though some performance comparisons with respect to specific phenomena are reported in Hirschberg 1991, the problems of getting sub-system comparisons sufficiently informative to provide leverage for system development is a recognised problem even if, in the end for a given task, it is only whole-system performance that matters. The idea that it should be possible to construct truly superior systems by combining the best elements from alternative systems is clearly attractive, and may be reasonable given the nature of individual tasks; but component comparison may be an ignis fatuus for systems based on radically different principles and of the complexity required for demanding NLP tasks.

Thus though there have already been gains from having several rounds in a group, and there may be further mileage to be got from future rounds, the characteristics of the evaluations may limit their informativeness. It is also probable that some specific applications may not be rich enough, whether for task or, as in the ATIS case, domain reasons, for significant further work. Indeed the very nature of the main evaluations up to 1993, i.e. MUC and SLS, raised important questions about the 'extensibility' or 'portability' of these evaluations. They were tied not merely to a task type, but to very specific instance applications. The materials and methodologies may be further used, and used thus competitively, in their own right. But just as with an IR test collection, the data themselves cannot be reused in any strict sense elsewhere, even for similar message processing and database tasks. The key question therefore is what, apart from the general experience of taking care, is exportable to other S&LP evaluation situations. Specifically, are there what might be called test and evaluation *standards*, in any substantive sense, that can be exploited and hence have a part to play in NLP evaluation in general?

Standards here is interpreted to refer on the one hand to those for test methodologies, i.e. *test standards* specifying a set of descriptors for characterising the properties of tasks and domains together constituting applications, and consequently a set of conditions or requirements for obtaining proper test data. The analogue in IR would be standards specifying minimum request set makeups and sizes. Standards refer on the other hand to those for evaluation methodologies, i.e. *evaluation standards* specifying the nature of evaluation criteria, measures and methods, Thus in IR these requirements include e.g. the use of recall and precision, the use of average of ratios across requests, and so forth. The TREC Conference is to a considerable extent implicitly if not explicitly, though with varying degrees of rigour, using test and evaluation standards developed in the IR community: the latter are illustrated, for instance by the way the competing teams' performances will be computed using procedures established by Salton's SMART Project (Salton and McGill, 1983). It is of course focussing in this on the 'core' perspective of IR associated with retrieving relevant documents: other perspectives, like economic ones, are not being considered.

The MUC and SLS evaluations up to 1993 represented early steps in the possible development of well-founded standards, though for only some perspectives. The 'train-and-test' paradigm used for these test is important here, given the nature of NLP tasks and the state of the S&LP art. It is less crucial in IR. However these evaluations were weak on any explicit analysis of the factors defining their tasks, including properties of the sources of their test materials which determined the environments of the tested systems, and in consequence were also weak on issues of realism and of statistical representativeness. Again, though 'recall' and 'precision' were imported from IR into the DARPA evaluations, they have been given distinctive and distinct meanings, and it is not clear how generally applicable they could be across NLP tasks.

More generally, it is not clear how far the notions of test and evaluation standards can be given, for S&LP, a form more concrete than rules of good

150

practice along with routine statistical guidelines, particularly if standards are sought for application across task types. IR testing practice, particularly from the core perspective, has perhaps imposed more uniformity on the varieties of retrieval than is actually there. NLP tasks are much more varied than these so it is unlikely that cross task standards are a realistic goal. What is, however, worth addressing is the question of whether useful standards can be obtained for task types.

Conclusion on the DARPA evaluations

In summing up the lessons to be drawn from the DARPA evaluations by 1993, one important general property of the evaluations has to be borne in mind. This is that they were directed towards S&LP evaluation within a global context of S&LP system development where, on the one hand, the capabilities of current systems were and still are much less than is desired and where, on the other, the S&LP tasks being attempted are very demanding, so a high degree of tailoring to the individual application is required. This has led to the emphasis on the notions of benchmarks and of training and test sets, and also to concerns with testing for transportability though this is clearly difficult to achieve both because the system implications of tasks are poorly understood and because much more tailoring to individual applications than is required than in, say, porting statistical indexing techniques in IR.

Overall by 1993, the DARPA MUC and SLS evaluations clearly marked progress in the S&LP field in addressing systematic testing, and thus also in tackling underlying issues of proper test collection design and construction. There were nevertheless deficiencies in MUC and SLS in that the need to identify and characterise performance factors, and to ensure reality and representativeness, was not sufficiently recognised. There is a great deal more to do on this and, as noted, on test and evaluation standards and on providing collections to assess system performance and potential utility for individual applications, as will be considered further in Chapter 3. Progress in this area is particularly important for the development of generic systems: to be efficient, transportability testing needs to be well targetted on the crucial, distinctive properties of individual applications.

Since writing our earlier report, the DARPA evaluation effort has been extended both 'vertically' over time for given task types and 'horizontally' into new task areas. This extension makes it easier to assess this effort and to identify significant points about NLP evaluation that emerge from it, while the scale of the effort indeed makes it imperative to try to draw lessons from the work for the field. Overall, the points just made about DARPA still apply (a comment in itself bearing on the amount of work necessary to progress NLP evaluation), though there has been considerable and valuable effort extending the DARPA evaluations in various ways as mentioned in Section 1, for example in system transportability to different applications (MUC), more concern with glass box tests (MUC, ATIS), task variation (TREC).

First, general observations, and starting with the good side:

1. There has been a clear growth in recognition of the need for evaluation, of understanding of what is required in evaluation, and of how to meet these requirements, so there has been a general improvement in evaluation methodology. Collectively, the DARPA conferences can be seen as a large scale study of, or experiment in, how to do NLP evaluation, from which a great deal has been learnt that can be applied, in a virtuous spiral, to new tests. This holds in particular for the way the central triangle of evaluation: how the evaluation subject, data, and measures, should be related to one another. The development of measures and procedures that are pertinent and definite is clearly visible, for example, in the history of MUC.

2. Much of this reflects the imposition of discipline deriving from the sponsoring agency which, while disagreeable from some points of view, has had the effect of forcing those working in the field to pay attention to evaluation while also allowing them, through the continuity of the whole, to do this in a consistent and coherent way. The common framework and (at least to a considerable extent) accumulated comparable results, are of enormous value in themselves because they make it easier to relate work by one player in the NLP field to that of another. The DARPA evaluations have done, rapidly, for the NLP community what the IR community had to find out (and thus could only discover more slowly, for itself.

3. Indeed, while the common style running through the DARPA conferences obviously stems from their common promoter (DARPA)'s concerns, it has also had the effect, enhanced by the participation of individual teams in more than one task area conference, of spreading this approach to evaluation more widely.

4. The extent of the DARPA programmes has also just by requiring, in the interests of control and progress evaluation, a continuing framework for each task, raised the issue of what the structure of large scale, mega-evaluations should be, and has offered some forms for trial.

5. The DARPA conferences have at the same time brought home the enormous cost of conducting serious evaluations, both in the primary costs, especially of gathering answer data, and in the secondary costs of participating. They have therefore emphasised the need for planning, particularly in data gathering, not just to meet technical desiderata, but to maximise data productivity and re-use.

6. Thus one of the most important outcomes, apart from the NLP task findings themselves, has been in the gathering of evaluation materials and their recording for future use. The buildup of resources, including indeed not only the test data itself. but the actual participants' results in standard forms, along with evaluation software (as for MUC and TREC), is an extremely valuable byproduct of the work, from which the wider community can benefit.

7. These resources, like the actual results, are enhanced in value because they stem from the systematic character of the evaluations themselves.

8. Thus the DARPA evaluations emphasise the value of rigorous and organised evaluation, not just because it can deliver improved system performance, but because it can make it possible to understand (via the evaluation conditions) why the systems perform as they do. The standardisation characteristic of the DARPA evaluations, not just in the actual measures used but in the recording of system output, etc, is very important here.

But now the less good points:

9. Using the EAGLES categorisation of evaluation types (see Section 2.3 below), the DARPA evaluations have been primarily 'adequacy' and 'progress' ones (both collectively for a task type and individually for any system), much less diagnostic ones.

10. More importantly, they have been adequacy and progress evaluations of a highly constrained type where the system boundaries have been tightly drawn and there has been no thorough investigation of environment influences on NLP operation, in particular of factors outside the obviously relevant ones to do with type of language material constituting system input.

11. There is an especially large deficiency on the human side, where system users are concerned, whether as information-providing partners in some tasks (e.g. inquiry), or as direct consumers of system outputs. In general the the role and character of human users has been assumed rather than directly studied for its impact on system performance and assessment. This stems from the emphasis on technology development, but underplays the importance of environment factors on system behaviour.

12. Again, there has been little interest in other aspects of evaluation, for example economic ones.

13. Finally, the promoter's constraints as well as internal community influences, but also the evaluation designs themselves with their tight forms and numerical metrics, have encouraged system tuning, perhaps even tweaking. Tuning to applications is not objectionable in itself, is indeed desirable in practical implementations, but it is damaging to research aimed at generic technology and systems and thus requiring generalisation across applications.

Second, evaluation methodology:

1. (As already remarked, but deserving note under this heading) the DARPA evaluations were primarily adequacy and progress ones, with little explicit treatment of setups that surround systems; however as series of controlled experiments, with tight feedback loops between test results and technology development, there has been a relatively orderly population of test grid slots along with useful actual performance improvement.

2. There have been some particularly sound practices, notably

   a) the clear separation of training and test data sets;

   b) the use of pretesting for evaluation measures and methods;

   c) the habit of conducting dry runs for the real tests.

   All of these may seem obviously desirable, but are not always done.

3. However there have been weaknesses especially at the data level, for instance in not controlling data gathering at different sites adequately (ATIS), or in using arbitrary compilations of data (TREC), with consequences for the interpretation of test results.

Third, substantive points for NLP:

1. The evaluations have been distinguished by the use of very tough materials, as well as difficult tasks: the use of real text material in the MUC and TREC cases is noteworthy.

2. However, as already mentioned, the role of the user as a task participant in the strong sense of information provider via language, has not been a primary consideration; thus while humans figure in the tasks underlying SLS and TREC especially, they have not been a direct focus of study.

3. There have been severe limitations in the performance measures used, which have centred on 'recall' and 'precision' notions, with various specific definitions. As the ATIS end-to-end trial showed, there is a great need for other, and broader-scope, measures, but equally great difficulty in defining them.

Fourth, some points on the management and politics of evaluations:

1. The DARPA evaluations have heavily involved their communities; and while this might seem to introduce biases in favour of tests and performance outcomes favourable to the community rather than addressing objective or external needs, it has the advantage of increasing technical solidity through evaluations that are rational and practicable given the technology state of the art and of making the whole enterprise accessible and important to the community, thus encouraging participation and hence more system comparisons.

2. The effort required to conduct data gathering, especially to ensure consistency, is very large, as is the effort required to administer such collective evaluation conferences.

3. Overall, one of the most important features of the DARPA evaluations is in demonstrating the value of long-term programmes, both in developing methodology and in getting extended sets of results.

2.2 Evaluation tutorials

As evaluation has become more important, tutorials on it have appeared. Bates and Weischedel's (1987) tutorial on database front ends has already been considered in Section 1.3. This subsection provides a brief account of a more broad-ranging tutorial by Oviatt and Cohen. This is not tied to a particular type of task and also, as it is focussed on evaluation in the context of multimodal communication between man and machine, brings out new issues. Thus this is an area where evaluation can be very complex, not only for the relatively straightforward reason that replication is very difficult in dialogue situations (as in tests of interactive searching in IR). There is the more important challenge of a lack of comparable reference points in human-human communication. This may be because, on the one hand, the constraints and possibilities of the man-machine interface make it much more impoverished than any human-human analogue. However it may on the other hand, and more interestingly, be because the communicative situation is novel, with properties stemming from the nature of the machine which do not figure in the prior human case. (An analogue would be attempting to evaluate the merits of a man-machine interface based on writing when the human user had only communicated with other humans in speech: the different means of communication would be associated with other factors, like the permanence of a record.)

a) Evaluation of NL Modalities

This was a tutorial at the Third ACL Conference on Applied Natural Language Processing (Oviatt and Cohen, 1992). The following is a summary of the tutorial notes.

The tutorial begins with alternative philosophies of evaluation, namely: no evaluation, evaluation as marketing, evaluation as 'benchmarking' among systems, or iterative evaluation for definition and improvement of individual systems. The form of evaluation or design then depends on the research goals, which may be:

1. identify undiscovered linguistic phenomena (eg. conversation analysis);

2. quantify prevalence of linguistic phenomena (eg. corpus collection);

3. isolate and manipulate factors that drive language;

4. interpret language in relation to other phenomena to leverage explanation and prediction;

5. enhance objectivity by adopting hypothesis testing and other scientific conventions.

All five of the above research goals are achievable by experimentation, and the basics of experimentation are for example, the requirements of a good experiment, sampling techniques, laboratory versus field studies, and so on. Oviatt and Cohen discuss the common misconceptions that data is data is data, and that more data is better data.

Early evaluations such as some of those we discuss are covered e.g. Jarke et al (see Section 1.3.), followed by mentions of the Flickinger HP test suite (see Section 1.3.) and Neil-Montgomery Evaluation procedure (see Section 2.4) as worthwhile catalogues of linguistic phenomena. There is also mention of the proposal (see 2.2.1) for evaluating the syntactic performance of parser/grammars of English using the Treebank set of hand-annotated parses as a reference data.

The next part of the tutorial concerns experimentation on modality differences in interactive communication, as performed by Chapanis and reported in *Scientific American* 232(3) 1975 and *Human Factors* 19(2) 1977. The modalities considered were face-to-face, speech, handwriting, keyboard and combinations, and the tasks were object assembly and geographical orientation. The experiments outlined modality differences, such as that speech is faster, more verbose, more tightly interactive, less planned, more repetitive and dysfluent, uses less varied vocabulary, uses more pronouns, less syntactically complex and well integrated and more indirect than non-speech. In addition, handwriting is faster, less verbose, has fewer pronouns and verbs, and has longer turns with fewer interruptions than using a keyboard. Compared to human-human communication, human-computer communication has clearer pronunciation, slower delivery, briefer utterances, is more precisely specified, uses simplified grammar and vocabulary, is cautious and conservative in style, involves less presumption of "common ground", comprises more limited and stereotyped dialogue and lacks confirmatory and explanatory language. Further research is needed to systematically compare modalities and human-human and human-computer differences, as well as to take account of the "gross structural factors" such as channel and partner characteristics that influence interactive communication. There should be more emphasis also on the discernment of patterns, explanations, and critical parameters, and the construction of a theoretical framework for prediction and modelling of multimodal communication.

The section on evaluation of interactive spoken language systems looks at several of the experiments comprising the DARPA Speech and Language Systems Programme. The is also a section on handwriting/pen systems. The issues of dialogue evaluations follow, accompanied by accounts of experiments by Oviatt and Cohen on modality effects on dialogue. Their summary of dialogue evaluations to date concludes that there aren't any! There is no true specification of dialogue behaviour even in one task.

Multimodal systems are finally presented, along with an example, as potentially advantageous due to improved error correction and avoidance, enhanced flexibility, enhanced efficiency and expressive power through parallel use of modes, and an accomodation of a broader user population and range of tasks. They should combine modalities complementarily i.e. optimising individual strengths.

2.3 EAGLES

The EAGLES project work is an important attempt to provide an organised account of, and guidance for, NLP evaluation. The project as a whole (European Commission Project LRE-61-100, cf ELSNEWS, 1995) covers a range of activities concerned with 'resources' of various sorts: evaluation methodologies, corpora, lexicons, and formalisms. These are viewed as constituting the infrastructure, both in terms of actual physical resources and of more abstract ones such as standards, for work on individual systems or tasks. In this section we consider the report of the Evaluation Working Group (EAGLES, 1994), which in part follows on from the Edinburgh Workshop, for example in some adoption of terminology, but also has elements of the tutorial; at the same time, the overall concerns and treatment are much broader than the particular methodologies considered in the next section. We have already considered this Report under the specific heading of machine translation in Section 1.1: we examine it here from the point of view of evaluation methodology in general.

It must be emphasised both that the EAGLES Report is a very substantial document, of great value from many points of view, and that our discussion here is only a summary one aimed at picking out the main, relevant features of Report's treatment of evaluation, shown in overview in Figure 8. It is also the case that the Report is an interim one and thus cannot be assessed as if it were complete. Finally, the Report has its own terminology, with some terms associated with a relevant International Standard, ISO 9126, (ISO, 1991), some with the same meaning as ours, some different. To avoid confusion, common words with different EAGLES interpretations to ours will be flagged by quotes, e.g. 'grid'.

The Report is intended to establish a framework, and 'toolkit' for those wanting to evaluate NLP systems, but approaching this from a particular point of view in relation both to what evaluation is for and to what sorts of things are being evaluated. The work starts from the distinction between *progress, adequacy* and *diagnostic* evaluation: progress evaluation aims to establish present system performance in relation to some goal, typically via established criteria; adequacy evaluation assesses system performance in relation to intended use; and diagnostic evaluation addresses system failures. Comparisons between systems (or system states) play an important role in the first two in particular. The EAGLES work is restricted to adequacy evaluation (though of course there are lessons in it for the other types). It further approaches adequacy evaluation under the 'Consumer Report' (CR) paradigm, i.e. evaluation with respect to particular functional capacities. This is of course a quite general strategy from a logical point of view: it is essentially that represented by evaluation with respect to system objectives, from some user-based angle, in our account. However the overall slant is more specific, with the CR approach treated in the more concrete form: 'I'm a customer: which of these market products are good buys for what I want?', so translation systems, for example, are to be considered in the same style as, say, washing machines. This approach partly reflects the encompassing language engineering *zeitgeist*, but is more generally valuable in emphasising an

```
[meta-aim    :  standardise NLP product evaluation]

evaluation
  nature    :  adequacy
  type      :  e.g. benchmark
  format    :  Consumer Report
   ''grid''  :  reportable attribute values
                against NLP task systems

  stages :

    preparatory - define
      a) quality characteristics
         (task specialisation of general,
            via task model)
      b) attributes for characteristics
            with value sets
         especially consumer-pertinent
         reportable attributes
      [a+b constitute featurisation]
      c) measures for values
      d) methods for measures
         (including choice of test material)

    [proceed by applying or developing checklists]

    execution -
      a) conduct evaluation
      b) present results for reportable attributes
```

Fig. 8. Summary of EAGLES evaluation methodology (EAGLES, 1994)

important viewpoint in evaluation and in forcing attention on the detailed analysis required in evaluation for proper justification of 'purchasing' decisions. At the same time, the detail is illuminating for NLP evaluation in general.

The Report develops its general treatment of evaluation primarily through very detailed case studies of system evaluation for three NLP tasks, specifically chosen as leading examples because, since there are market systems available for these tasks, the CR approach is particularly apposite and can be properly implemented to illustrate the overall methodology. To support the Report's stance, such CR evaluation for NLP can be taken as a legitimate field for the application of international standards for product evaluation, as exemplified in International

Standard 9126 for software, though this Standard clearly needs some tailoring to the NLP area; and the Report exploits the ISO notions and terms.

As a general framework, the Report considers the design for an evaluation as involving four steps:

1. defining the relevant [product] *quality characteristics*;

2. defining the *attributes* pertinent to each characteristic;

3. defining the *measures* to provide *values* for each attribute; and

4. defining the *methods* for applying the measures to determine actual values.

This leads to a 'grid' notion with attributes and systems axes, and values in the cells. The ISO 9126 Standard groups attributes under the broad quality characteristics of 'functionality'; 'reliability'; 'usability'; 'efficiency'; 'maintainability'; and 'portability' with subcharacteristics as shown in Figure 9.

```
Functionality :
    suitability, accuracy, interoperability, compliance, security

Reliability :
    maturity, fault tolerance, recoverability

Usability :
    unedrstandability, learnability, operability

Efficiency :
    time behaviour, resource behaviour

Maintainability :
    analysability, changeability, stability, testability

Portability :
    adaptability, installability, conformance, replaceability
```

Fig. 9. Summary of quality characteristics for software, ISO Standard 9126 (ISO, 1991)

Then, for a specific task, an appropriate attribute specialisation is required so, for instance, functionality for spellchecking might be interpreted as (a) detecting misspellings and (b) proposing corrections. Such specialisations are then further specified as individual attributes, e.g. for (a) misspelling means not in dictionary,

159

and for (b) correct word among set of proposed possible alternatives. Clearly the crux is in the definition of attributes, at an appropriate level of granularity. They may be of different types - facts, features, tests, judgements, and have values of different types e.g. qualitative, quantitative, the latter absolute or relative, etc. Measures for the attribute values have to valid and reliable so, e.g. the measure for (b) could be percent correct proposal not included in response set. Finally, the methods for the measures provide the 'how to' (thus we may imagine for case (b) a specification covering what to do when the response set is empty as well as when it contains at least one word).

The Report includes some notes on test material, i.e. test suites, test corpora and test collections, and on some specific techniques like the use of rating scales and error analysis; and it provides some context for NLP evaluation per se by referring to some past evaluations.

However by far the major part of the Report, and where its value is greatest, is in the detailed presentation and discussion of the case study task areas: these are Writers' Aids, Translators' Aids, and Knowledge Management Systems, specifically document management systems. We have already commented on the treatment of translation aids, in Section 1, and document management systems are both largely outside our scope and only partly treated in the interim Report. We will take the treatment of writers' aids as an example here to illustrate the Report's approach to evaluation methodology in general. It should be noted however, as the earlier discussion of the evaluation of translators' aids makes clear, that while the general approach to evaluation in these two EAGLES example cases is the same, there are some differences of detail. Thus the translators' aids discussion refers to the business of choosing attributes and value sets for a system evaluation as *featurisation*, and approaches this via the construction and use of *checklists*. Note too that in practice value sets may be such that the notion of measure is pretty minimal, for example with simple presence/absence features.

The Report discussion of Writers' Aid evaluation begins with a context-setting summary of the development and general nature of grammar checkers, and of some past reviews of such systems. The main development of an evaluation methodology is accompanied by some case studies using actual systems as *test beds*. This development involves considering how to specialise the ISO quality characteristics, for example functionality or reliability. The specialisation is done in terms of a 'task model' i.e. a model of the task setup, for which the task is taken as a user revising a writer's unproofed text, via system advice, for a proofed text. Supporting input models are therefore required of the task 'subjects', i.e. the writer, the system, and the user, and output models of the task 'objects'. i.e. the unproofed text, the advice, and the proofed text. Writer types can be modelled by characteristics like language proficiency, training, etc; systems by e.g. advice language; user types by language proficiency, etc. Text types can be modelled by such properties as language, genre, and so forth, while advice is characterised in terms of properties like the use of flags only, or flags plus suggestions, error names, also different sorts of suggestions, etc. The important point about the task model, however, is that there are relations between the constituent models, in particular that between the two text forms from which an error taxonomy for a grammar checker can be derived. But the other relationships need to be explicitly defined as they are the basis for, first, the detailed model building and second, the formulation of the evaluation. For example, there is a relationship between user-type and advice-type, since the form of advice has to be judged, both for intention and achievement, for propriety for user type.

The next stage combines the general statement of task functionality for a grammar checker with the task model in order to provide more specific definitions of functionality, in terms of which the evaluation testing and reporting is done. Thus for example, if part of the general functionality requirement is that the system should show errors in such a way that the user can correct them, then this general requirement, involving a relationship between the writer, advice, and user models and the error taxonomy, is specialised into an explicit tabulation characterising writer properties against error types, system properties (form of error report etc) against error type, and so forth. The nature of the tabulation should be such that it can be done in a comparable manner for the different writers' aids being evaluated. (Of course analogous specialisation would be required for the other quality characteristics.)

Detailed analysis of the kind just described has to be supported by methods for obtaining the necessary information, and in particular with how test material is obtained which provides the types of error the writer's aids are supposed to detect. One obvious possibility is test suites. (The EAGLES concern with standardisation makes the idea of standard test suites for writers' aids an obviously attractive idea, because of the way they can concentrate as well as isolate error occurrences.) There are also details about scoring procedures to be supplied to implement the computation of performance measures like 'recall' or 'precision'.

The application of the CR paradigm draws attention to an important practical consideration in evaluation, often lost in researchers' and developers' concentration on systems themselves within their own technical framework, remote from that of consumers. This is the nature and choice of *reportable attributes* for characterising systems to consumers, i.e. supplying the columns in the CR. The task modelling just described is based on a technical analysis and terminology which is not necessarily meaningful to the consumer. In the writers' aid case this might lead, for example, to a high emphasis on, and more detailed treatment of, text and user properties, alongside some grouping under single heads of error types. As the Report notes, this reporting has to be related to an analysis of the system setup. It also motivates the choice of performance measures, e.g. 'recall' and 'precision'.

Finally, this very detailed discussion of writers' aid evaluation is supported by a description of tests on the test bed systems, intended as a validation of the approached just summarised though in fact presented (at least in the present interim report) in informal, commentary style.

It is useful to relate the overall EAGLES approach to evaluation methodology to ours. In fact the framework adopted for EAGLES has much in common with ours, and we share the emphasis on detailed *decompositional* analysis as a prerequisite for satisfactory evaluation. At the same time, the EAGLES focus on adequacy evaluation, and generic angle of approach from the consumer point of view, give the whole a particular flavour. The Consumer Report paradigm, and consequent concern with matters like the notion of reportable attributes, are both instructive.

One important distinction is in the subtly different interpretations of the term 'grid'. For us, a grid is defined by system parameters against environment variables, a natural account from a research point of view where internal system works are of interest and the focus of attention is on modifications of a given system, generating different parameter settings. Our notion of grid can perfectly well accommodate, however, alternative settings that are in fact associated with different actual systems, and can equally allow any arbitrary degree of generalisation or abstraction over parameters. So in the limit entire systems can be taken as irreducible, black box, wholes with their particular combination of parameter settings viewed as a single 'meta-parameter' setting different from that for some other system involved in a cross-system task comparison. Doing this disregards the issue (so fraught for DARPA) of whether system comparison in the finer grain of constituent parameters can be meaningful.

For EAGLES, a grid is attributes against different systems. However while in the translators' aids case discussed in Section 1.1 the attributes are fairly clearly system ones, in the writers' aids case the attributes cover, in our terms, both computational system parameters proper (e.g. advice language for writers' aids, error types addressed) and also system environment variables (e.g. input and output text languages, writer and user competences). This implies that the writers' aid evaluation is really, in our terms, not just of systems, but of setups, i.e. systems proper with their immediate environments. The EAGLES Report discussion of reportable attributes and measures indicates that it is also necessary to consider the wider, encompassing environment, if not as a formal element in evaluation. However the fact that environment variables and system parameters are not separatelty laid out in opposition to one another means that environment effects on system performance are covert rather than overt.

(To avoid confusion, it should be noted that for EAGLES the grid attributes are its columns and the systems its rows, following a common CR layout. We have tacitly assumed a convention with environment factors as columns and system parameters as rows.)

In conclusion, the EAGLES Report yet again demonstrates how much is involved in serious evaluation: whether or not specific, concrete evaluation resources, i.e. particular sets of (reportable) attributes, checklists etc, or particular test data sets, can be established as standard, and hence as public tools, must depend to a very considerable extent on the richness and variety of the task. Thus it is significant that, so far, EAGLES has addressed relatively limited NLP tasks.

2.4 Particular methodologies

Particular evaluation methodologies have naturally already figured in the earlier material in this chapter. This subsection is devoted to some specific methodologies which are important, for one reason or another, in the current NLP evaluation scene.

The first of these is the Wizard of Oz (WOZ) approach. This may be used either as a means of gathering data as a base for system design, its main use, or alternatively as a method of carrying out operations being evaluated: this would be plausible for instance where only part of an intended system had been implemented and evaluation was intended to address its contribution to the performance of the larger whole; the remainder of the system could them be simulated. The stimulus for WOZ approaches in data gathering, test and evaluation is quite clear: as computational systems are both expensive and limited, there is every incentive to see, via prior simulation, how they might behave. This seems particularly appropriate for NLP systems designed for human interaction. The first part of this section is therefore devoted to a brief review of WOZ, using the proceedings of a Workshop in which it was a major topic.

We then consider the Neal-Montgomery System Evaluation Method, since this has been explicitly put forward by its authors as a general-purpose evaluation technique for NLP systems: however it is clear that anything developed and publicly disseminated on this basis has to be treated with care.

a) The Wizard of Oz experimental method

The Wizard of Oz (WOZ) method is a means of performing simulations in order to collect data of use to the design of language and dialogue systems (Ahrenberg, Dahlback and Jonsson, 1992). There are various questions associated with this. Firstly, why use simulation as a method of data collection? Secondly, of what use is such data in the design process? And thirdly, what are the problems to be faced in the practical execution of such simulation experiments?

1. Why use simulation as a method of data collection?

The main arguments in favour of using WOZ data collection methods relate to the tailored use of language in certain communication contexts and with particular application domains. It seems a reasonable assumption that interactions between users and their machines will be different from interactions between humans for the same purpose. People generally can be shown to modify their language when talking to children for example, or foreigners. The aim is to be maximally understood with the least effort, and this requires adjustment in different contexts. However, it is impossible to predict precisely how users will modify their language with a particular computer application. Will aspects of language such as using indirect utterances for politeness, or assuming areas of common knowledge and so on, be dialogue phenomena that a particular NL application system will need to understand? Perhaps the fact that the interface requires text as input instead of speech will affect the users' use of language? One solution to this problem of prediction is to simulate the required system and evaluate the simulation before designing the system itself. The only alternative to this is to design and build prototype systems which are then iteratively evaluated and improved. The latter is bound to be the more costly option, as well as being a less effective one. As was pointed out by Tennant (1979), people always adapt to the limitations of an existing system. Such an experiment does not therefore tell you what they ideally would need.

2. Of what use is the data in the design of NL interfaces?

Fraser, Gilbert and McDermid (in Ahrenberg, Dahlback and Jonsson, 1992) identify five uses for simulation data:

(a)   Theory testing on previously formulated hypotheses, such as whether a user will respond with politeness formulations if the system generates these.

(b)   Theory generation. Data can be used to induce generalisations. For example, the use of 'hesitation items' such as 'erm' before periods of silence indicate that the speaker is not yet finished with her turn.

(c)   Specification construction. A series of simulations need to be carried out in order to iteratively converge upon an appropriate and feasible design. The first will have a relatively unconstrained Wizard, but then further simulations should replace this with the aim of eventually determining a specification for a technically feasible system.

(d)   Testing of particular 'modules' of a dialogue system, to determine whether they perform according to their specifications. This involves simulating only those modules not being tested, making up a 'bionic wizard'. For example, the front end and linguistic processors of the intended system could be used to generate probable syntactic strings as text. The human wizard then composes appropriate replies and types these as input to a text-to-speech system.

(e)   Evaluation to determine whether the system provides an adequate level of performance. 'Adequacy' is externally defined e.g. a given percentage of users being satisfied with the system, or in a given percentage of dialogues the user is able to carry out the task successfully. The design as well as the specification must meet with evaluation requirements.

Fraser, Gilbert and McDermid justify distinguishing these objectives by pointing out that the different objectives of a simulation will influence its design, the data collected, and the most appropriate analysis.

3. What are the problems?

First and foremost, the success of a WOZ experiment depends upon its human 'subjects' being convinced that they are in fact dealing with a computer system and not a human being. This means that for example, if using speech, the wizard's voice should be synthesised. It also means that the wizard should not understand utterances too complex for a (state-of-the-art) parser or those in overlap with the system's speech, or utterances dependent on real world knowledge unavailable to the system. These constraints can be quite difficult for the wizard. The wizard must also behave inflexibly like a computer, must respond very fast like a computer, not make spelling mistakes, and so on. Some of these problems can be solved by using an experimental environment especially for running WOZ simulations. Pre-formulated standard calls to the background application system can then speed up response times. There can also be stored answers and canned texts which can be accessed by pull-down menus. All this makes the simulation experiment a costly business, however. The simulation environment firstly has to be customized to the particular application. And the background system must be well tested and working properly. For the collection of valuable data, the task cannot be too simple. The instructions about how to interact with the system should also neither be too specific or too open-ended. Different wizards should be used so that the language the subjects use does not reflect any one particular person's behaviour. Overall, WOZ simulations are difficult, labour intensive, and time consuming.

There has been some criticism of WOZ experiments on ethical grounds because its human subjects are being deceived. Ahrenberg, Dahlback and Jonsson (1992) argue against this. They have given debriefing sessions to subjects following the experimental session, in which explanations are given of what occured and why, and an offer is made for data collected to be destroyed if the subject wishes. They found that their subjects were always happy with what had occurred. Such sessions also give feedback as to whether the subjects were successfully 'fooled' by the wizard.

Oviatt and Cohen (1992) also refer to the difficulties of carrying out properly controlled WOZ experiments, and data collection for the DARPA ATIS application was in some cases done in this way without sufficient regard for its implications. The problems are very well illustrated by the speech case since it is extremely hard to predict the performance of a putative speech recogniser in sufficient detail (e.g. for unknown speakers over telephone lines, in free dialogue) to design an accurate simulation. For test and evaluation purposes, therefore, even more than just design data gathering, the WOZ approach needs great care.

b) The Neal-Montgomery System Evaluation Methodology

The Neal-Montgomery System Evaluation Methodology (Neal, Feit and Montgomery, 1991; Walter, 1992), described also in Section 2.1(b) as the Benchmark Investigation/Identification Program, was intended by its authors to be *the* standard evaluation tool for any NLP system. Specifically, it is a methodology for producing quantitative, objective profiles of NLP system capabilities without requiring system adaptation to a test domain or text corpus. It thus consists essentially of a careful categorisation of linguistic features requiring processing capabilities, along with instructions for the formation of suitable domain-relevant sentences with these features and for scoring system output for this test material. The Methodology is thus one for constructing and using test suites for English grammars. The Methodology is designed as an neutral, replicable procedure which should give consistent results for independent human evaluators; it has already undergone some testing on existing NLP systems, and is now available from Rome Laboratories.

Firstly, each identified linguistic (lexical, syntactic, semantic or pragmatic) feature is defined and explained in order to establish a standard delimitation of that feature. Illustrative language patterns and sample sentences then assist the human evaluator to formulate input which tests the feature on the NLP system within the system's native domain. Scoring is of the system's responses to the user's input as S (success), C (correct but the stated criterion was not met), P (partially correct), F (incorrect response), and N (unable to accept input or form a response). Each feature is tested by several Methodology items, each of these examining only one linguistic capability. Thus (as illustrated in Walter, Feit and Montgomery, 1991), if the feature is relative clause postmodification of noun phrases, and specifically with relative pronoun as subject, this in turn has to be tested as three different Methodology items for three different forms. One important point is that each item is designed to test a new capability in isolation, given an established ability to handle the other phenomena also represented in the test sentence. Individual test scores are then aggregated into percentages for classes of linguistic capabilities that are hierarchically organised. This means that quantitative, descriptive profiles are obtained which can then be viewed at varying levels of granularity.

The total apparatus covers a large list of phenomena. There are (in Walter, Feit and Montgomery, 1991), twelve feature classes ranging from basic sentences via adverbials and quantifiers to the semantics of events, and there are, for instance, fifteen individual capability items for postmodifying relative clauses.

The Methodology appears to be the most thorough early attempt at this type of enterprise: compared for instance with Gamback's similar 'array'-type approach to test suite construction (in Thompson, 1992), this is much more explicitly and elaborately specified. It is, however, of interest that initial testing with the Methodology showed considerable divergence among test scores; and the whole Methodology so far has been essentially limited to sentential syntactic phenomena: it is not clear how readily it can be extended in semantic and pragmatic directions, and into task contexts say involving dialogue. Indeed in this connection it should be noted that while scoring presupposes answers, the Methodology seems to assume that what the answers are is obvious (e.g. what successful system processing is), or that they will be explicitly provided. But there are clearly weaknesses in this, for instance in the implied separability of syntactic from other processing, or in the difficulty of evaluating different systems on the same answers. The Methodology as so far developed has not escaped the limitation to syntax which was a conspicuous feature of discussions of evaluation during the eighties, and does not really tackle the issue of what true comparability across projects implies in terms of ability to handle phenomena when this requires an explicit definition of answers. Attempts to grapple with the latter raise the problems on the one hand of having reference answers for generic systems like the Treebank parses, or on on the other of having application-specific ones like the MUC templates. It is thus somewhat premature to regard the Neal-Montgomery Methodology as *the* NLP evaluation methodology.

Oviatt and Cohen (1992) also comment on the limitations of the Methodology, partly on the operational grounds of evaluator training, partly on the theoretical grounds of knowing what correct responses are or imply, though they note the value of such 'consumer reports'.

In addition, any attempt to use the Methodology for comparisons between systems, as opposed to evaluating individual systems, would present very serious problems and would indeed be of doubtful legitimacy. The Methodology is precisely designed to allow systems to be tested within their own domains, to avoid the cost of domain customisation for test purposes. But there is no reference to, or control of, the domain properties, so comparing performance for different systems, each with their own domain data, would not allow for any effects of domain differences, certainly not in any explicit or quantifiable way.

2.5 Corpora, test suites, test collections, and toolkits

Many points about test and evaluation resources of these various kinds have been made in the previous sections, in the context of specific evaluations or of general discussions of test and evaluation methodology, and some specific individual resources have been mentioned, for instance the DARPA data sets and the SAM materials. In this section we first describe, briefly, a further individual effort in the area not so far mentioned, and then review the current picture as a whole and its implications for evaluation.

We consider some later test suite work in the next section.

a) Specific test and evaluation resources

The Natural Language Sourcebook

The Natural Language Sourcebook (Read et al, 1990, 1988, Baker et al, 1991) was a research component in the development of the Artificial Intelligence Measurements System (AIMS). The objective of the AIMS project was to explore methodology for investigations comparing AI system with human performance in a way which would place AI systems on a continuum of human performance. It would then be possible to roughly benchmark systems under development. Originally, the project was to focus on the area of natural language understanding (NLU), taking human performance in reading comprehension tasks as the source of benchmarks for evaluating NLU systems. Other areas also investigated, however, included expert systems and machine vision. Our concern in this report is only with the natural language studies.

The Sourcebook was designed to act as a base for the benchmark task specifications by supplying an explicit and organised descriptive classification of natural language phenomena, viewing these as problems for (human or machine) NLP. Thus the Sourcebook characterises and maps the field to provide a consultative resource in which problems in NLU are identified and categorised by example, with an overall ordering on complexity or intractability. The Sourcebook is seen as a means for developing empirical benchmarking procedures to compare system output with human performance, relative to task difficulty, because it makes it possible to specify language-using tasks in terms of particular processing problems in a way which is common to those setting human performance tests and those defining NLP system capabilities. The whole thus assumes that suitable tests exist or can be devised which will establish human performance benchmarks for the evaluation of individual NLP systems, and also allow comparative evaluations between systems adopting different approaches to the same problem(s). The Sourcebook comprises 197 processing problems to be addressed by intelligent computer systems, classified into an AI scheme with cross-reference to a linguistic scheme and to a cognitive-psychological scheme. Each entry is called an 'exemplar' and consists of one or more sentences, a fragment of dialogue or piece of text to illustrate the conceptual issue, a bibliographic reference, and a discussion of the requirements a system might have to meet in understanding the example. There was an electronic Hypercard version.

Some experiments were done on human benchmarking and system assessment against this, but these were quite limited and it is not clear that there has been any significant further development of this approach to NLP testing and evaluation. It would certainly be difficult to convert the quite informal descriptions and categorisation of the Sourcebook exemplars into actual task specifications. There are other serious obstacles too, notably the fact that current NLP systems are quite unable to tackle some of the problems listed, and the challenge of testing NLP systems on some of the problems either without recourse to domain knowledge or with a clear distinction between the respective roles of application-independent and application-dependent system capabilities. A systematic compilation like the Sourcebook thus has more immediate value as a developer's checklist for determining a system's objectives and design.

b) General state of test and evaluation resources

We have already noted the distinctions between corpora, test suites and test collections (and also toolkits). By *corpora* we mean bodies of naturally-occurring linguistic material, like running text or recorded dialogue; by *test suites* selected natural or artificially-constructed material designed to have certain properties; and by *test collections* material subsuming both input data and required output data or *answers* constituting *reference* data for evaluation. All of these can be labelled *test data* in a broad sense. All raise issues, in the context of legitimate testing and evaluation, of *realism* and *representativeness*, though in varying degrees depending on the purposes for which they are to be used and hence needs they have to meet. These may be quite complex: thus for corpora we distinguished *coverage* from *distribution* corpora, precisely to allow for the role of statistical information about linguistic phenomena in relation to representativeness. Test suites in particular, as designed for exhaustive system testing in the interests of transportability for example, have to be representative in the sense of being linguistically justified; but they need not be realistic, as with syntactically correct but semantically futile or nonsensical sentences for parser testing.

Test suites may be of a kind that can also be used, at least for some purposes, as test collections even though they do not include explicitly defined answers. This occurs where the data specification is such that the answers though implicit are obvious, as for instance in a speech case providing pairs of sounds for discrimination where the required answers - 'the members of the pairs are different' - are manifest. Speech test suites consisting of text to be read, or corpora including recorded and transcribed speech, similarly embody their answer data. However it is essential, in relation to what NLP is primarily about, to recognise the importance of test collections which include explicit answer data defining, for each input, what the system ought to give as output. This answer data is necessary because, for NLP tasks in general, answers are not obvious or unequivocal, those responsible for systems have no inside track to them, and objectivity in testing is crucial. Thus while, say, testing a language analyser in the usual style to see whether it delivers the parse trees or logical forms the system designer labels as correct, i.e. thinks it ought to get, may be called evaluation, the lack of objectivity and control means that this activity is only informal testing, not true evaluation.

When independently-vetted answers, e.g. parse trees, are provided for controlled data like test suites, these might be seen as test collections. However the fact that the material is controlled means that it is better to make an explicit distinction between test collections and these artificial *checking collections*.

The DARPA evaluations, as illustrated by the TREC one, manifestly involve test collections. Test collections constitute *evaluation data* in a strong sense, and while checking collections do this too, the difference between them is that test collections are (or simulate, at any rate approximately or notionally) natural input and output data for the activity in question, which is not a requirement for checking collections and may indeed be precluded by a checking collection's specific purpose, particularly if built on top of a highly artificial test suite. Test collections are naturally, though not necessarily, associated with complete tasks, like database query or information retrieval; this is primarily because task performance as such is of interest, but also because it may be difficult to define meaningful intermediate or partial processing outputs. However given the continuum of subjects for evaluation from sub-components to whole setups, it is reasonable to label material intended for subtask evaluation, for instance sentences from a natural corpus with accompanying answer parse trees, as a test collection.

It will be evident that under the general heading of test data we have two broad classes: what we here call *working data*, which consists only of input material for some data gathering or processing purpose, and evaluation data, which consists of input data and correct answers for the process to which the input data is being subjected (i.e. *not* actual processor output, whether this consists of transformed input - e.g. spellcorrected text - or derivatives of the input - e.g. word frequency statistics). The data in itself is what we earlier called *reference* data for evaluation. In general such data can include ancillary output material as well as answers in the strict sense.

As we regard our data categorisation as significant for our purposes, we will summarise it for use in the subsequent discussion as follows:

```
test data
  working data : input only
    natural      ---> corpus
    artificial   ---> test suite
  evaluation data : input and output (ie working + answer data)
    natural (task or subtask)         --->  test collection
    artificial (subtask especially)   --->  checking collection
```

It should be noted here:

1. That the way we use "test data" is *not* that which is common in the DARPA community, whose test data, or test set, is our evaluation data.

2. Further, that a distinction is commonly made between training data and test (= evaluation) data. This is natural for those working for example in speech recognition and in the DARPA context (e.g. MUC, TREC). Training data specifically refers to 'precompetitive' evaluation data, i.e. specially supplied or, as usually in TREC, old evaluation data. We will use training data, and more specifically, as before, *training set* only in this sense appropriate to evaluation, though the notion is often interpreted more broadly in the sense of working data used to determine system parameter settings. (We will also continue, when the old/new contrast is important, to refer to new evaluation data as a *test set*.)

3. It has recently become customary to refer to annotation, and *annotated corpora*, especially in the context of providing common data resources. The relevant point here is that the notion of annotation may be very widely interpreted so the annotations may range from low-level administrative information to answer information in our sense. "Corpus" may also be used more widely than in our sense. However we may note that depending on the use made of the annotations, an annotated corpus may constitue evaluation data (e.g. a tagged corpus for testing a tagger), whether or not the annotations were originally and explicitly thought of as providing answer data (as e.g. relevance assessment labels on a document set would be).

In reviewing, now, the current state of the art in the provision of test and evaluation data, it is thus necessary to ask:

1. how far these data distinctions have been understood, so their implications are recognised, i.e. whether what may be called the *data sort* of test and evaluation material is clear;

2. how far representativeness has been addressed; and

3. how far legitimacy of use for test or evaluation has been established.

Representativeness is a major issue for all test data and even more for evaluation data: what is the data meant to represent, and how is it known that it does indeed represent this? As noted in the context of the DARPA evaluations, data may be representative without being realistic from some task point of view. Whether data is *realistic* is a separate point which has to be expressly considered. But it is also desirable to refer explicitly to *legitimacy* because though in the individual case a properly representative test collection for a task would would be legitimate test or evaluation data for a system to do that task, attempts to exploit data that is already available mean that legitimacy needs to be considered. For instance while an IR test collection may be quite representative of one IR situation, or a type of IR situation, it does not follow that it is legitimate data for any IR system testing. This point is important because there is a danger, particularly in investigations with a narrow linguistic focus, to treat any body of data, and particularly a large corpus, as both representative and legitimate, and to neglect environment factors. All of the three issues, of data sort, representativeness and legitimacy, collectively characterising data *status*, are important for individual evaluations; they are vital for data intended for general-purpose, community use.

Corpora

There have recently been rapid developments in the collection of large corpora and other linguistic materials proffered for community use, for example those being accumulated under the aegis of the Association for Computational Linguistics's Data Collection Initiative (DCI), and by the Linguistic Data Consortium (LDC) (cf DATA). These materials are naturally mainly written ones, though the large British National Corpus (cf BNC), for example, includes spoken as well as written material. The corpora are indeed predominantly large bodies of machine-readable text(s) that happen to be available, more or less formatted and described. In the most obvious sense their representativeness as data is clear: a large mass of the Wall Street Journal, for instance, is a fair sample of the WSJ itself and is also, though not in a very well-defined sense, a sample of 'quality' newspaper data.

This material, as running text, is a *data source*, for instance of word frequencies; and there is a general assumption that large and heterogeneous bodies of miscellaneous material - like the DCI texts taken together, - can be deemed representative of language usage as a whole, at least for some linguistic phenomena like function word behaviour. Whether or not this assumption is reasonable with respect to the material as an information source is not of concern here, but some reserve is needed with respect to the use of the material for testing. These corpora collectively are very attractive as devices for testing purportedly general-purpose processors, if only for economic and project comparability reasons, and they can clearly be very useful, if only informally, to system developers (e.g. one can learn something from many parser collapses, though how often it ought to succeed is another matter). But from the point of view of evaluation rather than testing, these data files have severe limitations, since their representativeness is not defined and there are usually no accompanying answer specifications, e.g. for whether sentences should be parseable, what senses words have, what meanings sentences have, etc. The bulk files in particular lack answer data, though annotated material providing answers to some kinds of question, for instance part of speech tagging, is now available. The files also normally lack answers in relation to any language-using task, with some notable exceptions like the Canadian Hansard data, which can be very reasonably taken as defining translation inputs and outputs (for that domain), or where the data is in fact derived from evaluations like DARPA ones.

The particular representativeness problem with this textual material, even collectively, is that its status in relation to genre sampling is completely unclear. This issue has been addressed within the framework of the British National Corpus initiative (cf BNC), but again the fact that this material has been assembled with the specific interests of lexicography in mind mean that it may have limitations for other purposes. The problems of defining or determining genres (text types etc) are, moreover, so difficult that this initiative cannot be expected to overcome them even within its own frame of reference. However the more general question of representativeness applies to 'natural' as well as artificial, designed corpora like the Brown Corpus, and in various ways, not only the obvious one of sampling from a larger source. Thus even where a natural corpus is a large solid block, perhaps representing all the source over some substantial period, like the materials used in the TREC evaluations, there is often little information about the original selection criteria for these natural corpus sources: for instance how does something enter the TREC DoE data source?

Rayner et al (1993) report on an interesting strategy designed to construct representative test corpora for system developers in an economical but systematic way. Given an overall corpus, this can be partitioned into equivalence classes by generalisation using explanation-based learning driven from chosen criteria; representative examples can then be selected to form a subcorpus.

(The material available from the LDC and also from NIST (Pallett, 1992) includes speech resources with annotative information providing some kinds of answer specifically for speech-processing purposes. The points just made refer primarily to non-speech test materials or to data like the ATIS corpus which is relevant to language as well as speech processing, as more relevant for this report.)

Test suites

Some existing test suites and ones under development have already been mentioned, for example those described by Gamback and Gibbons in Thompson (1992). Those for the speech area as illustrated, notably, by the SAM materials described by Gibbons, appear to be designed with more care than that used for language processing. In general it seems to be the case that language test suites, for instance sentence sets designed for parser testing, are not very systematically designed or rigorously controlled. They are more often simply accumulated in an adhoc way, though this is not surprising since, as Gamback points out, the effort of constructing exhaustive and discriminating sets providing a completely classified data is a major effort. However the Alvey Natural Language Tools (Briscoe, 1992) include a test suite of a quite organised kind, designed to match the wide coverage grammar supplied, and to support coherent testing under grammar modification or development.

More importantly, the recent TSNLP project (Balkan et al, 1994; Balkan, Arnold and Fouvry, 1995) has been devoted to test suite design and construction.

In motivating TSNLP, Balkan et al (1994) provide a useful summary review of the nature and value of test suites, especially in relation to the EAGLES (1994) treatment of evaluation under the headings of 'evaluation purpose' (diagnostic, progress, adequacy), 'evaluator type' (user, developer), 'evaluation basis' (suite, corpus), 'system type' (module, compound) and 'evaluation method' (black box, glass box). Suites are distinguished from corpora by their control, systematicity and parsimony, by the inclusion of negative examples, and annotations. However as annotations can include e.g. frequency data, suites can serve some of the functions for which corpora are normally deemed necessary. Moreover while suites are conventionally seen as primarily serving system developers interested in glass box diagnosis, or perhaps progress assessment, and as mainly pertinent at the module rather than system level, Balkan et al argue that suites can be of value to users and in adequacy evaluation, and can be used in black box mode as well as (under suitable conditions) serve larger system as well as individual component assessment. They thus emphasise the need to be clear about intended suite applications and about the encoding of relevant information, especially as annotations.

The major design issues to be considered are therefore in the choice of phenomena e.g. particular grammatical forms, and of their combinatorial (i.e. context setting) range. Should the suite treat adverbs, for instance, and in combination with both intransitive and transitive verbs? In the choice of phenomena for coverage, practical factors (e.g. likelihood of occurrence) are as important as theoretical ones (i.e. formal linguistic status). Decisions have also to be made about the granularity with which generic phenomena have to be treated, and coverage at any grain level. In the treatment of combinations the issue is how to achieve control by isolation and systematic variation without a suite explosion, so decisions have to be made about what cases are central or exemplary and about how contextual factors (e.g. the lexicon in relation to syntactic structures) are treated (selected, simplified, marked etc) to ensure that phenomena of interest are correctly characterised in terms of their (in)dependence relations. The requirements for adequate suites clearly imply a range of annotation types from the formal linguistic to more informal classificatory and comment points. Such annotations would indeed allow concrete linking between test suites and corpora, notably by marking corpus frequency for suite phenomena, so for example a general-purpose suite could be placed in relation to an application-specific corpus. This would make it possible to extend the use of test suites from their primary role as benchmarking tools for system developers to serve application-oriented evaluation.

Balkan, Arnold and Fouvry (1995) reports briefly on the technical details of the actual suites produced under the TSNLP project, covering three languages and providing substantial data with extensive annotations primarily intended for checking syntactic analysers (and hence with a deliberately restricted lexicon), validated by some testing with real systems. The TSNLP work emphasises the value of systematic (i.e. automatic) generation of examples, of negative examples, and the need for suite construction tools.

Outside speech processing, the main area for test suites has been to test syntax analysers, and the problems of designing test suites for semantic, pragmatic or generic task purposes (like database inquiry) have not been significantly addressed.

Test collections

The DARPA initiatives have meant that test collections, which were scarcely heard of in NLP research before, have been much more seriously adopted and carefully provided. However progress in meeting the onerous demands of really well-founded test collections from which suitable general inferences can be drawn has been very slow, not surprisingly in view of the nature of the NLP tasks with which DARPA initatives have been concerned and the consequent challenge of providing adequate collections.

Thus when reviewing the general state of DARPA data collection for our report in 1993, we found many deficiencies. Considerable effort had by then gone into establishing what were intended to be bona fide collections, i.e. ones of a suitably representative and legitimate, as well as realistic, character, at least from a qualitative if not quantitative point of view. However even so, it appears that the data collection was not very rigorously controlled. The ATIS collection, for instance, included material obtained by Wizard of Oz means, and the methods of collection varied across the different sites involved (MADCOW, 1992). This material indeed ilustrates the problems of NLP data collection very well since system limitations are so great that human material (in this case inquiry dialogues) cannot be directly used, while until systems have been developed they cannot be exploited to obtain more relevant material. At the same time, as mentioned in the earlier section on this technique, there are considerable difficulties about WOZ simulations. There are particular problems in this situation about obtaining data which illustrates usage patterns reliably, since this really requires large, unconstrained samples.

But there were also, and still are, much more serious deficiencies in the DARPA evaluation test collections. They are in general very limited in task *instances*, in the sense of user requirements of needs, as illustrated for example by the size of an IR test collection query set. Thus MUC initially had just one task instance, i.e. message topic: 'terrorist incident', progressing since to joint ventures and microelectronics. The ATIS test material used in February 1992 (Pallett, 1992) represented 42 inquiry scenarios, i.e. air travel needs. TREC in 1992 used 100 document queries, and enlargement on or variation of these sets has been relatively slow and modest.

It is important to recognise these instance limitations, since they may be obscured by the richness of the data in other respects. Thus the MUC terrorist topic is a broad one and may be met in different detailed ways in different messages, and might thus be deemed to be decomposed into a topic set. In the ATIS case the 1992 scenarios are associated with 971 query utterances, covering 687 paired with answers. Moreover, though there are only 42 source scenarios, there are actually 122 subject scenarios representing variants for the task recorded by different speakers. However while the evaluation refers to the quite large query set, this has to be seen in the context of a quite small original scenario set. In the TREC case the queries were divided into two subsets for two forms of retrieval task, making instance sets of respectable but not striking size by IR standards; and while the later TREC tets have made use of further queries, these have still formed distinct sets, typically of 50. These real limitations are important because while other data components of these evaluations may be very large (for example the enormous TREC document sets), and these other components may be significant environment checks on system performance, the scope of the task evaluation is set by the smallest data component, in both ATIS and TREC cases the query set sizes.

As a related point, bearing on realism and representativeness, while the TREC queries are at least 'quasi-real' (i.e. they were provided by persons familiar with their user community's requirements), the ATIS scenarios up to 1992 were not derived directly or even indirectly from a real user community, and indeed in some cases were motivated by quite other NLP concerns (MAD-COW, 1992, and L Hirschman, personal communication, 1992). Even allowing for the difficulty of obtaining real queries addressed to a non-existent system, the weakness of the foundations for the large ATIS evaluation edifice are rather striking, especially when seen from a broader task setup point of view.

The DARPA MUC and ATIS materials, though not the TREC ones, also illustrate the problems presented by the fact that the agreed answers (e.g. the MUC templates) are honed, consensual ones and are to that extent 'unnatural'. This follows from the need, when the NLP task is complex, for solid enough answers to allow numerical performance measurement. It is also a natural consequence of the fact that in these cases evaluation is being approached as a laboratory experiment: it is then appropriate to have fully explicit answer specifications. Whether it is necessary, or at least desirable, to have consensual answers to avoid individual biases (as in the definitions of MUC template fills) is a question that ought to be openly considered. It is one which has already been examined in IR, for instance in connection with whether there is a correct index description for a document providing a norm with which individual indexing system outputs can be compared (or, alternatively, whether a human indexer's description should be adopted as this). Consensual norms can be seen as compensating for individual idiosyncracies: thus a consensual set of relevant documents for an IR request (as determined by a committee of librarians) may be taken to represent what a bunch of users all putting the same expressed request would like to get.

But setting aside the question of whether such norms really exist or could be attained, the more important point is that the MUC and ATIS norms have been *substitutes*, much more fully than the library committee's relevance set, i.e. are deemed to be what is required for task performance, though what really matters is the delivered task functionality itself. Thus in the IR case the 'correct' index descriptions are deemed to be those that ought to select relevant documents in searching, where the true functional answers are the actual relevant documents a user identifies in relation to his need. In the MUC case the templates are deemed to be what an end user would find helpful, and similarly for ATIS, the database responses are those the user is presumed to find satisfactory: though here there is additional evidence for this in the recorded dialogues. However, bearing in mind the real functional requirement, a lesson from IR is that different substitutes may be equally satisfactory from this point of view. (The TREC answers are not very perniciously substitute ones, and are not consensual, being done by user lookalikes.)

The interest in task resources has continued since our original report, assisted on the one hand by more machine power and capacity, and the general availability of machine readable raw material, and on the other by the growing concern to provide proper test data, especially evaluation data, capable of supporting systematic investigations as well as well as a range of interests. The EAGLES project in particular covers considerable effort on resources (see e.g. ELSNEWS, 1995), and this has been an important aspect of the DARPA programmes.

Thus Dahl et al (1994) describes the collection of the ATIS-3 corpus of spoken dialogues, aimed at more realism, both through the use of a larger database than for the previous SLS corpora and through the use of automated dialogue systems, rather than simulations, for the collection (though system inadequacies sometimes produced glitches). As with the earlier ATIS corpora, user inputs were classified as 'context-independent' or 'dependent' or 'unanswerable' via the Principles of Interpretation, so altogether along with other annotations the material included speech waveform, session log, detailed transcription, query classes, and minimum and maximum query answers. It is noteworthy that the Principles document, while robust and comprehensive in relation to new material, was also ten pages long and based on no less than 10,000 utterances. Dahl et al note the intention of constructing common *development* test data, i.e. training data independent of previous evaluation answer data which encourages competition-winning performance turning or tweaking, but which is also common to all sites, allowing more objective system comparison.

Hirschman et al (1993) report on the rather more elaborate data collection for the ATIS end-to-end experiment. This involved, in a careful process, the choice of 2 sets of 4 travel scenarios with well-defined solution sets and then collection of actual dialogues from 8 subjects doing 4 sessions in a counterbalanced way. The sessions were recorded as log files with timestamping, and human evaluators annotated the classes of user input, system output and 'correctness' etc of response, using the Principles of Interpretation (see the the earlier discussion of this ATIS experiment in Section 1.3 for further detail). As Hirschman et al note, this more complex body of test data presented problems of cross-site variation in collection and also evaluator variation, and also raised the issue of extending the Principles for response characterisation by 'utility' as well as correctness.

At the same time, the effort of gathering complex template answer data of earlier MUCs has been one stimulus for the simpler treatment of templates in MUC-6, though the new range of different answer sets, as with the CSR Hub and Spokes and TREC-4 Tracks, require more answer effort in total.

The DARPA test collections are nevertheless, especially the 'heavy' NLP task ones, clearly limited as bases for performance extrapolation to other application domains for the same task, or even, perhaps, within the same domain, whether or not (as with MUC) participation in ther evaluations has successfully demonstrated transportability for the processing techniques used. The IR community's experience with collections demonstrates that anyone claiming a generic information extraction system needs to show his system performing successfully for a range (even if only limited, depending on the system style) of application message types and template types. Moreover, just as this implies, the more refined the NLP task the more difficult it is to define what a generic task processor, e.g. for message processing, should be capable of doing: if templates are different in kind, so they are much more elaborate for some applications than others, how much system transportability should one expect? The IR case is a useful comparison point here, since if system deliverables are as simple as term lists, transportability is more feasible. With TREC, successive evaluations have shown that (apart from the impact of request quality on performance), it is possible for systems to cope with very heterogeneous document sets, perhaps more arbitrarily heterogeneous than in real life, but this is largely a reflection of the coarse task that document retrieval usually is.

The other main area where what are in fact test collections are being provided is is in parsed sentence sets and corpora like the Pennsylvania Treebank (Marcus, 1991) and Sampson's SUSANNE (Sampson, 1992, 1995). These are promulgated as task neutral, and thus to avoid confusion might be called 'comparison collections'; but like the task-specific collections, have requirements for representativeness which appear not to have been examined in significant detail. It is also not clear, as the discussions of generic evaluation at the Edinburgh Workshop emphasised, how useful for formal rather than informal purposes the supplied parsing 'answers' are, especially when they are quite detailed, even if they are intended to be 'theory-neutral'. Parse trees cannot be taken as uncontrovertible, first-hand task-related answers in the way that user relevance judgements in IR can. This is indicated by the problems encountered in the parsing/grammar workshops described earlier. However careful and consensual they are, they are still only second-class answers, like the MUC templates, because they presuppose future use for some ultimate task purpose, but this is unspecified and also more remote than in the message processing case.

The input texts used for these collections do not appear to have been chosen with any strong regard for representativeness (indeed Marcus notes random external stimuli). Similarly, while there are good historical and comparative reasons for using Brown Corpus material (as in SUZANNE), its representativeness needs a fresh look.

There do not seem to be any significant checking collections based on serious test suites available.

Altogether, the various test collections referred to in this section show that there may be substantial differences of style in the way that answers are provided. They also show that even where there are good reasons for chosen styles, it is necessary to recognise the implications of different styles in interpreting evaluation results.

Tools and toolkits

Resources like the Pennsylvania Treebank are sometimes labelled "tools", and the UK Alvey Natural Language Tools (Briscoe, 1992) include a grammar. However we will consider primarily processors rather than data resources here.

The SAM apparatus for speech includes test and evaluation *tools* of this kind. However the NLP tools currently available, e.g. via the Consortium for Lexical Resources (cf CLR) or within the Alvey Tools are not primarily evaluation tools in King's sense (in Thompson, 1992), and the same applies to Carpenter's grammar toolkit ALE (Carpenter and Penn, 1993). Nor are they designed as test tools in our strong sense of supporting evaluation by carrying out operations and providing outputs suited to organised performance assessment, though parser output, for instance, may be used for formal assessment with little modification. Parseval (Harrison 1991, 1992) is an evaluation tool for parsers, with the same role as the Cornell IR evaluation program used for TREC; and the DARPA NLP evaluations have their own particular tools, like the MUC scoring program and the answer assessment program used for ATIS. There are also conceptual tools, like the ATIS 'Principles of Interpretation' (see Boisen and Bates, 1992) which have a potential utility outside a particular application domain, though they may still be tied to a generic task like database query and, with a yet broader intended utility, the Neal-Montgomery Methodology.

The problems of designing and applying such tools for the NLP case are suggested by the Parseval experience, and they are well illustrated by the Cornell IR package: this is very well-founded, but implements its evaluation criteria and performance measures through specific methods, for instance for averaging performance across request sets, with implications which anyone using the program may not appreciate.

Architectures and standards

Growing interest in language engineering (LE), as well as the experience of evaluation, has recently inspired work on *architectures*, exemplified by the TIP-STER (cf TIPSTER) and GATE (Cunningham, Gaizauskas and Wilks, 1995). These architectures are viewed as infrastructure specifications for NLP or LE which on the one hand provide a common framework for actual processors and on the other allow convenient data management and interchange through data form specifications: TIPSTER, for example, exploits the abstract notion of data document. Architectures so conceived thus have something in common with toolkits, especially where 'default', vanilla tools are are also supplied, but are aimed rather at providing a skeleton for 'plug and play', particularly for subtask modules, for system engineers or evaluators. However in imposing conventions for data characterisation they also address the important question of data reuse. Thus TIP-

178

STER (generalising on the MUC and TREC experience) adopts an annotation approach, and from this point of view architectures encourage the application of operating standards e.g. by implementing data description through the use of TEI-conformant SGML.

The key concerns in these architecture proposals are thus with system and data transportability and sharing, which are important both for system development and informal or formal evaluation. The architecture notions involved have still to be developed in detail and tested by extensive use, But they are clearly of potential value for promoting evaluation. The GATE architecture might, for example, be a useful framework for conducting mega evaluations with the 'braid' model, of the kind outlined later in this Section.

Conclusion

Overall, the conclusion to our 1993 report on the NLP test and, more significantly, evaluation resources currently available was that they had many limitations. However the issues of resource design and collection were being seriously addressed for the first time, and heroic efforts, especially where speech material is involved, were being made to obtain fair sized and reasonably objective data sets. However even where there was considerable prior experience, as in relation to the TIPSTER and TREC evaluations, practical considerations meant that the material did not meet proper standards of realism, representativeness, and legitimacy. Documentation was also often poor, so factor data was lacking.

Since then, however, adequate data provision has been increasingly recognised as vitally important, especially as a community-wide prerequsite in NLP research and LE development. The resources explicitly referred to here are only a few of those becoming available; understanding of what is required of test data is growing, and the quality of resources is rising. Thus in the speech area data collection continues on an increasing scale in data set size and also of variation (e.g. different speakers of the same material). At the same time, as mentioned earlier, there is a growing effort, both in the USA and Europe, in providing multilingual resources either of comparable status (e.g. newspaper stories in different languages), or of strictly related material, e.g. translations.

There is nevertheless much still to do, both a proper test (and especially evaluation) data specification and in its subsequent provision. Thus there typically needs to be a much more careful and explicit examination of the fundamental assumptions on which a whole evaluation rests than is at all common,, to establish what the data requirements on the three counts mentioned above are, and to ensure that they are met. Zue (in Ramsay, 1992), notes that much more consideration needs to be given to what test and evaluation data is *for*. All this implies that test collections in particular involve comprehensive analysis and detailed design examining all the points involved, especially in relation to environmental factors, of the kind initiated during the seventies for IR under the rubric of the 'ideal' test collection(s) (Sparck Jones and van Rijsbergen, 1976), for which a specific design study (Sparck Jones and Bates, 1977) was carried out.

The reasons for the state of NLP evaluation resources until recently, and to a considerable extent still, are not hard to seek. Much of the work has been influenced by the needs and experience of speech assessment; by the appearance of large volumes of text data; by the community's interest in natural language phenomena rather than NLP for task purposes; and by lack of experience in evaluation for NLP tasks. This has led on the one hand meticulous care about some aspects only of an evaluation, and on the other to a rather cheerful belief that enough stuff plus enough obvious and plausible variety (e.g. system designers assuming they can second guess end users in supplying database queries) will be satisfactory. More generally, the defects of many recent and current resources can be attributed to some uncertainty over the goal of evaluation itself, and specifically about the relation between the generic and the individual in NLP, and between general-purpose and special-purpose system evaluation: this is considered further in the next section.

There is nevertheless, as noted, a rising standard of quality in the provision or test and evaluation resources in the field. Experience in speech research has in particular had one beneficial effect. The need, in developing speech processors, for training material has led to a clear distinction, for data, between training sets and test sets, and this distinction has been propagated through the DARPA evaluations whether or not they involve speech processing. This is important for the relation between evaluation and prediction.

Predicting performance for some system (processing method etc) can be seen as applying over successively broader application and task ranges: from the past to the future for some specific application, for instance from old to new queries put to a specific database access system; from one application domain to another for the same generic task, for instance for different databases in database query; and from one task to another (whether or not the domain is the same), for example from query to translation. In IR only the first two really apply (even if document retrieval is a broad task with many variants). In practice training and test sets are often conflated on the tacit assumption that observed performance can be taken as predictable from past to future in the first type of situation: the only case where a strict training/test separation is made is where relevance information is exploited in searching. Alternatively tests may be made across quite different test collections, in practice with one or two as training sets and the others as test sets, though their respective status is not usually explicitly marked. The DARPA style is one which deserves wider use. On the other hand, the problem with the DARPA evaluations so far has been that there has not been enough variation in test sets, so there is a danger of somewhat incestuous, ad hoc tuning, which reduces predictive value.

2.6 Generic NLP system evaluation

We have distinguished generic systems from general-purpose systems. *Generic systems* are those intended, after suitable customisation, to be used for different applications, certainly for the same task in different domains and perhaps for different tasks. *General-purpose systems* do not require customisation. This is only a crude distinction, and applies primarily to whole NLP systems, or at least to the NLP subsystems of larger systems. At the level of individual components there may not be a material difference, since the individual component may be general-purpose but have to be supplemented or complemented by additional, normally application-specific, resources. A syntax component consisting of grammar and parser is an obvious example, since for any system at least a lexicon is also needed. At the same time, it is quite common to adapt such general-purpose components to individual applications, for instance by ordering grammar rules. As mentioned earlier, general-purpose systems with any significant NLP power do not exist: the main operational distinction is between processors intended to be capable of the complete range of NLP operations but needing further data provision, and ones covering only some operations. The amount of data provision required may vary: thus systems may come with 'core' lexicons. There is, moreover, really no sharp division between the two situations but rather a continuum, depending on such matters as the view taken of the range of a language processor, the processing philosophy (e.g. syntax driving), the allocation of data to one component rather than another (e.g. rules versus lexicon), etc. However as a working distinction we can separate generic systems, notionally supplied with full NLP processing capabilities but requiring data supplement and requiring or allowing other application customisation, and components, whether these might be more properly labelled generic or general-purpose.

The important point in relation to evaluation is that in both cases there is incompleteness, but the form this takes has rather different implications for how evaluation can be done.

As the earlier accounts of evaluation workshops show, attempts have already been made to address the problems of evaluating generic processors. However most of the methodological concern has been with the problems of evaluating components, like syntax analysers or language generators, where the component inputs and/or outputs are internal to the system as a whole and have no independent natural role. They have in particular no direct visibility for human users in some NLP task. It is clear that component testing and evaluation is primarily a system developer's concern, and also a laboratory rather than operational one. As the general state of NLP systems advances it should become possible to do some operational, black box component testing by plugging alternatives into running systems. But in general components are not yet isolable in this way, and there is indeed no reason to suppose that all systems would naturally or even could have a modular design of the required kind. The main point emerging from the earlier discussions of component evaluation is that very careful analysis of the presuppositions on which they are based is necessary, and that the informativeness of test and evaluation results for components is very limited and highly specialised. In particular, extrapolating from component performance to system performance is highly dangerous. At the same time, though progress is being made in understanding evaluation for components, much more work needs to be done on appropriate methodologies and techniques both for investigating individual components and for comparing alternative components with the same general function.

However though well-founded and tradeable components are clearly desirable, it is perhaps more important here to consider the state of generic system evaluation. There are now a number of NLP systems which can claim to be generic systems, at least for the sentence if not the discourse level, for instance those developed by BBN, SRI, and New York University: for the purposes of discussion SRI Cambridge's Core Language Engine (CLE) (Alshawi, 1992) can be taken as an illustrative example. These generic systems have already been used for different applications under less or more taxing conditions from an operational point of view, and thus have been, if only very informally, evaluated for both their individual performance and their transportability. They have also in some cases been evaluated rather more formally (e.g. Gamback in Thompson, 1992; Rayner et al, 1993), and some of the systems were tested with the Neal-Montgomery Methodology (Walter, 1992).

The Final Report on SRI's CLARE project (Alshawi et al, 1992) contains notes on a variety of studies testing CLARE (the Core Language and Reasoning Engine) both for language coverage and as a generic system customised to applications. Most of these were not rigorous as evaluations, but collectively they illustrate issues in evaluating generic systems and indicate the range of applications that is desirable for test purposes before a generic system can be said to be well-founded. For instance, DRA RSRE (Malvern) experimented with CLARE as a natural language front end to Autoroute, a commercial route-planning package. This on the one hand raised the problem of choosing an appropriate form of connection between the two subsystems, given various levels of sentence representation that CLARE provides and Autoroute's own internal query forms, and on the other the need to gather good data about the kinds of queries a large population of potential users would have. This would include not only typical query content and hence patterns to match, but also characteristic telegraphic query forms, as telegraphese occurs frequently in such applications. The initial tests with CLARE showed failures in both matching and parsing, and thus emphasised the importance of knowing what is required of a generic system for a given application.

The Autoroute package itself is a good example of what might be described as a utility application for testing NLP systems, and in fact also speech processing systems. Supplied with 'correct' answers, allowing formal evaluation, it could function like DARPA test materials; for though Wizard of Oz techniques are needed to get test data, it seems the package could be driven in this mode in a fairly straightforward way so a large sample of material could be readily obtained and draft answers provided.

The BBN, SRI etc systems typically have three important properties for our present purpose: they have a modular construction designed to separate their general-purpose from their application-specific elements; they have data specifications intended to facilitate customisation; and they have increasingly large permanent data resources which reduce the effort of, for example, lexicon provision for individual applications (this is a major motivation for the growth of interest in exploiting machine-readable dictionaries). There are also commercial, or regular operational systems, primarily for particular tasks (notably database query and translation), which are also generic: the SYSTRAN software is a major example. These have in a few cases been subjected to quite explicit evaluation, and are also open to the informal market assessment of potential purchasers: see the earlier sections on task evaluation.

As just suggested, generic systems may be evaluated either for their performance in a single application where, strictly, the fact that they are generic is irrelevant, or evaluated from the point of view of potential new applications where, in practice in particular, easy transportability is an important consideration in the evaluation. Thus the effort of customisation itself, as well as potential performance, matters. In relation to the discussion of predictive range in the previous section, that is, generic systems are sometimes evaluated within the narrowest range, for future performance in the same application, but evaluation for the wider ranges is of more importance, and while this can be from different points of view, transportability tends to loom large.

Clearly, evaluating a generic NLP system just as a shell without any data is impossible. However though generic systems are incomplete, like components, once they have some data resources evaluation is not necessarily subject to the difficulties of component evaluation, or not to the same degree. This is because with a natural language system one can have actual language input or output (as opposed to, say, parse trees), or inputs or outputs that are independent and can be externally validated: thus database queries can be assessed for their database propriety. This of course is not to imply that evaluation thus becomes easy: only that generic system evaluation is then like specific system evaluation. It is possible moreover, within this framework, to study the extent to which, say, the standard resources supplied with a generic system, like a core lexicon, are adequate for the specific task, just as one could test the adequacy of a specially-constructed lexicon.

Thus though their owners may be very concerned with the performance of their generic systems, and it is important for the field that large systems in which a great deal has been invested should be evaluated, from a task performance point of view they can only be evaluated like any other system. The distinctive evaluation issue with generic systems is customisation. What does this involve in qualitative and quantitative terms? How is this aspect of a system as a global 'object' evaluated? From this point of view, one might ask what the Neal-Montgomery Methodology might look like if it was applied to a system along with a new test domain, whether as a way of investigating individual system customisation or providing a controlled, because common, base for cross-system comparison.

Rayner et al (1993) report, for the CLARE system, on a customisation effort exploiting both both the fact that CLARE is highly modular in structure and customisation tools for new languages and new domains, allowing rapid test corpus formation to aid an application developer. It is also clear that many of the participants in the DARPA evaluations see these as much as evaluations of their systems from the generic point of view as for their specific value for the particular application: that is that those engaged in MUC, for example, would at least like their systems to be seen as suitable for other message processing applications, and possibly with rather different specifications. However, even where these new applications are being introduced (as in TIPSTER), and a good deal of information is being collected about the participants development and customisation work (as in TREC (Harman, 1991)), there is so much ad hoc work required for the successive tests, that it is impossible to treat the DARPA studies as systematic tests and evaluations of generic systems as such. The continuous improvement and modification the systems undergo, under the stress of the DARPA remits, mean that it is impossible to separate the generic from the specific contributions to overall performance even for the individual application, and therefore to have any basis for predicting the performance of the generic system resources for other future applications. For the same reason, it is impossible for those specifically concerned with transportability from an economic point of view to assess customisation effort in any rigorous way, for instance with respect to tradeoffs between performance and the locus, or amount, of customisation effort.

This is of course not to imply that information about customisation effort and cost has never been obtained in the field as a whole; and it may also, on the other hand, be noted that in the simpler IR case, at least one system in TREC has been run off the shelf, and in at least one case without any 'startup' phase. The relevant point here is that, in the relatively novel context of serious evaluation for objects as complex as NLP system that the DARPA evaluations supply, these have not so far included controlled assessments of the contributions of generic systems as such, in a way leading to informative predictions. Indeed one issue which the DARPA evaluations raise is the point at which it becomes rational to move to new data, simply because, even if the current task is not wholly well done, testing has become a matter not even of tailoring but of tuning by tweaking.

Engelien and McBryde's Report

As Engelien and McBryde (1991) are concerned with market systems, their review is in principle particularly relevant to generic system evaluation. However the points made are basically rather general: thus they note that it is hard to demonstrate generic systems to potential customers since they require an application before it exists (and BBN are quoted as saying that large clients are primarily interested in generic potential). They also emphasise the very considerable effort normally required for customisation, say six months, even if as little as a week is the claim for a simple database interface. Specifically, customisation is open-ended, and expensive, and leaving it to users is risky. The most successful systems are those where the customer is heavily involved as 'owner' (though this may mean the outcome is a redone, one-off system, as mentioned for one MT case), and where the user wants them to work: i.e. user goodwill and commitment are vital.

Engelien and McBride do not themselves tackle evaluation head on, and there is very little information in their report about systematic evaluation. There is considerable detail about individual systems which provides some information for informal assessment including, for example, timing data; and there are some lists of expected benefits from NLP task systems which are useful reminders. More importantly from the evaluation point of view, there are accounts of their experiences with NLP systems from nine major companies. These provide, even though only informally, a good deal of food for thought. They emphasise in particular the need to look at all aspects of the NLP system's environment, i.e. the entire setup, and their examples show how far this can extend. It includes, for instance, the ramifications for training requirements (e.g. not just to use the specific system, but computers at all, for translators); types of staff needed (e.g. not skilled programmers for database inquiry); machine requirements (e.g. loading implications for existing machines in database inquiry); management aspects (e.g. control from having translation done in house, security on data through restricting training in interface use, length of 'warm-up' time for staff adoption); staff work (e.g. machine consistency allows long document division among translators so work is more varied, automatic text categorisation reduces boredom); but also novel requirements (e.g. to filter material to determine what is suitable for machine processing, say for automatic correspondence generation; to have access to machine-readable input for translation); there is also an instructive list of the conditions one organisation found for MT.

There is however little evidence in these accounts of formal evaluation, though one in text categorisation found a similar level of performance to humans, but with different types of mistake, and one MT user has a test sentence corpus which is routinely applied after system updates. It is of course obvious that e.g. training is required with new systems: these descriptions are nevertheless useful in drawing attention to the sometimes less than obvious manifestations of setup factors. Otherwise, there is an overall message in the fact that as people are clearly buying systems, sometimes at considerable cost or in non-trivial numbers, the crudest sort of NLP evaluation, by willingness to pay, is taking place. In particular, there is enough information generally available about these market systems for it to be very unlikely that there is a continuous stream of ingorant new purchasers each of whom finds they have bought a pup.

2.7 Mega-evaluation

As mentioned in discussing the DARPA Conferences, these raise the important issue of how to design *mega-evaluations*: that is to say, evaluations extending over many participants and over long periods of time. Such evaluations can be seen simply as a rather visible version of grid filling, connecting across factor options (whether variables or parameters), or as an explicit, even self-conscious manifestation of normal science. But the focus on evaluation as such, rather than on discovery, and on the need to organise these evaluations simply because providing the evaluation data (especially answers), as well as conducting the evaluation itself, is so costly, suggests that there is an important topic in the form such evaluation programmes should take in order to optimise on results for effort.

In the ordinary way individual projects have their own research programmes, partly intended, partly fortuitous, often responsive to what others do; and communities may well, as over time in IR, share data. So de facto but also haphazardly, grid slots are filled in. However the DARPA initiatives force attention on the best way of organising evaluation so that as many as possible of the different evaluation needs can be met, as much data commonality can be achieved, and as much proper comparison between results can be assured. Thus even if evaluation funding agencies have their own specific remits, when the subjects of evaluation are as complex as they often are, economics and science alike suggest a 'multiplexed' design aimed at capitalising on the large effort and cost involved by meeting as many evaluation needs and satisfying as many participant interests as possible. Needs, interests, and hence tests can properly be black box or glass box, task- or (neutral) technology-oriented, under laboratory or operational conditions, remote from or involving real users, etc. Even if participants in the DARPA evaluations have shared a common desire to perform well, and the enforced concentration on specific evaluations has been claimed as a very effective technology driver (notably in speech recognition), the limitations of this strategy have led DARPA to the programme structures represented by the SR Hub and Spokes model and TREC Tracks model. These have a range of different evaluations - each individually properly conducted - with linkage, and hence comparability, achieved through common data and/or tasks and/or systems and/or metrics. In both cases, however, the global task remains the same - speech recognition and text retrieval respectively. Thus the highest-level difference between the two models has been at the management level, with the hub tests compulsory for SR evaluation participants, but no such compulsion for TREC in its first cycle with tracks (TREC-4). [6]

In both cases, the way the models have been instantiated for their particular conferences has been primarily based on what may be described as 'manifest need or interest' as a ground for a particular spoke or track, rather than on a view of how the spokes or tracks relate to one another to achieve most effective coverage of the empty grid slots. However as Kubala et al (1994) make clear, in the SR case, the detailed specifications for the spokes were designed to maintain informative relations between the different tests across the programme as a whole, notably through shared data, within a rather tight and tidy design for the whole set of tests. Thus both hub and spokes were targetted on particular constrasts between primary and secondary conditions for system operation, with the spoke tests examining various different test/training data mismatch problems not applying to the hub, for example language model and speaker adaptation. The hub tests allowed inter-system comparisons, the spokes normally only intra-system ones. With TREC on the other hand, there was less control of the overall instantiation, though this can also be explained by the fact that the overall scope of the text retrieval task is wider than the speech recognition one implying, among other things, the need for quite different evaluation criteria for different tests.

---

[6] TREC-5 has compulsory main tracks, precisely to balance coverage with concentration in evaluation.

However while the TREC-4 filtering and multilingual tasks, for example, were not designed for linkage, it would be possible in future to increase linkage by having non-English data filtering.

The real challenge for mega evaluation is in covering more than one task. This is necessary for political as much as intellectual reasons. As already noted, NLP tasks have their own particular conditions, while there are also limits on how far 'task-free' NLP system evaluation can be carried. But is is also unreasonable to expect any NLP research team to undertake any arbitrary task. Recent proposals drafted for the CEC (Crouch, Gaizauskas and Netter, 1995) have therefore been concerned with mega-evaluation structures that can connect different S&LP teams or approaches without imposing the constraint of any one task which would be either too taxing for some participants or too undemanding for others (for example translation for people with indexing engines, or vice versa). The proposals are also intended to address multingual evaluation, as a central concern in Europe, and also in the harder form of translation evaluation as well as of the weaker ability to operate successfully in different languages of the DARPA SR and TREC mega-evaluations, while recognising the problems of providing adequate multilingual data.

The mega-evaluation structure, 'braided chain', advocated in the CEC proposal, is therefore more open than hub and spokes (and tracks as so far interpreted, though less open than tracks as totally independent could in principle be), but still seeks to make comparability points of contact. The braided chain has a number of strands, with different data sharing points so, for example, one system's task output can offer other systems' task inputs, but where these data can be surface linguistic objects (words, texts) and not necessarily or primarily deeper language objects like predicate-argument structures. As one example, a task strand for extracting key passages from initial long documents which would exercise some peoples' systems could produce these passages not only as final output but also as input to a further translation stage, or for speech synthesis, since the braided model is intended to cover spoken as well as written language. Alternatively, either longer texts or passages, or transcribed speech, could be offered for 'fact extraction' in MUC style, delivering predicate argument units taken either as database entries or as 'deep' input to an output surface language generator to produce text reports.

As these examples imply, the braid need not be a tidy one, since strands can enter and exit at different points. The key motivation is to allow for work on different tasks (and also in principle the same task conducted in very different environments), without presupposing a global or universal NLP system model with well-defined 'modules' e.g. syntax, semantics, with its implication that all tasks require the same modular system structure (even if there can be alternatives for particular modules, e.g. coarse or fine parsers), and hence that system comparisons can be made by plugging alternatives into the module locations along the processing line (or perhaps leaving positions empty). Looking at a sufficiently wide range of tasks (and environments) involving NLP suggests that such module isolation is very difficult, as indeed the SemEval definitions (cf Moore, 1994) imply, since there are logical dependencies between different modules, for example in IR between indexing and searching. Thus quite apart from any practical constraints it may impose on the conduct of evaluations, e.g. through data transfer conditions, the universal architecture assumption is quite a strong theoretical one, presupposing a neutral but tidily customisable NL processor. The braided model is much less exigent. However while it does not impose a plug-in strategy, it allows it where appropriate. Thus as a practical matter, it can subsume tests on sub-system component alternatives, for example different syntax modules, wherever the encompassing task and processor conditions allow the necessary subfunction isolation.

Correspondingly, because the braided structure covers a range of tasks and subtasks, there are also different evaluation points which may not only provide different kinds of performance information but address different consumer needs, e.g. those of system developers, or end users. Similarly, the model makes it possible to vary task or subtask environments, as these affect particular points in the braid, without necessarily affecting other points.

Clearly, working out all the details in instantiating the model is bound to be very hard, especially in ensuring proper data sharing. But all of the various mega-evaluation structures raise the central issue of how to formulate good evaluation designs that cover wide area NLP rather than single tasks, i.e. can accommodate effectively, but not intolerably expensively, multiple *tasks*.

Some further, concrete illustration, of such a braided chain evaluation, is given in Chapter 3. The payoff from learning how, and being able, to conduct such mega-evaluations is nevertheless clear. This is not only economising on evaluation effort: it is also in demonstrating system or subsystem transportability, i.e., especially if application to different tasks is shown, in testing claims that particular approaches or processors to NLP are generic.

2.8   Speech evaluation

We have already considered, in the section on tasks, NLP evaluations involving spoken language. The accounts of the evaluation workshops also referred to speech assessment in its limited, technical sense of evaluating a processor's abilities to make correct word identification relying on no more linguistic knowledge than lexical and low-level syntactic information (as supplied, e.g. by tagging). In general terms, speech processing is viewed here as equivalent to accurate transcription, turning sounds into words correctly, independent of or indeed without any intention to do, NLU. For convenience we can label evaluation on this basis *transcription* evaluation.

As mentioned earlier, this is a large field of activity with its own characteristic problems and well-established test and evaluation methodology. It has its own well-defined performance measures like word error rate (WER) and sentence error rate, and style of system characterisation through receiver operating characteristic (ROC) curves. Measures like WER may be very useful in relation to the specifically speech modules of SU systems, but as has been pointed out in connection with ATIS, are of limited utility in terms of evaluating global system task performance, for instance in handling user queries acceptably. It is not clear that these comparatively simple and direct performance measures have useful analogues elsewhere for NLP; i.e. that there are either other aspects of NLP systems to which anything conceptually similar applies or, more importantly, are aspects to which they could be applied, however formally suitable, without gross and hence damaging oversimplification. It is essential that general notions like operating characteristic curve should not be picked up from some area in an attractively definite form and transferred without enough consideration to another: this point has already been made in connection with "recall" and "precision", but needs making again for speech notions like "error rate". From this point of view, the message of speech recognition evaluation is that while accepting that the operational application of these measures is not trivial, definiteness, objectivity and ease of application for evaluation criteria, measures and methods are inversely related to real informative utility.

The major lessons from speech, i.e. transcription, evaluation are rather those stemming from the care the speech community puts into data design and collection (e.g. what to do with "er"), and the proper treatment of numerical and statistical notions. Both of these could with advantage by taken on board by the NLP community, though sufficiently fully and not with the rather spotty effect of some of the DARPA work, where great care on points for which speech experience is obviously relevant is not matched by comparable care elsewhere.

3   Conclusions on evaluation to date

It is quite clear from the foregoing that S&LP evaluation has become a live issue in the last few years. This concern with evaluation has taken two forms: there has been much more actual system evaluation notably, but not exclusively, within the remit of the DARPA evaluations. At the same time, while these specific task evaluations have naturally promoted discussion about, and the development of, test and evaluation metholodogy, there has been a more general growth of interest in evaluation, closely related as both stimulus and response to the the development of corpora and other appropriate data sets.

In general terms, this growth of activity and interest in evaluation is to be welcomed. It is essential for the health and progress of NLP, and of its underpinning computational linguistics, both intellectually and practically. NLP - indeed S&LP - evaluation, whether it is a science or an art, is nevertheless still primitive and limited, and there are also specific dangers in some current trends.

In attempting to draw overall conclusions about the state of the art in NLP evaluation, we have two different types of information to consider. First, there are the actual evaluations: what methodologies, whether explicitly considered or just de facto implemented, have they applied? Second, there are the methodological discussions: what have they examined and advocated?

Comments on actual evaluations

Thus first, to summarise the salient features of actual NLP evaluation, we see these as follows:

A1   evaluation is strongly task oriented, either explicitly or implicitly;

A2   evaluation is focussed on systems without sufficient regard for their environments;

A3   evaluation is not pushed hard enough for factor decomposition.

Amplifying these claims:

1)   Most of the relatively solid evaluations have been carried out under the various DARPA headings. It is quite clear that while these DARPA conferences have made a serious attack on test and evaluation methodologies, this has been done from the bottom up in response to the requirements forced by the attempt to define and determine performance for the specific tasks involved. Some understanding of what is required for evaluation, and good practice, are slowly spreading from one task to others; and some test strategies - e.g. the use of training and test sets, and evaluation criteria - notably 'recall' and 'precision' are being applied, albeit in distinct particular forms, across tasks. However the individual task types are very different, and many aspects of evaluation are outside their frame.

2)   At the same time, the nature and implications of the frame are not sufficiently recognised or considered. In general, not enough attention is paid to the properties and characteristics of systems' actual or assumed environments, and in particular to the detailed analysis of environment factors for their specific consequences for system testing and evaluation. While some evaluations, like the DARPA ones, do in fact refer to specific environments through their test data, there is an underlying presumption even here that the pertinent features of the environment are encapsulated in the test data (for instance in the TREC queries and relevance assessments). However this assumption may not be inspected, and in any case the environment variables and their values may not be explicitly identified so their impact on system performance can be clearly determined. Alternatively, it seems to be often to be assumed, without the detailed analysis that a proper environment specification demands, that the conditions of some particular test are suitably representative of some larger - and itself unspecified - set of similar environment conditions.

3)   This failure to bring out the test and evaluation circumstances applies at all levels, as a decomposition failure. Thus while there are on the one hand conventional descriptions of NLP system composition, and on the other acceptance of the fact that the same linguistic resources and processes may be very differently distributed, there is not enough attempt to fully identify all the system elements that can figure as performance factors and consequently to establish, for any given case, what the environment variables and system parameters with their potential respective value and setting ranges are.

In general, these three broad features of the actual evaluations have been associated with a failure to consider adequately what and who evaluation is for, and hence to take the implications of evaluation aims into account in test and evaluation design.

One important consequence of these characteristics of actual evaluations is that generic system (or subsystem or component) evaluation occupies a somewhat uncertain position. Generic evaluation is a matter of concern, particularly for components like parsers and grammars but also for more comprehensive subsystems like those represented by SRI's Core Engines, for some members of the NLP community. But most of the actual evaluations done have not been aimed directly and systematically at investigating the performance of the whole system from a generic perspective, so as to be able to attribute performance results clearly either to the fixed, generic elements or to the application-specific elements of the whole, or so as to be able to measure customisation effort and effects. Many of those involved in actual evaluations, for instance within the DARPA framework, are of course viewing their systems or some component of these as generic, and are informally evaluating their performance under individual application stresses. But this is not usually organised, overt evaluation. One obvious reason for this is that most putative generic systems are still actually being developed, but the lack of explicit definition means that generic system or component evaluation as such has not yet been sussed out.

Thus the observed main feature of generic evaluation is closely related to those listed for individual system evaluations. This is that

A4   generic evaluation is often inadequately delimited.

That is, it is frequently not clear precisely what is being assumed about the role of, and hence requirements on, a generic system or component, whether from the point of view of their simple embedding within an individual application system without any adaptation, or from the point of view of customisation operations.

Comments on methodology discussions

Turning now from the evidence actual evaluations supply about the state of NLP test and evaluation methodology to that supplied by explicit discussions, these clearly show that exploration of what is involved, rather than definition of what should be done, has usually been the order of the day. Thus methodologies in the general discussions we have reviewed, like those of the Edinburgh Workshop for example, tend to have the same properties as the actual evaluations we have considered. That is,

M1   the methodology is primarily task stimulated and motivated;

M2   the methodology is more concerned with systems (or subsystems etc) than environments;

M3   the methodology is not decompositional enough.

and, with respect to generic systems,

M4   the methodology fails to define what is meant by a generic system (subsystem, component).

The later workshops, like the Edinburgh one, show much more sensitivity than earlier ones, as they are well grounded in actual NLP system R&D and direct experience of the complexities of NLP and its use. Again, recent methodological discussions, like the EAGLES report, are more sophisticated than earlier ones, and engage constructively with detail: EAGLES indeed is much more of a specification of what should be done - within the framework of a certain type of evaluation, - than earlier discussions, and is much more sensitive to environment and setup. But there is still a long way to go in translating first-hand experience into solid comprehensible guidelines, and procedures, for the design and conduct of evaluations.

Major issues

Thus the main issues for NLP evaluation which our survey of Chapter 2, following on our earlier conceptual analysis in of Chapter 1, has served to emphasise are:

I1   What is evaluation *for*? That is, is an evaluation intended as a means of demonstrating scientific merit, or of determining commercial viability, or of aiding development? And then who - directly or indirectly - is it for?

I2   Is evaluation comparative or predictive? That is, is an evaluation competitive for the same task, or justificatory for new applications?

I3   Can evaluation criteria, measures and methods be generalised? That is, is an evaluation necessarily task - even application - dependent, or can specific evaluation techniques, as opposed to abstract notions, be applied across individual cases?

I4   How do fixed exemplars and artificial constraints help? That is, what role do benchmarks, or laboratory experiments, play?

Finally, as a pervasive, underlying issue,

I5   Should NLP evaluation be linguistically or computationally oriented? That is, how far is NLP 'just' serving the machine simulation or emulation of present human language use, so evaluation refers to this, and how far is it serving new uses, so novel reference bases for evaluation have to be defined?

In the next, and final chapter, we take these questions as the starting point for our view on how NLP evaluation should be approached.

Chapter 3

Strategies for Evaluation

In this concluding chapter we attempt to show how, drawing on our earlier analysis and description, we believe NLP evaluation should be approached. In Section 1 we make our recommendations. For the reasons mentioned there these are in fact rather modest and informal: but if only, disappointingly, mice from a mountain, we hope at least healthy, vigorous, rapidly breeding and colonising mice. Thus in Section 2 we try to show what our recommendations imply, by developing some detailed illustrative evaluations, working from a guiding checklist of questions constituting a framework for designing tests and evaluations which should be methodologically sound. These examples, in particular, are intended to indicate how design decisions need to be both grounded in good general principles and in the natural dependencies between the answers to the different questions. (A summary of our whole evaluation framework, with two of the examples focussing on the narrower NLP aspects, appears in Sparck Jones (1994).)

1 General recommendations

In fact, the major issues for NLP evaluation listed at the end of Chapter 2 are open issues. We cannot assert that NLP evaluation *must* be thus and so: evaluation is not necessarily *of* the same sort of thing, *for* the same sort of reason, and thus *with* the same sort of use. In consequence, criteria etc cannot be generalised, and while fixed exemplars and controlled experiments have a vital role this is not a universal one. One cannot, moreover, say NLP evaluation should be linguistically, or alternatively computationally, oriented.

So if we take our implicit original question: are there any magic bullets for NLP evaluation, the answer is no; not because we do not know how to make them, but because they would not do the job. It is evident that there is far too much variety in the situations and subjects of evaluation to come up with a definite scenario. We cannot offer instructions along the line: "Take 14 texts consisting of 14 messages from the UP wires ...". Just hypothesising concrete instructions of this sort shows what a mistaken idea this would be, even if some of the evaluation literature suggests that it might be both desirable and feasible. On the contrary, evaluations have to be designed for the individual case, just as the good cook treats each meal as unique, but equally is good because she is familiar with proper principles and sound practice, and has some appropriate tools to hand, even if others have to be improvised or adapted.

Thus our Recommendations are just two:

1.   Unpack the evaluation by working systematically through the series of relevant questions (cf Figure 1), pushing into the necessary detail and decomposing the evaluation subject in corresponding detail for proper answers;

2.   Envisage the evaluation from the start as a programme of coherently-related component evaluations based on a performance factor grid.

Or, Divide and Rule!

In the next section we present the questions summarised in Figure 1. Then in Section 2 we show how they are applied using extended examples.

1.1   Question framework

We can approach evaluation in an organised way by asking a series of questions which gradually *decompose* the *subject* of the evaluation - component / (sub)system / setup - in response to the *unpacking* process which designing and conducting an evaluation requires. We will present these questions below. However is must be emphasised that though they are given here in a tidy and sequential fashion, deciding on the answers to later questions will in practice lead to revision of those given to earlier ones: there are dependencies among the questions, and it may also prove impractical to act on some decision because, for instance, the required data is unobtainable or too costly to obtain. It is nevertheless essential to make these *constraints* explicit since they carry over in assessing the *informativeness* of the results. In general, every decision in answering a question has to be *justified* on methodological grounds in relation to the motivation for the evaluation and the nature of its subject. The major questions we list of course subsume many lower-level ones that have to be gone through for any individual evaluation, as we hope to illustrate in Section 2.

Thus first (cf Figure 1), what is the *motivation* for the evaluation: why is it being undertaken? What is the *perspective* being adopted: achieving the task as such, financial, scientific, etc? What is the *interest* prompting the evaluation: that of a system developer, or funder, etc? What is the explicitly recognised *consumer* of the evaluation results: manager, user, scientist, funder, etc? What, then, is the particular *goal* of the evaluation: what is the evaluation intended to determine? In consequence, what is the *orientation* of the evaluation to be: intrinsic or extrinsic? What *kind* of test is it to be: an investigation or experiment? What *type* of evaluation: black box or glass box? What *form* of *yardstick* is to be used: ideal performance, attainable performance, exemplar performance, performance comparable with some given alternative? What is the appropriate *style*: is the evaluation to be suggestive, indicative, or exhaustive? What is the *mode* of the evaluation to be: quantitative or qualitative, or perhaps a hybrid?

194

```
EVALUATION REMIT : to establish

   motivation - why evaluate
     perspective - task/financial/administrative/scientific ...
     interest - developer/funder
     consumer - manager/user/researcher

   goal - what discover

   orientation - intrinsic/extrinsic
   kind - investigation/experiment
   type - black box/glass box
   form (of yardstick) - ideal/attainable/exemplar/given/judged
   style - suggestive/indicative/exhaustive
   mode - quantitative/qualitative/hybrid

EVALUATION DESIGN :

   to identify
     subject's ends - what's subject for
     subject's context - what's it in
     subject's constitution - what's it of

   to determine
     performance factors
       environment variables
       'system' parameters

     performance criteria
       performance measures
       application methods

   evaluation data

   evaluation procedure
```

Fig. 1. Framework questions for evaluation scenario determining test and evaluation programme on subject

The answers to this first set of questions, on the evaluation remit, lead to the second set, of evaluation *design* questions. These fall into three classes. The first class defines the evaluation subject at the level of detail necessary to conduct the evaluation. Thus the questions here ask what the subject's *ends* are, for instance for systems their objective or function; what the subject's *context*, inanimate or animate, is; and what the subject's *constitution*, as structure and process, is? The characterisation of ends is needed on the one hand to validate the remit, and on the other to validate the evaluation criteria. With the characterisation of context and constitution the necessary questions about *performance factors*. i.e. about *environment variables* and *system parameters*, can be answered. The second class of design questions therefore addresses the choices of evaluation *criteria*, and then *measures* and *methods*. The third class of questions deals with the choice of evaluation data, i.e. its *sort* and *status*, and in the light of the other classes, its specific *nature*. Clearly, the answers to these various questions have to be related to one another in a way that ensures proper connectivity between the various elements and, in particular, proper *linkage* between the subject, via the data, and the measures. The fourth, again related, class of questions is what the *procedure*, i.e. action sequence, for the evaluation is?

Thus the outcome of the analysis of remit and design is a strategy, or *scenario*, for conducting the evaluation subsuming a *programme* for *testing*, to determine what the subject is doing and to gather the results data, and for *evaluation*, working on the results data, to determine how well the system is doing. In practice, things are unlikely to be as smooth as this, if only because of unexpected problems and findings, so *cycling* will probably be desirable, but thinking of the evaluation as a whole in this way helps to provide and maintain the *grid* design which makes individual *runs* and groups of runs useful and the evaluation as a whole informative.

2 Evaluation illustration

As we cannot simply provide instructions on how to evaluate NLP systems, and in particular cannot supply ready-made performance criteria, measures and methods, we believe that the most useful thing to do in this chapter is to illustrate what we see as rational evaluation practice through some extended examples, which will complement the opening examples illustrating the potential complexities of evaluation in Chapter 1. Thus we will try to show how the analyses of issues, concepts, and experience we have presented in the report could be applied in designing and conducting well-founded evaluations for some different cases. These will still only be indicative sketches, as exhaustive accounts would be far too bulky. But we hope they will provide enough detail to show how appropriate and informative, because methodologically sound, NLP system evaluations should be conducted. We will in particular attempt to demonstrate how some of the key notions and distinctions covered by the questions just listed apply.

For this presentation we will use one hypothetical system and consider various different evaluations for it. We will go into detail for some of these, to try to show what evaluation in its real complexity involves, and use the others, given in less detail, to suggest other possibilities and the distinctions they call for. As we are dealing with an imaginary NLP system we will not be concerned with whether such a system could currently be built, or with precisely how it would work if it could. More importantly, as we have to characterise the system for the purposes of our illustration, we will simply assert that it has the properties we mention, without any regard for whether the system's design as thus specified is particularly sensible or well-motivated. For the same reason, as we have an imaginary system context with human users and so forth, we will simply state that this has certain features, that there are such and such evaluation needs, etc, without attempting to explain or justify these.

2.1   Illustrative examples: scene setting

For our illustration, we will take a hypothetical architectural design application, namely a student training program called "PlanS". We will describe this initially in a quite informal way, using expressions like "the intention is to teach students" for purely descriptive reasons: of course a major requirement in conducting an evaluation is knowing what such intentions are.

The general idea with PlanS is that students at a School of Architecture, say, are set house design requirements and can develop their designs using various data sources, interacting with the system which acts both as a supplier of factual information and as critic of the completed designs. We are not concerned here with whether this hypothetical system is sound in its details from either a pedagogical or architectural point of view: we will just suppose it is plausible enough to support our discussion of evaluation.

The house design requirements that are set deal with three aspects of house specification: layout, as subject to specified total floor area, building orientation, and number and type of rooms e.g.

```
1000 square feet;
SW facing;
3 bedrooms, 2 kitchens;
```

materials, as subject to exterior wall and roof specifications e.g.

```
yellow brick;
black tile:
```

and cost e.g.

```
less than 30,000 (pounds).
```

Of course some categories may be left unspecified, e.g. orientation, or cost, and as illustrated, only some properties in a category given e.g. number of bedrooms but not of any other rooms. For simplicity we assume the houses have to be single-storied, and the repertoire of room and material types is straightforward.

The intended way of using PlanS for training is that the user submits the specification which is filed for reference and then sets about planning the house themselves, using simple graphics with supporting annotations giving compass orientation and room labels, filling in an accompanying box with choice of materials and perhaps their own computed cost. To help in this design activity the user can ask for information about available materials and their prices, and about building regulations, which we will suppose are rather simple e.g. every room above a certain size must have a window and there must be at least two doors. We will however suppose that the user cannot seek criticism during the planning process: they have to develop their complete design and the system then offers comments, on two levels: a lower one of fact, on whether the design meets the set specification and also building regulations, e.g. Bedroom 3 needs a window; and a higher one of quality, on whether the design is sensible or not, e.g. all the rooms face north (undesirable in the UK), or the hall is larger than is needed for room access. PlanS also produces its own design(s) for the given specification and the user can ask what its merits are deemed to be. The initial specification is input in natural language, and all the inquiry and criticism is conducted in natural language. This is also genuine NLP in both input and output: there are no text templates at this level, only for some 'packaging' (e.g. acknowledgements, prompts).

Overall, PlanS is based on the assumption that the basic concepts involved are ones the user either knows already or can easily relate to what they know. Thus for example users know about conventional names for rooms in houses, the types of material available for walls and roofs and so forth, though they are not required to use a fixed vocabulary or to know precisely what materials are available to the system. Similarly, they have the essential idea of what a house plan is like: the system is for constructing and assessing particular plans. PlanS is also fundamentally user driven: it can only respond to what the user does or offer its own solution to the problem posed by the starting specification. PlanS is not itself a teaching system in the sense of having its own programme of instruction, e.g. for setting specifications of increasing difficulty, say: this is left to the human teachers responsible for the students. The general mode of working is also quite simple, in that there is a design cycle: specify, draw, assess; there is no assessment during drawing. A complete plan can be revised after assessment, but this is taken as a new cycle. [1]

We also assume a straightforward user screen interface with specialised subtask windows: for the initial specification display; for data display on materials, regulations; for the user plan drawing; for the user system NL dialogue; and for the system's own plan(s). There is a separate window for higher-level session commands (e.g. start a new cycle). (We will disregard matters like editing, filing etc.)

Thus the kind of simple session a user might have could be something as

---

[1] Note, however, that we are arbitrarily - but quite realistically given the characteristics typical of packages - assuming that the user cannot query the system's critique of their plan, or critique the system's plan.

follows (with items which would actually be in the command rather than dialogue window marked *):

```
                [startup sequence]
S    *   Please enter specification.
U        4 bedrooms, combined kitchen-dining, blue bricks, SW
             facing.
S    *   Please draw your plan.
             [U draws, labels, redraws etc]
U        How much are rustic tile?
S        10 pounds per square foot.
U        What other sorts are there?
S        Redland Composite, Roman concrete ...
             [U draws etc]
U        Do french doors count as doors?
S        Yes.
             [U draws etc]
U    *   Done
S        Your design costs 27,500 pounds.
         You have 5 bedrooms, but specified only 4.
         There is no door to the kitchen.
         The sitting room faces north.
         Your plan, with the cheapest materials (London Common
             brick, Southend plastic tiles), would cost 22,750
             pounds.
         Alternative plans, with these materials, for your
             specification, would cost less than 24,000 pounds.
             [S displays its plans]
U        What's good about your plan 2?
S        Sitting room and bedroom 1 face south.
U    *   Restart, modify specification (in specification
             window)
U        Is a bath required?
S        No, as long as there is a shower.
             [continued ...]
```

This notional system is far from trivial, but its internal capabilities are limited and its interaction facilities constrained. Specifically, looking at it as a dialogue system, everything is done within a rather simple task structure assumed familiar to the user, and is strongly anchored in the user's own single current design. Thus the linguistic exchanges are treated as ahistoric, with at most local anaphor and ellipsis, and they are interpreted in the known (sub)task context in relation to well-defined objects determined by the task and its structure. For instance, "Bedroom 3" must refer only to a named room on the user's plan, or to one in a system plan, according to the current task phase. (The system does not allow combined modalities, for example for deixis in linked mouse pointing and natural language dialogue utterances.)

Thus to characterise PlanS using our earlier terminology, its *task* is architectural design development, with housing as the particular *application domain*. The system's *function* is to help the user to produce completed designs meeting the set specification and satisfying both explicit individual building regulations and general criteria for good (house) design; its own *objective* is to provide information, assess designs, and provide plans meeting specifications well.

The system itself consists, first, of a core knowledge-based system which we will suppose is of an orthodox rule-based kind able to produce and evaluate house designs; this depends on a domain model for houses along with a set of design criteria, building regulations, costing rules, and data on materials (we assume simple multiplication by floor square feet for roof costs, by external wall linear feet for walling costs).

The interface part of the system has three constituents dealing respectively with overall interaction control, graphics, and natural language which are essentially separate from one another, managing their various windows (e.g. the systems own plan output is on a window under the global controller).

In our earlier terms, therefore, the PlanS *system* consists of a substantial non-natural language *subsystem*, the *n-system*, with various *component* modules, most importantly the expert system, but also the graphics interface component and the global controller; and the natural language interface component, or *l-system*. The controller and expert system are of course linked to one another and to the graphics and natural language components. The various screen windows and keyboard constutute the *terminal* part of the interface; there is no *apparatus* outside the system just described.

The l-system itself obviously has its own components including input parser / interpreter and output generator, grammar, lexicon. There are of course links for message communication, presuming some form of representation for natural language expressions, between the l-system and the expert system, and for using the graphics component plan labels. We are not concerned here with the details of the system's internal operation, and will refer to these (as hypothesised) only to illustrate particular points.

We will now suppose, for the purposes of some possible evaluations, that the PlanS is already installed and has been in use for some time in the Architecture Department at Poppleton Polytechnic: [2] we will not consider its evaluation as a potential purchase. For convenience we will now take this hypothetical installation as actual fact, and talk accordingly. Thus PlanS is used for full-time, first-year students, in their second term following initial introductory courses on the elements of building design, basics of construction materials, etc, and induction into computing. The students are shown what PlanS does and gain practice with it partly by being given set specifications and partly by being encouraged to set some themselves. In the classes the teachers may, and we suppose often do,

---

[2] with acknowledgements to Laurie Taylor

set specifications which differ for individual students, tying in with their particular work. Halfway through the term the students are given two assessed practical sessions based on a series of increasingly challenging specifications, where their designs are recorded and subsequently marked by their teachers for quality; and the students' experience in house design is also tested indirectly in end of term written examinations. There are on average 20 students in the class, and there are 2 teachers responsible for this training, who are themselves thoroughly familiar with the system. (We will disregard here everything to do with low-level problems in using the system e.g. faulty startup, misunderstood commands etc.)

With the scene thus set we can now examine what various evaluations would require, and how they could properly be carried out. We will choose examples to illustrate the implications of various *levels* of evaluation, and consider these primarily in relation to the system's NLP operation. As indicated earlier, we will develop some of our notional evaluations more fully than others. It may not always be obvious what some of our discussion has to do with NLP evaluation: but as we hope to show, we will in fact be making points relevant to NLP evaluation. Some of the hypothetical background in Poppleton Polytechnic may not always appear very explicable: we will just take e.g. some of the putative evaluators' interests as given.

2.2 Examples: evaluations

The specific evaluation cases we will consider will be for two setups, one including both teachers and students, the others students alone; for the system as a whole; for the language subsystem; and for one component, the lexicon. We will label these as follows: Case E, the educational setup involving teachers and students; Case U, the setup with student users; Case S, for the system; Case L, for the l-subsystem; and C, for the lexicon component. We will thus be proceeding through a sequence of nested evaluation subjects with progressively narrower bounds, but it does *not* follow that the evaluations themselves are simply subcases since e.g. their motivations may be quite different. We will also, as mentioned earlier, treat some in more detail than others, in particular the first: this may not appear primarily concerned with NLP, which is our main concern, but the presentation serves both to make some important points indirectly bearing on NLP evaluation, and some of the detail is also exploited for later cases.

Finally, we must emphasise that with respect to the non-NLP aspects of these evaluations, we are not claiming that all the specific choices we make are sound, as we do not have the necessary domain expertise e.g. in educational matters. What we are trying to do is illustrate the kind of analysis that is required.

Case E

We will suppose that somebody, say the Department Chair, has been motivated to ask whether having training with PlanS is a good thing: is it educationally effective? (We consider implications of why they are asking later.) As described earlier, PlanS is used both formally and informally, and involves teachers in setting and assessing problems, and the students in doing these. It is also a fact that after the initial induction, teachers and students do not work together with PlanS, jointly developing and discussing problem solutions, with whatever educational consequences this might have. However we (i.e. the Chair) can still justify an evaluation of setup E as a whole because the teachers are responding to both PlanS's capabilities and the students' activities in posing and assessing problems, and are thus developing and modifying their own teaching. We thus can consider educational effectiveness as determined by the mutual interaction of teachers, students and system, even if the interaction is somewhat limited.

Thus trying to pin down educational effectiveness also serves to delimit the setup more clearly. We now must ask what the evaluation perspective is. This might seem obvious, but though the motivation is educational, the perspective could be e.g. financial or managerial. We will assume here that the adopted perspective is in fact, and exclusively, the task one, so non-task factors like staff time costs are deliberately excluded. The prompting interest in the evaluation is that of the Chair, which we can call managerial, and we assume the Chair along with the Department's staff as a whole including the two teachers directly involved constitute the consumers for the evaluation findings. Coming now to the specific goal(s) of the evaluation, the broad original motivation has to be reinterpreted, as determining whether E is educationally effective, or how effective it is. This may seem no more than paraphrase of the stated motivation, but it has to be taken further: what does educationally effective mean?

We are not as amateurs going to embark on this vast topic: but while whatever definition is adopted will eventually be operationalised through the evaluation criteria etc, leverage is required now from a definition of the evaluation goal. We will therefore assume that educational effectiveness means enabling teachers to promote and students to achieve an understanding of and ability to use the technical area concepts (in this illustration those of house design), with greater effectiveness associated with more solid grasp, more imaginative use, more sophisticated concepts etc.

Continuing to formulate the evaluation remit, what is the orientation of the evaluation to be? As we are considering the setup for its own educational effectiveness, we are really engaged in an intrinsic evaluation, rather than an extrinsic one relating to the Department's course as a whole, though the line is a fine one here. What kind of evaluation should we be seeking? We will suppose that consideration shows that (at least the initial) desire is simply to try to establish what level of effectiveness E has, not whether or how it could be made higher, which would depend on an evaluation designed to account for the existing level of performance. This means we are engaged in an investigation, not a series of experiments, with consequences to be examined later for the required data gathering. Then if we ask what type of evaluation, black box or glass box, as what is being looked for is essentially a 'report' on E, it seems more sensible to do black box than a glass box investigation: depending on the results, it might subsequently be useful to engage in a glass box inspection.

We now have to choose our form of yardstick: without a yardstick we will only get a description of E, e.g. listing how may problems on average students did etc. But there are difficulties of definition here. What, for instance, would ideal performance for E be: that staff be stimulated by PlanS to set many, interesting problems, that students solve at speed with plans needing no critiquing? How many problems, what is interesting? Alternatively, can some 'realistic' attainable level of performance be specified, e.g. using past experience? Are there exemplars or comparable setups elsewhere: however even if PlanS is used elsewhere, it does not follow the other setups are sufficiently comparable; and in fact we will assume that there is a crunch here, since there are no independent similar setups for close comparison. Groping for a viable choice, we will suppose we can adopt a baseline approach, because we think we can (as described later) obtain performance for PlanS problems from similar students without benefit of working with PlanS. With respect to the evaluation style, it seems in keeping with the Chair's interest to consider an initial fairly 'lightweight' evaluation, but indicative rather than merely suggestive in view of the fact that E is an established rather than novel setup. What, finally, is a suitable mode of evalution? It might appear that a qualitative approach, with questionnaires say, would be appropriate, but against this, as educational effectiveness is rather woolly already, it might be worth trying to have a more concrete evaluation of some quantitative kind.

All of this outlines the evaluation remit, clearing the undergrowth for the detailed evaluation and leaving a few identified trees to turn into timber. We now have to look at the actual design.

First, since we are engaged with an intrinsic evaluation, what are the setup's ends? What is it intended, in its own terms, to achieve? We have determined our evaluation goal, but we need to be sure it is fair in relation to, and can be tied into, the setup's ends. More specifically, as we are concerned with a setup involving humans as well as system, we have to identify E's (internal) purpose. E may in fact have a variety of purposes; but we believe they include ensuring a sound and thorough knowledge of basic planning, as evinced by house design, by promoting student practice in a hands-on, varied, and painless way. This is not obviously quite what we wanted to find out: our interest was in educational effectiveness seen as stimulating imagination. But we think the setup's purpose can thus be interpreted or harnessed, legitimately, via characterisation of the design problems set and their solutions. (Of course in practice the evaluation might have started by looking at the setup's 'declared' purpose and working from there.)

We now have to establish the evaluation givens: thus what is the setup's context? Some of the informal description given earlier refers to E's surroundings, which for the evaluation have to be taken as fixed. Thus the context includes e.g. the overall syllabus, the nature of the student intake, the staffing characteristics, what sorts of things buildings are, the existence of building regulations. Again, when we ask what the setup's constitution is, details about the modus operandi, e.g. way problems are set, time students have to tackle them, facilities of the PlanS system itself, are all relevant. It is important that when we are evaluating a setup, properties of the humans involved have to be treated just as objectively as those of the system, and a much longer list than that just briefly introduced needs to be explicitly examined. In particular it is necessary to ask specifically, but also to decide, whether any feature is to be allocated to context or constitution: in many cases this is an essentially arbitrary decision, because it is based on a view of whether it is immutable, but in practice rather than principle. Thus for example, setup E could be modified by having less experienced teachers involved. This would change it just as much as the kind or order of problems set.

But it seems sensible to adopt a liberal view of context, as relatively given, and a parsimonious view of constitution, to contain the evaluation, in order to address the immediately following, and crucial, question: what are the performance factors for E? What are the environment variables, and 'system' parameters (treating the setup as an abstract system), relevant to the evaluation? The variables, providing a definite and (appropriately) selective version of the context, must include the students' experience with architectural concepts, and with computing, for instance, which may be labelled e.g. as 'modest' for a variable value. The variables must similarly include the teachers' experience in setting and assessing problems, e.g. 'extensive' and 'practised', say. Finally, there are variables for the generic house design activity e.g. 'nontrivial'.

As the evaluation is black box, questions about the 'system' (i.e. setup) parameters appear otiose: everything is given and the 'system's' insides are opaque and inaccessible. However is may be useful to notice, as potentially but only informally relevant to interpretation of the evaluation results, the number and types of the problems set, relations between problems set and assessed, nature of PlanS comments on its own plans etc. It may appear odd that these pieces of information are not required for the evaluation, but they have the same only indirect relevance to the evaluation as, say, the nature of the thesaurus that an IR setup embeds would have to an investigative evaluation of this setup from the point of view of the whole setup's performance levels.

The next question is about the performance criteria. We will try to work with student success in providing designs with little system critiquing, and in handling novel problems in the formally assessed exercises, where the problems set by teachers are non-routine and grow rapidly in difficulty: the idea is that this takes account not only of the students' behaviour but also reflects the teachers' more dynamic response to what the system achieves for the students. What measures can we use to apply these still vague criteria, and what methods to apply the measures? The notions mentioned are hard to pin down, and we cannot explore what is needed in detail here. Much of the challenge is moreover in the data definition, considered below. We will suppose that student success can be measured in terms of the extent of PlanS's criticisms of their plans, and the difference between students' plans and the system's own. Thus we will measure by simple numbers of criticisms per plan, and plan difference on three grades: very like, not very like, and very unlike. These will be averaged over the students, and taken at points over time, in the two cases. The methods for the first measure will be the direct use of system output sentences.

We also need measures for non-routine problems, and for growth in difficulty, both for themselves and to support the student performance assessment: this evaluation is thus rather complex. For the former we will take proportion defined as 'challenging' as opposed to 'straightforward', and informally define more than 50% challenging as a norm; for the latter, say, increase in the expected (non PlanS) time to complete, taking 5% increase per problem in the sequence as norm. We will not pursue the precise form of this measure here insofar as it is used to determine the problems get more difficult, but only remark that student performance is measured relative to it, e.g. as percentage reduction. Note that the various different measures would have to be taken together (though they could not be numerically combined) for overall performance information; and clearly if the assessment of the teachers' problem setting showed the problems were not interesting or increasingly difficult, the rest of the evaluation might be abandoned. This part of the design must also choose statistical tests for the various component measures.

What, now, is the data to be? First, what sort and status of data do we need? Given the nature of the evaluation we are engaged with, we have to have a test collection, i.e. material with reference data, and also one that is realistic, representative and legitimate. We suppose that we are fortunate in having to hand entire records including log files of the last year's operation of E. This must have the right status for our evaluation, though we still have to make detailed decisions about precisely how it is to be used. Must we, for instance, use all of this material or is sampling sufficient? As e.g. the number of students is not large, it is better not to sample on them, as we are sampling on time points, say 5 over the total period. What we also need to ensure is student representation on all the points. (We are of course only using completed problems, however much we might otherwise learn from abandonment.)

Then, though we are trying to contain the effort of the evaluation since it is only an indicative one, we need human judgements both for the reference data to categorise the problems and to rate the plan differences. We will get these by using two staff members not involved in the PlanS teaching, seeking agreed judgements from them. The real problem is the baseline data for times. We want to allow for growth in design experience, so are obliged to gather data at comparable real time points from our benchmark students: we are fortunately able to find these at our sister University of Poppleton's Architecture School. Each of our own set problems at our sampling intervals are given to one of their students: this only gives one time per problem but we deem it sufficient after averaging. All of this includes a lot of careful recording to correlate the various pieces of information.

Supposing we have followed through the decisions we have sketched, we have our evaluation scenario: it gives a programme for the evaluation embodying our choice of choice of test methodology, primarily that of gathering and processing the log files, and our evaluation methodology, doing the assessment and getting the reference data, and then applying this in conjunction with the evaluation measures to give our various sets of performance figures. We also need at this point to apply statistical tests for differences over the baseline etc. Overall for E, we have a rather challenging evaluation motivation, but have decided that a rather crude and simplistic approach to the evaluation is fair for a first pass.

Of course as a result the evaluation may not be very informative. It may conclude, for instance, that performance is far from showing the improvement over the baseline we believed we would get, or alternatively, that there is a large percentage improvement. In either case there will be no exhibited means of determining why performance is what it is. All that we have is, given situation S we have performance P (absolutely and relative to baseline). But the explicit decisions we took about how to evaluate can then be examined and used to provide leverage for more discriminating further evaluations. Thus if we imagine performance is poor we can pursue further inquiries for instance changing the criteria, or the reference data, or modify the environment or explore the setup itself, perhaps changing parameter settings and thus engaging in more systematic analysis: all of these would lead to comparative investigations or experiments and thus start filling in a grid.

More pertinently from this report's point of view, though PlanS involves NLP and the setup's working thus exploits NLP, the evaluation we have just developed does not specifically address the NLP contribution to performance. Example E shows that it is quite possible, in trying to evaluate a setup as a whole, for worthwhile reasons and in a proper way, to learn nothing about a specific element of the whole however much it is playing its part. Something much more targetted would be needed to establish what part. Observation of the log files might show something about the NLP, but this is not part of the present evaluation. Certainly trying to draw any conclusions about NLP from the evaluation results would be very dangerous: thus it might be natural to conclude that as natural language is used for interaction with PlanS, if performance is high the NLP must be satisfactory. But it could rather be the case that there is very little interaction, beyond specification input which is not challenging for NLP. To learn about NLP performance for setup E implies, because setup E is so all-embracing, a different evaluation scenario, and in particular one which is much more decompositional of E itself. This would in fact amount to evaluation with the l-subsytem as subject, but within a very rich and full environment.

Thus the major point from this example is an indirect one. Any attempt to determine the NLP contribution to E could only be by a very extensive comparison changing the settings for a whole range of 'system' parameters, and well as of E's environment variables. It is thus preferable for practical reasons, even if at some potential cost in loss of information, to focus more narrowly on the l-system: but it is then necessary to try to cover as much as possible of the rich environment by changing its variable values, and this in turn will involve considerable effort. The illustrative evaluation we have just presented might indeed deem irrelevant to someone alertly concentrating on NLP. Our intention in going through it has been first, simply to indicate what a broad-bound evaluation of a setup embedding NLP might look like; and second, to draw attention to the fact that disengaging the NLP element may imply a dilution, or damaging loss, of information simply because the overall view of a complex whole and its internal interactions is lost. We will also use some of the detail in the remaining examples.

Case U

As we have gone into some detail for a setup evaluation with E, we will consider an illustrative evaluation for setup U, system plus its students users, more briefly, primarily to emphasise the consequences of different choices in creating the evaluation scenario.

Thus in developing a remit for U, suppose we were stimulated by a claim made for PlanS, that it enables students to get a good grasp of planning very quickly. So even if we still assume our motivation is educational effectiveness, we are now adopting a somewhat different perspective: do the students proceed rapidly? We assume that the interests and consumers for U are as for Setup E. But should the evaluation orientation be extrinsic or intrinsic? It seems intrinsic: we are interested in whether one of the setups's internal ends (i.e. purposes) is achieved. What kind of evaluation do we want? We would like to get a handle on rapidity, and as this may well be dependent on either prior training or the nature of the problems set e.g. their sequencing, this suggests experiment is required, not just investigation. However we may still accept black box experiments since we are not changing the setup itself, only varying some context (if we started studying the student user's activities within the setup, on the other hand - and supposing these separable - we would be embarking on a glass box evaluation.)

What form of yardstick: how rapidly might students work with PlanS, or alternatively work without PlanS at the same design task? It is not obvious there is any absolute or readily determined attainable speed, which suggests that we should try to find some comparable setup with the same task but with e.g. some other system or no system. However we cannot deprive some of our current students of PlanS to see how they perform, and finding a comparable task community elsewhere is difficult: in fact we assume it is impossible for this illustration. Thus we have to return to trying to define attainable speeds, which we will consider further in the discussion of the detailed design. If we have some comparison base, what should the evaluation style be: the apparent difficulties of getting a really robust comparison base suggest we should try only for an indicative evaluation since an exhaustive one could not be supported: so how to do this well? Finally, what mode of evaluation: it seems a quantitative one would be feasible, as we are dealing with times.

Now to the detailed design. This is an intrinsic evaluation again, so we have to validate the evaluation motivation against the setup purpose: one purpose of the setup is to promote fast learning. We suppose that this is a purpose of the setup embedding PlanS, as well as an objective of PlanS itself. Trying to characterise the context, that for setup U includes the contribution of the teachers, now outside the setup being evaluated, both in setting problems and also in carrying out the formal examination assessment. Other features of the E context, like the fact that these are first year students, also hold for U. The constitution of U is now the students activities in relation to PlanS specifically, but no longer their replies to examination questions, and PlanS itself.

What performance, and first environment, factors are relevant to our specific evaluation goal? They include the students' degree of familiarity with architectural planning concepts e.g. moderate; their experience with using a computer system, and with graphics, e.g. modest; the nature of the problems posed e.g. easy, medium, hard. What are the 'system' (i.e. setup) parameters? They presumably include helpfulness of the system's critiques; convenience of graphics system; also length of session; and 'workover' habits of the students, i.e. exploring related designs themselves. Then what performance criteria are appropriate in this case: they must be both absolute speed of problem solution and increase of speed, related of course to level of student performance on the problems. Thus a possible measure would be cycle time for acceptable solutions defined as those with no criticisms for breach of building regulations, lack of doors to rooms or other obvious faults, and failure to meet the problem specification: i.e. the measure is on basic planning capability, not style (thus it is assumed that if the input problems are ordered by difficulty, the measure automatically takes acount of this.) A method for the measure would identify and time cycles from input start to null critique delivery, average times etc.

The test data could be actual log files if they existed, as for setup E before. Alternatively, if these were not available, special selective records of input problems and end-cycle critiques could be recorded. But the reference data still needs to be obtained, and this depends on some notion of bad, average, and good times for the problems. On the assumption that the investigation is being done presently for this years students, the strategy for gathering the answer times is to take last year's already-trained best three students, give them the new problems, and average their times as 'good' times, or benchmarks.

Thus for setup U, the evaluation scenario defines a rather simple and basic programme of test and evaluation. It would only provide rather limited information, and is heavily dependent on a rather crude approach to determining reference times: it would thus naturally be followed up by further studies based on the one hand on a rather more careful treatment of reference times, and on the other on alterations in the 'system' parameter settings, and on changes in the most obviously important environment variables. The first two could be done as retrospective experiments, applied to the test session data; however decomposition to study e.g. the effect of session length (taking this as a parameter) would only be possible if the number of sessions, and perhaps also students, was large enough for valid samples sizes. Changing the environment variables, e.g. nature of the problems done, could be similarly studied by decomposition, though new problems would also be desirable; and new sessions, with all other factors held constant, would be needed to study problem ordering effects.

But finally, here again, there is no direct evaluation of the NLP contribution of PlanS, i.e. whether it helps to promote rapid learning, though as with setup E, inspecting complete session log files could show how much interaction there was. It would nevertheless be dangerous to infer that if degree of natural language interaction was correlated with speed, it was a causal factor.

It is however possible to envisage, for a more limited evaluation like this, what testing for the NLP contribution might require. Thus we could, for instance, conduct a parallel experiment with the natural language interface deleted and replaced by a specialised language one (assuming we could invade the PlanS code), and compare performance for two subsets of students from a neighbouring engineering course and were invited to undertake two weeks of 'extra' training. (The general design would be otherwise the same). This would nevertheless not be a very well controlled experiment, and might need to be interpreted only indicatively.

Case S

For this case we will start from a rather different motivation: we want to evaluation PlanS from the point of view of its plan assessment capabilities as reflected both in the critiques it offers for the students' plans and the alternatives it produces itself. This is again a task motivated evaluation, with a task perspective, but much narrower and more selective than before (though we assume the same interests and consumers as before). Thus the goal of the evaluation is to find whether the system assesses soundly and also instructively and informatively; and the orientation is intrinsic, since we are looking at the system doing its own job, not serving some external one.

What kind of evaluation is in order here? Our interest is specifically in what PlanS is like, not what it might be like. To follow up the latter would require comparative experiments either modifying PlanS itself, or, say, conducting WOZ studies simulating a notional alternative PlanS. In the present case an investigation is appropriate, to determine how good the assessment is. But it could usefully be a glass box investigation since it would be sensible to decompose the analysis into the critiques of the user's own plan and the system alternative(s). But for both, what form of yardstick can be found? It is not obvious there can be a yardstick in any of the senses previously defined, except possibly for the factual correctness of the critiques, but these are not the aspects of them that seem most important. Thus it looks as if the evaluation will have to 'bootstrap' from judgements on intuitive notions like 'helpful' or 'sound'. This suggests the style is best seen as indicative, given that the mode of evaluation can hardly be other than qualitative: that is, we will have the concluding system contributions for each design cycle with PlanS rated by a panel of judges for helpfulness and soundness on simple scales e.g. poor, fair, good.

Continuing into the design phase, we are primarily looking under ends at one of the system's objectives, to provide constructive feedback, not at its external function, to train by offering feedback. The context is the problems and the student users, and the constitution is the system with its various parts: the expert system and the natural language interface, and also the component of the interface used to present the system's own plans. The content of critique and alternative plan(s) is clearly most important, but presentation also matters in both cases. Then identifying relevant performance factors in these, the specific environment variables are the set plans, which we may for this evaluation simply lump together without regard for ordering or categorisation by difficulty, and the students' own solutions, though these might be categorised as e.g. earnest, perfunctory. The system parameters, though not subject to experimental change, are the expert system's interpretation capacity for plan specifications, its student drawing interpretation capability, its assessment apparatus, its own plan formation capacity, and its linguistic and drawing expression capabilities.

Now for the criteria: for the critiques, degree of completeness in covering the problem specification, degree of centrality in relation to main design concepts; for the alternative plans, degree of plausibility, degree of difference from the students. To measure these, for a qualitative evaluation, we will simply have three levels, as indicated earlier, and compute averages over all problems for the two aspects separately.

Thus the data gathering will be done by taking a random sample of all completed cycles over the whole period of use of PlanS for a year, assuming this gives adequate coverage of the environment variables. For assessments, we use two competent judges not otherwise involved with PlanS, so without knowledge of its specific habits but given instruction in its general level of competence and concepts (e.g. it is not capable of critiquing on x), and for each problem require their agreed ratings.

The programme and test and evaluation methodology is thus fairly straightforward, though the evaluation is not very analytical: a natural related investigation would be to decompose the problems by hardness classes, to see whether PlanS assessment is at the same level for all. This could require all plans produced, perhaps for more than one year, to get large enough samples, and an independent panel of problem categorisers. Even so, it is not clear whether the effects of the students' own learning are adequately covered.

The problem with this evaluation is again, as before, that it is not discriminating enough in relation specifically to NLP. That is, it does not distinguish the natural language processor's abilities to express its critiques satisfactorily, as opposed to the expert system's ability to provide appropriate and helpful message content. To evaluate the system's natural language expressive powers needs a more tightly focussed evaluation.

Case L

(see Figure 2)

The illustrative evaluations so far have all in one way or another been motivated by an interest in educational effectiveness. We start from this point here too, and suppose that our motivation is to find out whether the natural language interaction capability is the most effective means of interaction with PlanS for student training purposes. The perspective is thus a direct, task-related one, and for simplicity we assume the teachers involved as both interests and consumers. We assume that the l-subsystem is working properly itself, and that it can meet whatever expression and communication requirements the rest of the system has. Thus the goal of this evaluation is to determine whether natural language is the best interaction medium to support the house design activity from alternatives which, for present purposes we will limit to one, namely the

```
REMIT

   Motivation : NL interaction best for PlanS ?
      Perspective : task-oriented
      Interest    : teachers
      Consumer    : teachers

   Goal : NL better than menus ?

   Orientation : extrinsic
   Kind        : experiment - compare 1- and m-modules
   Type        : black box
   Form        : (direct comparison)
   Style       : exhaustive
   Mode        : hybrid


DESIGN

   [Ends          : function - support of training
    Context       : student users
    Constitution  : competing 1- and m-modules]

   Performance factors :

      Environment variables : planning problems, students, system
      System parameters     : communication media, 1- and m-modules

   Evaluation criteria    : plan quality
      Measures   : three grades on plans
                 : convenience of interaction
      Methods    : all completed problems
                   self-administered questionnaires

   Evaluation data  : real problem sample over time
                      independent student sessions
                      several time points

   (Test procedure      : install m-module)
   Evaluation procedure  : gather problems
                         : apply to students
                         : give questionnaires
                         : assess plans
                         : assess questionnaires
```

Fig. 2. Summary of evaluation scenario for Example L

211

use of fixed tabular/menu displays. Thus it has been suggested by one of the teachers involved with PlanS that as natural language is used only reactively by the system in response to the user's input, queries, or plans, too much weight is placed on the student's own initiative: a student is not prompted, as they might be with a menu or checklist, to think about all aspects of what they are doing. Specifically, while the system could be more proactive and still use natural language, interaction would be simpler, clearer and more comprehensive with tabular displays etc. (The underlying presumption is therefore that the nature of student inputs would not make such an interface impracticable.)

The orientation, concentrating on the NLP contribution to interaction, is extrinsic. It is evident that this evaluation ought to be an experimental one, to constrain the comparison enough to be informative. But it is also black box, since it seems appropriate to try two alternative modules, the existing l-subsystem which we will here label the l-module, and an alternative menu-based or m-module. But what form of yardstick is right (and available) for evaluating alternative interfaces as contributors (along with the rest of the system) to educational effectiveness? It seems reasonable to use plan quality in some way, since better interfaces should, where all else is constant, lead to better plans; but of course there are no answer plans (it would not obviously be reasonable to take the system's own candidates as such). So bootstrapping is again required, as for the evaluation of U. It would be desirable to attempt a fairly exhaustive evaluation, to try to allow for different aspects of interface use, distinguishing specification input, user query during plan formation, and concluding system assessment. At the same time, as part of the overall strategy, the users could be asked for their view on the two interfaces, giving a qualitative evaluation along with the quantitative one within a hybrid whole. The evaluation remit is thus to conduct comparative experiments with the two modules.

The evaluation design is therefore, in relation to the existing l-system's ends, focussing on its contribution in support of training, i.e. on its external function rather than internal objective. But the context is not just the surrounding system: it is the entire setup involving student users as well as system, as with Case U. The evaluation subject's constitution is the various subparts of the two modules and the processes they carry out: we will take it that globally the general procedure is as originally described, with cycles, and it is only the modes of information submission and presentation that differ.

The environment factors are the properties of problems and students, and also those of the rest of the system, specifically the intrinsic capabilities of the knowledge-based subsystem. The system, i.e. subsystem, parameters are the (external interface's) communication medium - sentences versus headed boxes with bits of natural language or sub-natural language, and the content information types - expressed in natural language or manifested in table headings etc (these are tricky to define). In practice the two modules would be two distinct objects: however from the logical point of view what we have is a single high-level parameter, called interface modality, with two different settings: these subsume distinct lower groups of parameters we are not directly concerned with here. We will sometimes refer to alternative modules, sometimes to to different parameter settings, as locally convenient.

The evaluation criteria for the quantitative evaluation will be much like those used earlier: ability to produce satisfactory, or perhaps high quality, plan designs, measured by judge's ratings on a simple three-level scale, averaged over all completed plans. The qualitative criteria will be ease of expression for user inputs, clarity of information for system outputs, and general comfortableness, on simple scales, averaged over users whose plans are also covered by the quantitative evaluation. The method, e.g. for the qualitative assessment, chooses the time of completion of the questionnaire as at the end of each session, and self-completion by the user alone. Note that while the qualitative assessment refers to user attitudes to convenience etc, it is oriented towards determining system effectiveness rather than acceptability in the evaluation.

However for this evaluation, because it has explicit comparisons, the data gathering is rather more complex. It indeed presupposes the existence of the alternative m-interface. Thus it is essentially part of the test methodology to obtain the m-interface, and specifically to ensure that it is strictly comparable with the l-module. For this evaluation, that is, it is not proper to take another complete system with a non-natural language interface, because the other capabilities of the system may be different: even if the design problems set were the same, there are no correct answers and no guarantee the two systems have the same design and assessment powers. The m-module has to be specific for this evaluation. It may either be actually constructed, which has the advantage of control but the disadvantage of cost, or simulated by WOZ, which is cheaper but less controllable. Fortunately, the Poppleton Computing Centre has some existing software which can be adapted without too much difficulty by the Department hacker, and used after testing to ensure that it is properly connected with the knowledge-based subsystem: the presumption is that the latter has available, or can use, the same information for both alternatives, though the actual use can differ.

But now how to get the problem sample? As the m-module might be less educationally satisfactory than the existing l-module, it is undesirable to give it to real new students. But simply copying observed real student inputs submitted to the l-version, with the necessary minimal translation, into the m-system would not be satisfactory because the different possibilities offered by the two systems could affect direct user inputs. The approach adopted is therefore to take some students from another department, induct them sufficiently into the necessary building design concepts, and divide them into two groups for the two interfaces, supplying them with real problems as set for the genuine architecture students. These problems will be a random sample, over time, from the total real set. In order to capture some of the longer term effects, while accepting that these test students are not being concurrently educated with the architecture courses the real students are getting, the test students have a succession of sessions at weekly intervals for several weeks. Their submitted plans are recorded for the subsequent evaluation, and they are also at the end given the questionnaire.

The overall evaluation procedure is thus to install and test the m-module, obtain the sample of real problems, adminster them to the new students, assess the results and also grade the completed questionnaires for positive or negative flavours. The complete scenario is given in summary form in Figure 2.

It has of course to be recognised that this evaluation, though quite comprehensive and exhaustive, is limited by not being done for the real students. It also does not constitute a detailed evaluation of the different features and elements of the natural language processor: it only determines whether it as a whole does better or worse than its non-natural language competitor. To do this, developing a careful grid-style comparative evaluation, would require comparable modifications of the two modules designed, for instance, to test syntactic flexibility in the l-module against hopefully analogous menu item ordering and grouping in the m-interface; or again, to compare vocabulary scope in the l-module with more or less restricted concept labels in the m-interface. These would be glass box studies, but it is clear from the suggestions just made, it would be difficult to ensure enough control to provide clear evidence of the relative roles of different natural language powers.

Case C

We will consider evaluation for our illustrative component, the lexicon, only briefly.

Our deemed motivation here is to discover how far the system's limitations, as indicated by interpretation failures and the consequent tailoring habits the users develop, and by incomprehensible or opaque output critiques, are attributable to lexicon inadequacies. The perspective here is, we suppose, that of the task itself, and we take it that the interests are those of the teachers involved and the computing staff who act as system developers (actually customisers), these two groups also constituting the consumers for the evaluation findings. It is possible to examine the lexicon and so discover whether words are in the vocabulary, but there may still be poor lexical entries, and in relation to system output it may not even be obvious that a wanted word is missing. For the purposes of illustration we suppose that the lexicon is the only accessible system component within the l-subsystem, but that there is a vocabulary entry system (e.g. of a TEAM-like character). We therefore have an evaluation goal of discovering whether the lexicon is responsible for perceived imperfections in natural language input or output.

This is essentially an extrinsic evaluation, since the lexicon is being assessed for its response to external demands. The appropriate kind of evaluation appears to be an experiment, to try to isolate possible lexicon effects, and it we also have a black box evaluation, in fact not only for the lexicon itself but for the whole system though we hope that we can design the experiment to achieve an indirect glass box view here by being able to attribute effects to the lexicon as opposed to the rest of the system. The style is to be indicative at least, and quantitative. Thus the challenge of the remit is how to determine specifically lexical effects.

The evaluation design is thus focussed on the component's function in relation

214

to the rest of the system, though for a passive data source this cannot really be distinguished from its internal objective which may be defined as supplying good coverage correct information. However the emphasis on function does guide the evaluation design. The context is the entire system plus its inputs, both planning problems and user queries. The problems figure not only through their natural language submission, but also because they underpin the system's own critiques: thus the user's plans and the knowledge based system's assessments of them are inputs to the natural language generator exploiting the lexicon for output. The constitution of the evaluation subject proper is just the lexicon content and lookup mechanism.

The rather different uses of the lexicon for natural language input and output suggest that it is desirable to consider the two separately. The performance factors are very similar, but not identical. The environment factors for input are the sentence words, grammatical forms and also their conceptual content, if this can be characterised, since some of the perceived failings may in fact be associated with domain modelling or expert system limitations rather than language ones. The environment factors for output are the language generator and the conceptual content of output messages. The 'system' parameters for the lexicon itself are its content and style of definitions.

What are the evaluation criteria to be? They seem to be lexical as opposed to grammatical failures in the input and similarly for the output. But these are insufficient, since they do not take account of inappropriate conceptual mappings, whether these are word-local or sentence-global. So the criteria need to be lexical versus grammatical failure and also what we will call lexical versus structural distortion (including incompleteness). We will use as measures ratios of word to sentence failures of each of these two types, normalised for sentence length, say. The method for applying the measure will be to limit 'sentences' to full ones, not partial phrases.

Clearly the problem is in data gathering and providing the references: how are conceptual distortions to be identified? It is certainly not sufficient to simply gather user session data. The need is for a test suite. Thus we can start by gathering a large sample of actual session data and extracting from it one set of dubious inputs and another of dubious outputs. As these are not necessarily marked by actual system rejection, i.e. explicit failure, identifying duds from e.g. later system behaviour for inputs, or from earlier system inputs for critiques, will be very laborious and requiring extensive checking. However, given some such sets of 'inadequacy triggers', they can then be used to generate two test suites. One, for inputs, will consist of a whole set of variant forms for each trigger, covering lexical, grammatical and conceptual paraphrases. The other, for outputs, will consist of a set of variant plans (because these are critique triggers), which could be submitted as if they were user productions to PlanS. These variant sets have to be designed as far as possible to discriminate among the system's responses when they are offered to it, so lexical failings are distinguished from syntactic and conceptual ones.

Then the actual experimental procedure is to offer all the inputs, within as far as possible very low-demand sessions in order to avoid generating noise when the system's response is only manifest much later, and then to notice whether the responses are in fact faulty or not. Thus the grid design is given by the varying values for the environment paramters represented by the three types of variant.

All of this lexicon evaluation is still very sketchy: it is a hard one to do. An alternative strategy would be to build up a very large set of test design specifications of very gradually increasing complexity, in one respect or another, and to assess whether the treatment of input and output matched the problem needs with increased sophistication or flexibility.

It must be emphasised, again, that the presentations of all our examples are only indicative ones. In each case, much more detail about the specific procedures - e.g. decisions about the methods for the evaluation measures - is required for proper evaluations, even when they are only intended to be indicative investigations. It is also always necessary, in considering the evaluation findings, to bear both the identified and unidentified performance factors in mind for the influence they will have had on the results even if, as will be the case for many evaluations, this influence is not understood. Then in trying to understand these influences, one individual evaluation will naturally call for further comparative ones, where it is essential to design for control on factor differences.

Sketch of a mega-evaluation

As we referred in Chapter 2 to the idea of mega-evaluation as organised multi-strand evaluation sharing processors or data but over different tasks (i.e. evaluation with a wider scope but also tighter structure than the typical evaluation programme), we conclude this chapter of illustrations with a brief sketch of how PlanS might figure in such a mega-evaluation. This is, however, only an indicative note since the whole idea of mega-evaluation needs developing from its present proposal state in the light of actual experience.

Thus, for example, those interested in evaluation for the quite different task of text retrieval and with a system which might be applied, under the label 'BuildTR', to a collection of building texts, could use the whole Poppleton environment as a testbed, but also more specifically consider whether, if PlanS were supplemented with BuildTR, students' design performance would improve. In the first of these cases BuildTR would need its own evaluation data; however in the second, existing PlanS evaluation results could supply the control (non-BuildTR) side of the comparison as a baseline, say, while the same PlanS inputs would be taken to obtain new performance data for students armed with BuildTR to supplement PlanS. It might also, for the pure retrieval case, be appropriate to take existing PlanS input specifications simply as search queries for BuildTR as an autonomous text retrieval system, and use PlanS's own responses to these to calibrate the relevance of the output texts retrieved by BuildTR. In the pure retrieval case BuildTR is a parallel strand for the whole of PlanS and its immediate U setup. In the supplementing case the most straightforward view is to see a complete system parallel strand, but within the same setup. But it would also be possible to have some local 'linking strands' in data sharing for testing, for example using the PlanS vocabulary to provide a search vocabulary as an alternative to some other candidate set of search terms, when evaluating BuildTR as a general facility for the germane student body.

PlanS could, as another different possibility, be used as a testbed for natural language generators, to explore ways of varying the presentation of the system's plan critiques, for example to compare PlanS's own generator 'PGen' with 'My-Gen'. The two generators would have exactly the same internal message inputs as content for their output. One form of evaluation could be a direct one requiring new criteria etc to assess performance, whether e.g. of ability to actually deliver sentences or of comparative output 'quality', the other an indirect one to see whether any differences in generated critiques affected student design: in this case, as above, evaluation data would be partly shared and partly have to be newly formed. In the first case there is 'short-strand' parallelism, in the second case in fact local system parameter alteration but longer-strand parallelism as far as evaluation is concerned, since the two versions of PlanS are taken as wholes.

It would clearly be possible, with due care, to try other alternative l-systems or components within the PlanS framework. PlanS's inputs could also be used as inputs for quite other tasks, for example as material for a house agent or yellow-pages inquiry system, at least for study purposes; and its inputs or outputs could be tried as material for translation (for laboratory purposes even if there was no practical translation requirement), just as its input could be used in spoken form for a recogniser or output for a synthesiser. In such cases much of the PlanS context or resource set could be cannibalised for assessment purposes, though without assuming too much setup reality in the stricter sense for the new task. If we extended PlanS with the capability to describe (as opposed to just critique) the students' own designs or, similarly to provide a text summary of its own plans, we could exploit these text outputs for testing candidate information extraction systems since the underlying PlanS design representations could be taken as embodying the desired extraction'answers'. In all of these cases, points along PlanS's processing are being treated as end or start points for other NLP activities.

All of this sketch must be treated with caution, since it is essential to avoid the danger we have repeatedly emphasised in this book, of evaluation that is improper because it rests on illegitimate assumptions about the characteristics of tasks and environments and hence makes inappopriate use of processors or data that happen to be available, and creates unjustified linkage between evaluation subjects and evaluation gauges. In general the mega-evaluation idea may turn out to have most utility either in facilitating exploration or preliminary checking for NLP systems, by reducing test and evaluation data gathering costs and (as illustrated for the PlanS case above) by offering at least some anchoring setup examples, or in encouraging well-organised multi-purpose evaluations in some specific context. Correctly approached, therefore, and with much more careful analysis, we believe that mega-evaluation can promote better NLP systems.

3 Conclusion

Our conclusion, both to this chapter and to our book as a whole, is thus really a slogan: in evaluation it is always essential to look at the environment factors. So the implication is that while NLP evaluation as such is fine, it is of limited value: what matters is the setup.

References

1. L. Ahrenberg, N. Dahlback and A. Jonsson (Eds), *Proceedings of the Workshop on Empirical Models and Methodology for Natural Language Dialogue Systems,* Third Conference on Applied Natural Language Processing, Trento, Italy, 1992; (Natural Language Processing Laboratory, Department of Computer and Information Science, Linkoping University, 1992).
2. D. Allport, 'The TICC: parsing interesting text', *Proceedings of the Second Conference on Applied Natural Language Processing,* Austin, Texas, 1988, 211-218.
3. P.M. Anderson et al, 'Automatic extraction of facts from press releases to generate news stories', *Proceedings of the Third Conference on Applied Natural Language Processing,* Trento, Italy, 1992, 170-177.
4. I. Androutsopoulos, G.D. Ritchie and P. Thanisch, 'Natural language interfaces to databases: an introduction', *Natural Language Engineering,* 1, 1995, 29-81.
5. H. Alshawi (Ed), *The Core Language Engine,* Cambridge MA: MIT Press, 1992.
6. H. Alshawi et al, *CLARE: A Contextual Reasoning and Cooperative Response Framework for the Core Language Engine,* Final Report, SRI International, Cambridge Research Centre, Cambridge, England, 1992.
7. E.L. Baker and F.A. Butler, *Artificial Intelligence Measurement System, Overview and Lessons Learned,* Final Project Report, Centre for the Study of Evaluation, University of California at Los Angeles, 1991.
8. L. Balkan, M. Jaschke, L. Humphreys, S. Meijer, and A. Way, *Declarative Evaluation of an MT system: Practical Experiences,* Working Papers in Language Processing 25, Department of Language and Linguistics, University of Essex, 1991.
9. L. Balkan, K. Netter, D. Arnold and S. Meijer, 'TSNLP : test suites for natural language processing', *Proceedings of the Language Engineering Convention, 1994,* ELSNET, Centre for Cognitive Science, University of Edinburgh, 1994, 17-22.
10. L. Balkan, D, Arnold and F. Fouvry, 'Test suites for evaluation in natural lenguage engineering', *Convention Digest, Second Language Engineering Convention,* Department of Trade and Industry, 1995, 203-210.
11. M. Bates and D. Ayuso, 'A proposal for incremental dialogue evaluation', in S&NLW 1991, 319-322.
12. M. Bates and R. Weischedel, *Tutorial: Evaluating Natural Language Interfaces,* 25th Annual Conference of Association for Computational Linguistics, Stanford University, 1987; (Bolt, Beranek and Newman, Cambridge MA).
13. BNC: Information about the British National Corpus, from Oxford University Computing Service, via natcorp@oucs.ox.ac.uk or http://info.ox.ac.uk/bnc.
14. S. Boisen and M. Bates, 'A practical methodology for the evaluation of spoken language systems', *Proceedings of the Third Conference on Applied Natural Language Processing,* 1992, 162-169.
15. E. Briscoe, 'Extended development of the Alvey Natural Language Tools', Computer Laboratory, University of Cambridge, 1992.
16. J.G. Carbonell, 'Discourse pragmatics and ellipsis resolution in task-oriented natural language interfaces', *Proceedings of the 21st Annual Meeting of the Association for Computational Linguistics,* 1983, 164-168.
17. B. Carpenter and G. Penn, *ALE: The Attribute Logic Engine, Version 2.0 - User's Guide and Software,* Laboratory for Computational Linguistics, Department of Philosophy, Carnegie Mellon University, 1993.
18. N. Chinchor, 'MUC-3 evaluations metrics', in MUC-3, 1991, 17-24.

19. N. Chinchor, L. Hirschman, and D.D. Lewis, 'Evaluating message understanding systems: an analysis of the Third Message Understanding Conference (MUC-3)', *Computational Linguistics* 19, 1993, 409-449.

20. N. Chinchor and B. Sundheim, 'MUC-5 evaluation metrics', in MUC-5, 1993, 69-78.

21. CLR, 'The Consortium for Lexical Research', in S&NLW 1991, 393-394.

22. P.R. Cohen, 'A survey of the Eighth National Conference on AI: pulling together or pulling apart', *AI Magazine* 12 (1), 1991, 16-41.

23. R.A. Cole et al (Eds), *Survey of the State of the Art in Human Language Technology*, sponsored by the National Science Foundation and Directorate XIII-E of the Commission of the European Communities, in press.

24. S. Cookson, 'Final evaluation of VODIS', *Proceedings of the 7th FASE Symposium* (Speech 88), 1988, 1311-1320.

25. A. Copestake and K. Sparck Jones, 'Natural language interfaces to databases', *Knowledge Engineering Review* 5, 1990, 225-249 (also as Technical Report 187, Computer Laboratory, University of Cambridge, 1990).

26. H. Cunningham, R. Gaizauskas and Y. Wilks, *A General Architecture for Text Engineering (GATE) - A New Approach to Language Engineering R&D*, Research Memo CS-95-21, Department of Computer Science, University of Sheffield, 1995.

27. R. Crouch, R. Gaizauskas and K. Netter, *Interim Report of the Study Group on Assessment and Evaluation*, Prepared for Directorate General XIII, European Commission, Luxembourg, 1995. (Available from the Computational Linguistics archive cmp-lg via http://xxx.lanl.gov/cmp-lg.)

28. D.A. Dahl et al, 'Extending the scope of the ATIS task: the ATIS-3 corpus', in HLT 1994, 43-48.

29. F.J. Damerau, *The Transformational Question Answering (TQA) System: Description, Operating Experience and Implications*, Report RC8287, IBM Thomas J. Watson Research Center, Yorktown Heights, NY, 1980.

30. DATA: Information about the Data Collection Initiative (DCI), Linguistic Data Consortium (LDC), and similar efforts appears at intervals particularly in newsletters, e.g. the Association for Computational Linguistics' *Finite String,* the European Network in Language and Speech's *ELSNews,* etc. The LDC (Director: Prof M Liberman, University of Pennsylvania), has initiated its own newsletter.

31. G. DeJong, *Skimming Stories in Real Time: An Experiment in Integrated Understanding*, Research Report 158, Computer Science Department, Yale University, 1979.

32. G. DeJong, 'An overview of the FRUMP System" in *Strategies for Natural Language Processing* (Ed Lehnert and Ringle), Hillsdale NJ: Lawrence Erlbaum, 1982.

33. EAGLES, *EAGLES : Evaluation of Natural Language Processing Systems*, Draft report, EAGLES Document EAG-EWG-IR.2, Eagles Secretariat, Istituto di Linguistica Computazionale, Pisa, 1994.

34. ELSNEWS, *Newsletter of the European Network in Langauge and Speech*, 4.1 January 1995, Centre for Cognitive Science, University of Edinburgh.

35. B. Engelien and R. McBryde, *Natural Language Markets: Commercial Strategies,* Ovum Ltd, 7 Rathbone Street, London, 1991.

36. B. Everitt, *Cluster Analysis*, 2nd Ed, London: Gower, 1986.

37. K. Falkedal, *Evaluation Methods for Machine Translation Systems. An Historical Overview and Critical Account*, Report, ISSCO, Universite de Geneve, 1991.

38. D. Flickinger, J. Nerbonne, I. Sag, and T. Wasow, *Toward Evaluation of NLP Systems*, Hewlett Packard Laboratories, Palo Alto, CA, 1987.

39. D.P. Frost, *The Design of a Natural Language Interface for Medical Expert Systems*, PhD Thesis, University of London, 1989.

40. J.R. Galliers and K. Sparck Jones, *Evaluating Natural Language Processing Systems*, Technical Report 291, Computer Laboratory, University of Cambridge, 1993.

41. R. Grishman, C. Macleod and J. Sterling. 'Evaluating parsing strategies using standardised parse files', *Proceedings of the Third Conference on Applied Natural Language Processing*, 1992, 156-161.

42. R. Grishman, 'Whither written language evaluation', in HLT 1994, 120-125.

43. B. Grosz et al, 'TEAM: an experiment in the design of transportable natural-language interfaces', *Artificial Intelligence* 12, 1987, 173-243.

44. G. Guida and G. Mauri, 'Evaluation of natural language processing systems: issues and approaches', in *Proceedings of the IEEE*, 74, 1986, 1026-1035.

45. S. Hanks, M.E. Pollack and P. Cohen, 'Benchmarks, test beds, controlled experimentation, and the design of agent architectures', *The AI Magazine* 14 (4), 1993, 17-42.

46. D. Harman, *Text Retrieval Conference*, Call for Participation, 1991; (National Institute of Standards and Technology, Gaithersburg MD).

47. D. Harman, 'Overview of the Second Text Retrieval Conference (TREC-2)', in IP&M 1995, 271-289 (1995a).

48. D. Harman, *Call for Participation. Text Retrieval Conference*, 1995; (National Institute of Standards and Technology, Gaithersburg MD) (1995b).

49. P. Harrison et al, 'Evaluating syntax performance of parser/grammars of English', in Neal and Walter, 1991, 71-77.

50. P. Harrison, 'Notes for the Grammar Evaluation Interest Group meeting', Boeing Computer Services, 1992.

51. G. Harvey, *Mastering Q&A*, Alameda CA: Sybex Computer Books, no date.

52. P.J. Hayes, L.E. Knecht and M.J. Cellio, 'A news story categorisation system', *Proceedings of the Second Conference on Applied Natural Language Processing*, Austin, TE, 1988, 9-17.

53. Hemphill, C., 'TI implementation of corpus collection', *Proceedings of the Speech and Language Workshop* (DARPA sponsored, June 1990), San Mateo CA: Morgan Kaufmann, 1990.

54. L. Hirschman, 'Comparing MUCK-II and MUC-3: notes on evaluating the difficulty of different tasks', in MUC-3, 1991, 25-30.

55. L. Hirschman et al, 'Multi-site data collection and evaluation in spoken language understanding', in HLT 1993, 19-24.

56. L. Hirschman, 'Human language evaluation', Session Summmary, in HLT 1994, 99-101.

57. HLT 1993, *Human Language Technology; Proceedings of a Workshop*, San Francisco: Morgan Kaufmann, 1993.

58. HLT 1994, *Proceedings of the Human Language Technology Workshop*, San Francisco: Morgan Kaufmann, 1994.

59. E. R. House, *Evaluating with Validity*, Sage Publications, Beverly Hills, CA, 1980.

60. L. Humphreys, *User-Oriented Evaluation of MT Systems*, Working Papers in Language Processing 16, Department of Language and Linguistics, University of Essex, 1990.

61. L. Humphreys, M. Jasche, A. Way, L. Balkan and S. Meyer, *Operational Evaluation of MT, Draft Research Proposal*, Working Papers in Language Processing 22, Department of Language and Linguistics, University of Essex, 1991.

62. W. J. Hutchins, *Machine Translation*, Chichester: Ellis Horwood, 1986.

63. W. J. Hutchins and H. L. Somers, *An Introduction to MT Systems*, London: Academic Press, 1992.

64. IP&M 1992, *Information Processing and Management*, Special Issue on Evaluation Issues in Information Retrieval, 28 (4), 1992, 439-528.

65. IP&M 1995, *Information Processing and Management*, Special Issue on the Second Text retrieval Conference (TREC-2), 31 (3), 1995, 269-448.

66. ISO, *International Standard ISO/IEC 9126. Information Technology - Software Product Evaluation - Quality Characteristics and Guidelines for their Use*, International Organisation for Standardisation, International Electrotechnical Commission, Geneva, 1991.

67. M. Jarke, J.A. Turner, E.A. Stohr, Y. Vassiliou, N.H. White and K. Michielsen, 'A field evaluation of natural language for data retrieval', *IEEE Transactions on Software Engineering*, SE-11, 1, 1985, 97-113.

68. JTEC, *Machine Translation in Japan*, Panel report, Japanese Technology Evaluation Centre, 1992 (loyola College, MD); reprinted as Part III of *Advanced Software Applications in Japan* (Ed E. Feigenbaum, E. Rich, G. Wiederhold and M. Harrison), Park Ridge NJ: Noyes Data Corporation, 1995.

69. M. King, 'Evaluating natural language processing systems', *Communications of the ACM*, 39(1), 1996, 73-79.

70. D.H. Klatt, 'Review of the ARPA Speech Understanding Project', *Journal of the Acoustical Society of America* 62, 1977, 1345-1366.

71. F. Kubala et al, 'The hub and spoke paradigm for CSR evaluation', in HLT 1994, 37-42.

72. LD 006, 'Speech input processor and workstation', Alvey Large Demonstrator Project, *Alvey Programme Annual Report 1985, Poster Supplement*, IEE Publishing, Stevenage, UK, 1985, 242.

73. W. Lehnert and B. Sundheim, 'A performance analysis of text-analysis technologies', *AI Magazine* 12 (4), 1991, 81-94.

74. D.D. Lewis, 'Evaluating text categorisation', in S&NLW 1991, 312-318.

75. MADCOW, 'Multi-site data collection for a spoken language corpus', in S&NLW 1992.

76. M. Marcus, 'Very large annotated database of American English', in S&NLW 1992, 430.

77. R.C. Moore, 'Semantic evaluation for spoken language systems', in HLT 1994, 126-131.

78. MUC-3, *Proceedings of the Third Message Understanding Conference (MUC-3)*, San Mateo CA: Morgan Kaufmann, 1991.

79. MUC-4, *Proceedings of the Fourth Message Understanding Conference (MUC-4)*, San Mateo CA: Morgan Kaufmann, 1992.

80. MUC-5, *Proceedings of the Fifth Message Understanding Conference (MUC-5)*, San Francisco: Morgan Kaufmann, 1993.

81. M. Nagao (Ed), *A Japanese View of Machine Translation in the Light of Considerations and Recommendations Reported by ALPAC, USA*, Japanese Electronic Industry Development Association, 1989.

82. J.G. Neal and S.M. Walter (Eds), *Natural Language Processing Systems Evaluation Workshop*, University of California, Berkeley, CA, 1991; Report RL-TR-91-362, Rome Laboratory, Griffiss AFB, NY, 1991.

83. S. Oviatt and P. Cohen, *Tutorial: Evaluation of Natural Language Modalities*, Third Conference on Applied Natural Language Processing (Trento, Italy), Association for Computational Linguistics, 1992.

84. D. Pallett, 'Session 2: DARPA Resource Management and ATIS benchmark test poster session', in S&NLW 1991, 49-58.

85. D. Pallett, 'Speech corpora produced on CD-ROM media by NIST', in Ramsay, 1992, 173-195.

86. D. Pallett et al, 'DARPA February 1992 ATIS benchmark test results', in S&NLW 1992.

87. D. Pallett et al, 'Benchmark tests for the DARPA spoken language program', in HLT 1993, 7-18.

88. D. Pallett et al, ' 1993 benchmark tests for the ARPA spoken language program', in HLT 1994, 49-74.

89. M. Palmer, T. Finin and M. Walter, *Workshop on the Evaluation of Natural Language Processing Systems*, Wayne, PA; Report RADC-TR-89-302, Rome Air Development Centre, Griffiss AFB, NY, 1989.

90. M.Q. Patton, *Qualitative Evaluation Methods*, Sage Publications, Beverly Hills, CA, 1980.

91. A. Ramsey (Ed), *Integrating Speech and Natural Language: Workshop Notes*, (ELSNET Workshop, Dublin, 1992), European Language and Speech Network, Centre for Cognitive Science, University of Edinburgh, 1992.

92. L.F. Rau and G.R. Krupka, *Issues in the Evaluation of Text Extractions Systems*, Technical report, GE Research and Development Centre, Schenectady, 1992.

93. M. Rayner et al, 'A speech to speech translation system built from standard components', in HLT 1993, 217-222.

94. W. Read, M. Dyer, E. Baker, P. Mutch, F. Butler, A. Quilici, and J. Reeves, *The Sourcebook*, Project Report 13, Centre for the Study of Evaluation, University of California at Los Angeles, 1990.

95. W. Read, A. Quilici, J. Reeves, and M. Dyer, 'Evaluating natural language systems: a sourcebook approach". *COLING 88- Proceedings of the International Conference on Computational Linguistics*, Budapest, 1988, 530-534.

96. S.E. Robertson and K. Sparck Jones, 'Relevance weighting of search terms', *Journal of the American Society for Information Science* 27, 1976, 129-146.

97. L. Rutman, *Evaluation Research Methods: A Basic Guide*, Sage Publications, Beverly Hills, CA, 1984.

98. S&NLW 1991, *Speech and Natural Language; Proceedings of a Workshop* (DARPA sponsored, February 1991), San Mateo CA: Morgan Kaufmann, 1991.

99. S&NLW 1992, *Proceedings of the 5th DARPA Speech and Natural Language Workshop*, (February 1992), San Francisco: Morgan Kaufmann, 1992.

100. G. Salton and M. McGill, *Introduction to Modern Information Retrieval*, New York: McGraw-Hill, 1983.

101. G. Sampson, 'The SUSANNE corpus', *ELSNews* 1(2), 1992, 8.

102. G. Sampson, *English for the Computer*, Oxford: Oxford University Press, 1995.

103. T. Saracevic, 'Evaluation of evaluation in information retrieval', *SIGIR 95, Proceedings of the Eighteenth Annual International ACM-SIGIR Conference on Research and Development in Information Retrieval*, 1995.

104. J. Slocum, 'Machine translation: its history, current status and future prospects', *COLING 84- Proceedings of the International Conference on Computational Linguistics*, Stanford University, CA, 1984, 546-561. 1984.

223

105. SLTW 1994, *Proceedings of the Spoken Language Technology Workshop*, (March 1994), San Francisco: Morgan Kaufmann, 1994.

106. SLTW 1995, *Proceedings of the Spoken Language Technology Workshop*, (January 1995), San Fransciso: Morgan Kaufmann, 1995.

107. K. Sparck Jones and C.J. van Rijsbergen, 'Information retrieval test collections', *Journal of Documentation* 32, 1976, 59-75.

108. K. Sparck Jones and R.G. Bates, *Report on a Design Study for the 'Ideal' Information Retrieval Test Collection*, (British Library R&D Report 5428), Computer Laboratory, University of Cambridge, 1977.

109. K. Sparck Jones (Ed), *Information Retrieval Experiment*, London: Butterworths, 1981.

110. K. Sparck Jones, *A Note on Robustness*, Computer Laboratory, University of Cambridge, 1988.

111. K. Sparck Jones, 'What sort of thing is an AI experiment?' in *The Foundations of Artificial Intelligence: A Sourcebook* (Ed Partridge and Wilks), Cambridge: Cambridge University Press, 1990.

112. K. Sparck Jones, 'Towards better NLP system evaluation', in HLT 1994, 102-107.

113. K. Sparck Jones, 'Reflections on TREC', in IP&M 1995, 291-314.

114. B.M. Sundheim, *Third Message Understanding System Evaluation and Message Understanding Conference (MUC-3)*, Call for Participation, 1990; (Naval Ocean Systems Centre, San Diego CA).

115. B.M. Sundheim, 'Overview of the Third Message Understanding Evaluation and Conference', in MUC-3, 1991, 3-24.

116. B.M. Sundheim, 'Information extraction system evaluation', in HLT 1993, 403 (1993a).

117. B.M. Sundheim, 'TIPSTER/MUC-5 information extraction system evaluation', in MUC-5, 1993 (1993b), 27-44.

118. B.M. Sundheim and N.A. Chinchor, 'Survey of the Message Understanding Conferences', in HLT 1993, 56-60.

119. B.M. Sundheim, *Sixth Message Understanding System Evaluation and Message Understanding Conference (MUC-6)*, Call for Participation, 1995; (Naval Ocean Systems Centre, San Diego CA).

120. W.R. Swartout, 'Evaluation criteria for expert system explanation', *AAAI Workshop on Evaluating Natural Language Generation Systems*, 1990.

121. H. Tennant, 'Experience with the evaluation of natural language question answerers', *IJCAI-79, Proceedings of the International Joint Conference on Artificial Intelligence* 1979, 874-876.

122. H. Thompson (Comp), *The Strategic Role of Evaluation in Natural Language Processing and Speech Technology*, Record of the ESPRIT DANDI/ELSNET/HCRC Workshop, Edinburgh 1992, Human Communication Research Centre, University of Edinburgh, 1992.

123. H. Thompson, 'Parseval Workshop', *ELSNews* 1(2), 1992, 7. (1992a)

124. TIPSTER, Architecture information, Department of Computer Science, New York University, via http://cs.nyu.edu/tipster.

125. TREC-1, *The First Text Retrieval Conference (TREC-1)*, Special Publication 500-207, National Institute of Standards and Technology, Gaithersburg MD, 1993.

126. TREC-2, *The Second Text Retrieval Conference (TREC-2)*, Special Publication 500-215, National Institute of Standards and Technology, Gaithersburg MD, 1994.

127. TREC-3, *Overview of the Third Text Retrieval Conference (TREC-3)*, Special Publication 200-225, National Institute of Standards and Technology, Gaithersburg MD, 1995.

128. M. Walker, 'Natural language in a desktop environment', *Proceedings of HCI '89*, Boston, 1989.

129. S.M. Walter, 'The Neil-Montgomery system evaluation methodology', in S&NLW 1992.

130. D.L. Waltz, 'An English language question answering system for a large relational database', *Communications of the ACM* 21, 1978, 526-539.

131. A. Way, *Developer-oriented Evaluation of MT Systems*, Working Papers in Language Processing 21, Department of Language and Linguistics, University of Essex, 1991 (1991a).

132. A. Way, *A Practical Developer-oriented Evaluation of MT Systems*, Working Papers in Language Processing 26, Department of Language and Linguistics, University of Essex, 1991 (1991b).

133. J.S. White, T.A. O'Connell and L.M. Carlson, 'Evaluation of machine translation', in HLT 1993, 206-210.

134. J.S. White and T.A. O'Connell, 'Evaluation in the ARPA machine translation program: 1993 evaluation', in HLT 1994, 135-140.

135. S. Whittaker and M. Walker, *Comparing Two User-Oriented Database Query Languages: A Field Study*, Technical Report HPL-ISC-89-060, Hewlett Packard Laboratories, Bristol, 1989.

136. Y. Wilks, *SYSTRAN: It Obviously Works, But How Much Can It Be Improved?* Report MCCS-91-215, Computing Research Laboratory, New Mexico State University, 1991.

137. W.A. Woods, 'Progress in NLU - An application to lunar geology', *AFIPS Conference Proceedings* 42, 1973, 441-450.

138. S.J. Young, *Final report: Alvey/SERC Project MM1003, Voice Operated Database Inquiry Systems, Speech Input*, Engineering Department, University of Cambridge, 1989.

Index

abstract measure, 97
acceptability, 60
activity, 13
adequacy evaluation, 157
aim, 14
angle, 39
annotated corpus, 170
answer, 59, 69, 139, 168
antecendent variable, 60
apparatus, 11, 200
application, 10
application domain, 200
architecture, 178
argot, 5
ARPA, 65, 69
attribute, 85, 159

baseline, 26, 58, 139
behaviour, 14
benchmark, 26, 58, 86, 139
black box, 26, 123

catalogue, 86
category, 13
checking collection, 169
checklist, 85, 160
comparison, 60
complexity, 6
component, 10, 200
composite, 61
computational, 76
constitution, 196
constraints, 194
consumer, 39, 137, 194
consumer report, 157
context, 196
corpus, 141, 168
coverage corpus, 141, 168
criteria, 19
criterion, 122, 196
criterion class, 61
customer, 135
cycling, 196

DARPA, 65, 68
data sort, 170
data source, 171
decomposition, 34, 162, 194
design, 196
design goal, 25
development data, 176
diagnosis, 136
diagnostic evaluation, 157
dialogue, 6, 107
distribution corpus, 141, 168
division, 8
domain, 10
dry run, 97

EAGLES, 66
eccentric, 45
economic, 73
effect, 23
effectiveness, 60
efficiency, 60
end, 60, 196
environment, 23
environment factor, 23
environment variable, 196
evaluation, 196
evaluation data, 59, 169
evaluation methodology, 144
evaluation standard, 48, 150
exemplar, 26, 60, 139
exigent processing, 5
experiment, 22
extrinsic criteria, 19

feature, 85, 160
featurisation, 85, 160
field evaluation, 98
form, 194
full processing, 5
function, 13, 71, 122, 200

general-purpose system, 10, 180
generic system, 10, 49, 180

glass box, 26, 123
goal, 39, 194
granularity, 26, 123
grid, 27, 122, 157, 196
guideline, 142

human performance, 96
hybrid system, 9

indicator, 61
informative, 63
informativeness, 194
instance, 174
interactive, 6
interest, 39, 137, 194
interface, 9, 200
intervening variable, 60
intrinsic criteria, 19
investigation, 22

kind, 194

l-system, 8, 200
language, 3
language system, 8
legitimacy, 171
level, 201
linguistic, 3, 71
linkage, 61, 196

measure, 20, 122, 159, 196
mega-evaluation, 185
method, 20, 159, 196
mode, 194
motivation, 194

n-system, 8, 200
narrow bound, 39
nature, 196
non-interactive, 6
non-language system, 8
norm, 26, 58

objective, 11, 122, 200
observation, 15
operation, 14
operational, 73

orientation, 194

p-setup, 13
parameter, 23, 122
partial processing, 5
performance factor, 23, 196
perspective, 39, 194
pretest, 83
principle, 122
procedure, 196
programme, 196
progress evaluation, 157
pseudo-language, 4
purpose, 11, 122

qualitative, 61, 122
quality characteristic, 85, 159
quantitative, 61, 122
quasi-language, 4

range, 50
rationale, 123
realism, 168
realistic, 171
reality, 148
reasonable, 45
reference, 58, 139, 168, 169
reliability, 60
remit, 196
reportable attribute, 85, 161
representative, 171
representativeness, 148, 168
richness, 6
role, 13
run, 27, 122, 196

scenario, 34, 196
scope, 14
separation, 6
serious material, 4
setting, 23
setup, 11
simple processing, 5
sort, 196
standard, 133, 150
statistical significance, 92

status, 171, 196
strategy, 34, 122
style, 194
subject, 30, 194
sublanguage, 3
substitute, 175
subsystem, 8, 200
system, 6, 200
system factor, 23
system parameter, 196

target, 139
task, 6, 200
terminal, 9, 200
test, 22
test bed, 58, 160
test collection, 26, 123, 168
test data, 56, 58, 122, 168
test methodology, 144
test program, 56
test set, 142, 170
test standard, 150
test suite, 123, 140, 168
testing, 196
tool, 55, 142
toolkit, 58, 142
training set, 142, 170
transcription, 188
transportability, 93
trivial material, 4
tuning, 95
type, 194

unpack, 34
unpacking, 194
usage, 71
user, 11
utility, 122

validity, 60
value, 23, 159
variable, 23, 122

wide bound, 39
working, 14
working data, 169

yardstick, 194

Springer-Verlag
and the Environment

We at Springer-Verlag firmly believe that an international science publisher has a special obligation to the environment, and our corporate policies consistently reflect this conviction.

We also expect our business partners – paper mills, printers, packaging manufacturers, etc. – to commit themselves to using environmentally friendly materials and production processes.

The paper in this book is made from low- or no-chlorine pulp and is acid free, in conformance with international standards for paper permanency.

Lecture Notes in Artificial Intelligence (LNAI)

Vol. 928: V.W. Marek, A. Nerode, M. Truszczynski (Eds.), Logic Programming and Nonmonotonic Reasoning. Proceedings, 1995. VIII, 417 pages. 1995.

Vol. 929: F. Morán, A. Moreno, J.J. Merelo, P.Chacón (Eds.), Advances in Artificial Life. Proceedings, 1995. XIII, 960 pages. 1995.

Vol. 934: P. Barahona, M. Stefanelli, J. Wyatt (Eds.), Artificial Intelligence in Medicine. Proceedings, 1995. XI, 449 pages. 1995.

Vol. 941: M. Cadoli, Tractable Reasoning in Artificial Intelligence. XVII, 247 pages. 1995.

Vol. 946: C. Froidevaux, J. Kohlas (Eds.), Symbolic Quantitative and Approaches to Reasoning under Uncertainty. Proceedings, 1995. X, 430 pages. 1995.

Vol. 954: G. Ellis, R. Levinson, W. Rich. J.F. Sowa (Eds.), Conceptual Structures: Applications, Implementation and Theory. Proceedings, 1995. IX, 353 pages. 1995.

Vol. 956: X. Yao (Ed.), Progress in Evolutionary Computation. Proceedings, 1993, 1994. VIII, 314 pages. 1995.

Vol. 957: C. Castelfranchi, J.-P. Müller (Eds.), From Reaction to Cognition. Proceedings, 1993. VI, 252 pages. 1995.

Vol. 961: K.P. Jantke. S. Lange (Eds.), Algorithmic Learning for Knowledge-Based Systems. X, 511 pages. 1995.

Vol. 981: I. Wachsmuth, C.-R. Rollinger, W. Brauer (Eds.), KI-95: Advances in Artificial Intelligence. Proceedings, 1995. XII, 269 pages. 1995.

Vol. 984: J.-M. Haton, M. Keane, M. Manago (Eds.), Advances in Case-Based Reasoning. Proceedings, 1994. VIII, 307 pages. 1995.

Vol. 990: C. Pinto-Ferreira, N.J. Mamede (Eds.), Progress in Artificial Intelligence. Proceedings, 1995. XIV, 487 pages. 1995.

Vol. 991: J. Wainer, A. Carvalho (Eds.), Advances in Artificial Intelligence. Proceedings, 1995. XII, 342 pages. 1995.

Vol. 992: M. Gori, G. Soda (Eds.), Topics in Artificial Intelligence. Proceedings, 1995. XII, 451 pages. 1995.

Vol. 997: K. P. Jantke, T. Shinohara, T. Zeugmann (Eds.), Algorithmic Learning Theory. Proceedings, 1995. XV, 319 pages. 1995.

Vol. 1003: P. Pandurang Nayak, Automated Modeling of Physical Systems. XXI, 232 pages. 1995.

Vol. 1010: M. Veloso, A. Aamodt (Eds.), Case-Based Reasoning Research and Development. Proceedings, 1995. X, 576 pages. 1995.

Vol. 1011: T. Furuhashi (Ed.), Advances in Fuzzy Logic, Neural Networks and Genetic Algorithms. Proceedings, 1994. VIII, 223 pages. 1995.

Vol. 1020: I. D. Watson (Ed.), Progress in Case-Based Reasoning. Proceedings, 1995. VIII, 209 pages. 1995.

Vol. 1036: G. Adorni, M. Zock (Eds.), Trends in Natural Language Generation. Proceedings, 1993. IX, 382 pages. 1996.

Vol. 1037: M. Wooldridge, J.P. Müller, M. Tambe (Eds.), Intelligent Agents II. Proceedings, 1995. XVI, 437 pages, 1996.

Vol. 1038: W. Van de Velde, J.W. Perram (Eds.), Agents Breaking Away. Proceedings, 1996. XIV, 232 pages, 1996.

Vol. 1040: S. Wermter, E. Riloff, G. Scheler (Eds.), Connectionist, Statistical, and Symbolic Approaches to Learning for Natural Language Processing. IX, 468 pages. 1996.

Vol. 1042: G. Weiß, S. Sen (Eds.), Adaption and Learning in Multi-Agent Systems. Proceedings, 1995. X, 238 pages. 1996.

Vol. 1047: E. Hajnicz, Time Structures. IX, 244 pages. 1996.

Vol. 1050: R. Dyckhoff, H. Herre, P. Schroeder-Heister (Eds.), Extensions of Logic Programming. Proceedings, 1996. VIII, 318 pages. 1996.

Vol. 1053: P. Graf, Term Indexing. XVI, 284 pages. 1996.

Vol. 1056: A. Haddadi, Communication and Cooperation in Agent Systems. XIII, 148 pages. 1996.

Vol. 1069: J.W. Perram, J.-P. Müller (Eds.), Distributed Software Agents and Applications. Proceedings, 1994. VIII, 219 pages. 1996.

Vol. 1071: P. Miglioli, U. Moscato, D. Mundici, M. Ornaghi (Eds.), Theorem Proving with Analytic Tableaux and Related Methods. Proceedings, 1996. X, 330 pages. 1996.

Vol. 1076: N. Shadbolt, K. O'Hara, G. Schreiber (Eds.), Advances in Knowledge Acquisition. Proceedings, 1996. XII, 371 pages. 1996.

Vol. 1079: Z. W. Raś, M. Michalewicz (Eds.), Foundations of Intelligent Systems. Proceedings, 1996. XI, 664 pages. 1996.

Vol. 1081: G. McCalla (Ed.), Advances in Artificial Intelligence. Proceedings, 1996. XII, 459 pages. 1996.

Vol. 1083: K. Sparck Jones, J.R. Galliers, Evaluating Natural Language Processing Systems. XV, 228 pages. 1996.

Vol. 1085: D.M. Gabbay, H.J. Ohlbach (Eds.), Practical Reasoning. Proceedings, 1996. XV, 721 pages. 1996.

Vol. 1087: C. Zhang, D. Lukose (Eds.), Distributed Artificial Intelligence. Proceedings, 1995. VIII, 232 pages. 1996.

Lecture Notes in Computer Science

Vol. 1053: P. Graf, Term Indexing. XVI, 284 pages. 1996. (Subseries LNAI).

Vol. 1054: A. Ferreira, P. Pardalos (Eds.), Solving Combinatorial Optimization Problems in Parallel. VII, 274 pages. 1996.

Vol. 1055: T. Margaria, B. Steffen (Eds.), Tools and Algorithms for the Construction and Analysis of Systems. Proceedings, 1996. XI, 435 pages. 1996.

Vol. 1056: A. Haddadi, Communication and Cooperation in Agent Systems. XIII, 148 pages. 1996. (Subseries LNAI).

Vol. 1057: P. Apers, M. Bouzeghoub, G. Gardarin (Eds.), Advances in Database Technology – EDBT '96. Proceedings, 1996. XII, 636 pages. 1996.

Vol. 1058: H. R. Nielson (Ed.), Programming Languages and Systems – ESOP '96. Proceedings, 1996. X, 405 pages. 1996.

Vol. 1059: H. Kirchner (Ed.), Trees in Algebra and Programming – CAAP '96. Proceedings, 1996. VIII, 331 pages. 1996.

Vol. 1060: T. Gyimóthy (Ed.), Compiler Construction. Proceedings, 1996. X, 355 pages. 1996.

Vol. 1061: P. Ciancarini, C. Hankin (Eds.), Coordination Languages and Models. Proceedings, 1996. XI, 443 pages. 1996.

Vol. 1062: E. Sanchez, M. Tomassini (Eds.), Towards Evolvable Hardware. IX, 249 pages. 1996.

Vol. 1063: J.-M. Alliot, E. Lutton, E. Ronald, M. Schoenauer, D. Snyers (Eds.), Artificial Evolution. Proceedings, 1995. XIII, 396 pages. 1996.

Vol. 1064: B. Buxton, R. Cipolla (Eds.), Computer Vision – ECCV '96. Volume I. Proceedings, 1996. XXI, 725 pages. 1996.

Vol. 1065: B. Buxton, R. Cipolla (Eds.), Computer Vision – ECCV '96. Volume II. Proceedings, 1996. XXI, 723 pages. 1996.

Vol. 1066: R. Alur, T.A. Henzinger, E.D. Sontag (Eds.), Hybrid Systems III. IX, 618 pages. 1996.

Vol. 1067: H. Liddell, A. Colbrook, B. Hertzberger, P. Sloot (Eds.), High-Performance Computing and Networking. Proceedings, 1996. XXV, 1040 pages. 1996.

Vol. 1068: T. Ito, R.H. Halstead, Jr., C. Queinnec (Eds.), Parallel Symbolic Languages and Systems. Proceedings, 1995. X, 363 pages. 1996.

Vol. 1069: J.W. Perram, J.-P. Müller (Eds.), Distributed Software Agents and Applications. Proceedings, 1994. VIII, 219 pages. 1996. (Subseries LNAI).

Vol. 1070: U. Maurer (Ed.), Advances in Cryptology – EUROCRYPT '96. Proceedings, 1996. XII, 417 pages. 1996.

Vol. 1071: P. Miglioli, U. Moscato, D. Mundici, M. Ornaghi (Eds.), Theorem Proving with Analytic Tableaux and Related Methods. Proceedings, 1996. X, 330 pages. 1996. (Subseries LNAI).

Vol. 1072: R. Kasturi, K. Tombre (Eds.), Graphics Recognition. Proceedings, 1995. X, 308 pages. 1996.

Vol. 1073: J. Cuny, H. Ehrig, G. Engels, G. Rozenberg (Eds.), Graph Grammars and Their Application to Computer Science. Proceedings, 1995. X, 565 pages. 1996.

Vol. 1074: G. Dowek, J. Heering, K. Meinke, B. Möller (Eds.), Higher-Order Algebra, Logic, and Term Rewriting. Proceedings, 1995. VII, 287 pages. 1996.

Vol. 1075: D. Hirschberg, G. Myers (Eds.), Combinatorial Pattern Matching. Proceedings, 1996. VIII, 392 pages. 1996.

Vol. 1076: N. Shadbolt, K. O'Hara, G. Schreiber (Eds.), Advances in Knowledge Acquisition. Proceedings, 1996. XII, 371 pages. 1996. (Subseries LNAI).

Vol. 1077: P. Brusilovsky, P. Kommers, N. Streitz (Eds.), Mulimedia, Hypermedia, and Virtual Reality. Proceedings, 1994. IX, 311 pages. 1996.

Vol. 1078: D.A. Lamb (Ed.), Studies of Software Design. Proceedings, 1993. VI, 188 pages. 1996.

Vol. 1079: Z.W. Raś, M. Michalewicz (Eds.), Foundations of Intelligent Systems. Proceedings, 1996. XI, 664 pages. 1996. (Subseries LNAI).

Vol. 1080: P. Constantopoulos, J. Mylopoulos, Y. Vassiliou (Eds.), Advanced Information Systems Engineering. Proceedings, 1996. XI, 582 pages. 1996.

Vol. 1081: G. McCalla (Ed.), Advances in Artificial Intelligence. Proceedings, 1996. XII, 459 pages. 1996. (Subseries LNAI).

Vol. 1083: K. Sparck Jones, J.R. Galliers, Evaluating Natural Language Processing Systems. XV, 228 pages. 1996. (Subseries LNAI).

Vol. 1084: W.H. Cunningham, S.T. McCormick, M. Queyranne (Eds.), Integer Programming and Combinatorial Optimization. Proceedings, 1996. X, 505 pages. 1996.

Vol. 1085: D.M. Gabbay, H.J. Ohlbach (Eds.), Practical Reasoning. Proceedings, 1996. XV, 721 pages. 1996. (Subseries LNAI).

Vol. 1087: C. Zhang, D. Lukose (Eds.), Distributed Artificial Intelliegence. Proceedings, 1995. VIII, 232 pages. 1996. (Subseries LNAI).

Vol. 1088: A. Strohmeier (Ed.), Reliable Software Technologies – Ada-Europe '96. Proceedings, 1996. XI, 513 pages. 1996.